x86 Software Reverse-Engineering, Cracking, and Counter-Measures

x86 Software Reverse-Engineering, Cracking, and Counter-Measures

Stephanie Domas
Christopher Domas

WILEY

About the Authors

With more than 10 years of ethical hacking, reverse engineering, and advanced vulnerability analysis as a defense contractor, **Stephanie Domas** has a deep knowledge of and passion for the hacker mindset. Pivoting her offensive skills to the defense, she built and led two cybersecurity businesses focused on defense of embedded systems, medical devices, and the healthcare industry. She currently serves as a prominent industry consultant and advisor with a broad range of tech companies and device manufacturers, from the newest startups to the industry giants, and is the CISO of Canonical, driving Canonical to be the most trusted computational partner in all of open source. Previously, she served as the chief security technology strategist at Intel where she owned the cross-Intel security technology strategy, formulating and implementing strategies that would accelerate Intel's strength, competitiveness, and revenue growth in the area of security. Stephanie is a passionate educator, strategist, speaker, advisor, and security enthusiast.

Christopher Domas is a security researcher primarily focused on firmware, hardware, and low-level processor exploitation. He is best known for releasing impractical solutions to nonexistent problems, including the world's first single instruction C compiler (M/o/Vfuscator), toolchains for generating images in program control flow graphs (REpsych), and Turing machines in the vi text editor. His more relevant work includes the sandsifter processor fuzzer, rosenbridge backdoor, the binary visualization tool ..cantor.dust.., and the memory sinkhole privilege escalation exploit.

About the Technical Writer

Howard Poston is a copywriter, author, and course developer with experience in cybersecurity and blockchain security, cryptography, and malware analysis. He has a master's degree in cyber operations, a decade of experience in cybersecurity, and more than five years of experience as a freelance consultant providing training and content creation for cyber and blockchain security. He is also the creator of more than a dozen cybersecurity courses, has authored two books, and has spoken at numerous cybersecurity conferences.

About the Technical Editor

John Toterhi is a senior security researcher specializing in embedded system reverse engineering, vulnerability research, and capability development. John started his career in 2010 as a civilian malware analyst for the United States Air Force, where he reverse-engineered malicious software threats to U.S. air and space assets. Since then, John has worked for multiple government and private organizations on large-scale software vulnerability discovery and CNO tool development. John is also a guest lecturer at Ohio State University, teaching reverse engineering and malware analysis, and co-leads a private offensive security bootcamp that helps prepare the next generation of cyber engineers to solve tomorrow's cyber challenges.

About the Technical Editor

Contents at a Glance

Contents

Introduction

Reverse engineering and software cracking are disciplines with a long, rich history. For decades, software developers have attempted to build defenses into their applications to protect intellectual property or to prevent modifications to the program code. The art of cracking has been around nearly as long as reverse engineers have been examining and modifying code for fun or profit.

Before diving into the details of how reverse engineering works, it is useful to understand the context in which these disciplines reside. This chapter describes what to expect from this book and dives into the history and legal considerations of software reverse engineering and cracking.

Who Should Read This Book

From security professionals to hobbyists, this book is for anyone who wants to learn to take apart, understand, and modify black-box software. This book takes a curious security-minded individual behind the curtain to how software cracking and computers work. Learning how an x86 computer works is not only powerful from a reverse-engineering and cracking perspective, but will make each reader a stronger developer, with advanced knowledge they can apply to code optimization, efficiency, debugging, compiler settings and chip selection. Then the curtain continues to pull back as readers learn how software cracking happens. Readers will learn about tools and techniques that real-world software crackers use, and they will set their newfound knowledge to the test by cracking real-world applications of their own in numerous hands-on labs. We then circle back to understand defensive techniques for combating software cracking.

By learning both the offensive and defensive techniques, readers will walk away as strong software crackers or software defenders.

What to Expect from This Book

This book is based on these three core tenets of reverse engineering:

- There is no such thing as uncrackable software.
- The goal in offense is to try to go faster.
- The goal in defense is to try to slow down.

Based on this philosophy, any software can be reverse engineered and have its secrets stolen and protections circumvented. It's just a matter of time.

Like other areas of cybersecurity, both offensive and defensive reverse engineers benefit from having a similar set of skills. This book is designed to provide an introduction to these three interrelated skill sets:

- **Reverse engineering:** Reverse engineering is the process of taking software apart and figuring out how it works.
- **Cracking:** Cracking builds on reverse engineering by manipulating a program's internals to get it to do something that it was not intended to.
- **Defense:** While all software is crackable, defenses can make a program more difficult and time-consuming to crack.

Both offensive and defensive reverse engineers benefit from the same set of skills. Without an understanding of reverse engineering and cracking, a defender can't craft effective protections. On the other hand, an attacker can more effectively bypass and overcome these protections if they can understand and manipulate how a program works.

Structure of the Book

This book is organized based on these three core capabilities and skill sets. The structure is as follows:

PART	TOPICS	GOAL
Part 1: Background	History and legal considerations	Understand x86 and learn to move quickly.
	x86 crash course	

PART	TOPICS	GOAL
Part 2: Software Reverse Engineering	Reconnaissance Key checkers Key generators Process monitoring Resource manipulation Static analysis Dynamic analysis Writing key gens Cracking software	Master the tools, approaches, and mindset required to take software apart and understand its inner workings.
Part 3: Software Cracking	Manual patching Automated patchers Advanced dynamic analysis Execution tracing Advanced static analysis Trial periods Nag screens More key gens More cracks	Master the tools, approaches, and mindset necessary to isolate behavior and modify software.
Part 4: Defenses, Countermeasures, and Advanced Topics	Obfuscation/deobfuscation Anti-debugging/ anti-anti-debugging Packing/unpacking Cryptors/decryptors Architectural defenses Legal Timeless debugging Binary instrumentation Intermediate representations Decompiling Automatic structure recovery Visualization Theorem provers Symbolic analysis Cracking extravaganza	Master defenses and counter-defenses. Evaluate defensive posture and tradeoffs. Explore advanced topics. Exercise reverse engineering and cracking tools, techniques, and mindset.

Hands-On Experience and Labs

The best way to learn reverse engineering and software cracking is by doing it. For this reason, this book will include several hands-on labs that demonstrate the concepts described in the text.

The goal of this book isn't to teach a particular set of tools and techniques. While the focus is on x86 software running in Windows, many of the approaches and techniques will translate to other platforms. This book will attempt to demonstrate a wide range of tools, including open-source, freeware, shareware, and commercial solutions. With an understanding of what tools are available and their relative strengths and weaknesses, you can more effectively select the right tool for the job.

Hands-on labs and exercises will also focus on reverse engineering and cracking a variety of different targets, including the following:

- **Real software:** Some exercises will use real-world software carefully selected to avoid copyright violations.

- **Manufactured examples:** Software written specifically for this book to illustrate concepts that are impractical to demonstrate with real-world examples.

- **Crackmes:** Manufactured software developed by crackers to illustrate a concept or challenge others.

Companion Download Files

The book mentions some additional files, such as labs or tools. These items are available for download from `https://github.com/DazzleCatDuo/X86-SOFTWARE-REVERSE-ENGINEERING-CRACKING-AND-COUNTER-MEASURES`.

History

Before diving into the nitty-gritty details of cracking and reverse engineering, it is useful to understand its history. Software protections and the tricks and techniques used to overcome them have been evolving for decades.

The First Software Protections

The first software copy protections emerged in the 1970s. Some of the early movers in the space were as follows:

- **Apple II:** The Apple II incorporated proprietary disk drivers that would allow writing at half-tracks, writing extra rings, and staggering and overlapping sectors. The purpose of this was to make the disks unusable by non-Apple machines and software that wouldn't know to read and write at these odd offsets.

- **Atari 800:** Atari 800 systems would intentionally include bad sectors in their disks and attempt to load these sectors. If these loads didn't return a "bad sector" error, then the software knew it wasn't a valid disk and would halt execution.

- **Commodore 64:** Legitimate Commodore 64 software was distributed only on read-only disks. The software would attempt to overwrite the disk, and, if it succeeded, it knew the disk was counterfeit.

These protections all depended on unusual behavior by the software, such as the use of invalid memory or attempting to overwrite the program's own code. Defeating these protections required an understanding of how the software worked.

The Rise of Cracking and Reverse Engineering

The rise of cracking and reverse engineering began in the 1980s. However, these early crackers weren't in it for the money. Cracking was a contest to determine who could figure out and bypass software protections the quickest.

Over the next several decades, the reverse engineering and cracking scene evolved. These are some of the key dates in the history of reverse engineering:

1987: Fairlight's formation in 1987 by Bacchus defines one of the first operational groups. Fairlight will later come to prominence in FBI crackdowns of the early 2000s. For more historic details visit www.fairlight.to and csdb.dk.

1990: Elliot J. Chikofsky and James H. Cross II defined reverse engineering as "the process of analyzing a subject system to identify the system's components and their interrelationships and to create representations of the system in another form or at a higher level of abstraction. ("Reverse Engineering and Design Recovery: A Taxonomy." *IEEE Software*, Vol. 7, Issue 1, Jan 1990).

1997: Old Red Cracker (handle +ORC) founds the Internet-based High Cracking University (+HCU) to allow everyone to learn about cracking. +ORC released "how to crack" lessons online and authored academic papers. +HCU students had handles that began with an +.

1997–2009: The "warez scene" emerges with groups competing to be the first to release copyrighted material. Insiders (aka "suppliers") provided early access to their groups, "crackers" broke the protections, and "couriers" distributed cracked software to FTP sites. Between 2003 and 2009, approximately 3,164 active groups were on "the scene", competing primarily for pride and bragging rights, not money.

2004: The FBI and other countries begin raids against "the scene". Operation Fastlink (2004) led to the conviction of 60 warez members, and Operation Site Down (2005) took down 25 warez groups.

The arms race between software protections and crackers continues to rage, and reverse engineering is an invaluable skill set on both sides. Crackers need to understand how a program works to manipulate it and bypass defenses. On the defensive side, it's important to understand the latest cracking techniques to develop defenses that protect intellectual property and other sensitive data.

Legal

The best way to learn is by doing. This is why this book includes labs and exercises with real-world software as well as manufactured examples and crackmes. We are not lawyers, and those with concerns should consult a lawyer. We recommend the Electronic Frontier Foundation (www.eff.org). Chapter 15 covers legal topics because we feel it's important for everyone to understand the US-based laws that affect this area. There are two main laws to be aware of: the Copyright Act and the Digital Millennium Copyright Act (DMCA).

The Fair Use Clause of the Copyright Act (Copyright Act, 17 U.S.C. § 107) states that reverse engineering falls under "fair use" when done for "...purposes such as criticism, comment, news reporting, teaching (including multiple copies for classroom use), scholarship, or research. ..." This exception is balanced against "the effect of the use upon the potential market for or value of the copyrighted work." In essence, reverse engineering used for educational purposes is legal if you don't share or sell the cracked software.

In October 2016, the DMCA also added an exception for good faith security research. It states, "accessing a computer program solely for purposes of **good-faith testing**, ...where such activity is carried out in a controlled environment designed to **avoid any harm** to individuals or the public, ...and is not used or maintained in a manner that facilitates copyright infringement."

The software examined in this book and used in exercises was carefully selected to fall under the fair use and DMCA exceptions. If you are planning to reverse engineer and crack software for anything other than self-education, you should consult a lawyer. The legal considerations of reverse engineering will also be explored in greater detail in a later chapter.

Software reverse engineering and cracking have a rich history, and this skill set has both offensive and defensive applications. However, it is important to understand the laws around these disciplines and ensure that your activities fall under the good-faith testing and fair use exemptions.

This book is designed to provide a strong foundation in the skills and tools used for software reverse engineering and cracking. Beginning with the fundamentals, the book will move on through sections on software reverse engineering and cracking to end with an exploration of advanced offensive and defensive techniques.

x86 Software Reverse-Engineering, Cracking, and Counter-Measures

Decompilation and Architecture

An effective reverse engineer or cracker is one who understands the systems they are analyzing. Software is designed to run in a particular environment, and if you don't understand how that environment works, you will struggle to understand the software.

This chapter explores the steps necessary to get started reverse engineering an application. Decompilation is crucial to transforming an application from machine code to something that can be read and understood by humans. To actually analyze the resulting code, it is also necessary to understand the architecture of the computers that it is designed to run on.

Decompilation

Most programmers write using a higher-level programming language like C/C++ or Java, which is designed to be human-readable. However, computers are designed to run machine code, which represents instructions in binary.

Compilation is the process of converting a programming language to machine code. This means *decompilation* would be the process of taking machine code back to the original programming language, recovering the original source code. When available, this is the easiest approach to reverse engineering because source code is designed to be read and interpreted by a human. The majority of this book will focus on the more typical case when decompilation is not possible. But for the purposes of learning, it is important to understand that sometimes you can decompile back to the source code, and when that is an option, you should take it.

When Is Decompilation Useful?

For many programming languages, full decompilation is impossible. These languages build code directly to machine code, and some information, such as variable names, is lost in the process. While some advanced decompilers can build pseudocode for these languages, the process isn't perfect.

However, some programming languages use what's called *just-in-time (JIT) compilation*. When programs written in JIT languages are "built," they are converted from the source code into an *intermediate language (IL)*, not machine code. JIT compilers store a copy of the code in this IL until the program is run, at which point the code is converted to machine code. Examples of JIT languages include Java, Dalvik (Android), and .NET.

For example, Java is well-known for being largely platform-agnostic, and the reason for this is its use of an IL (Java bytecode) and the Java Virtual Machine (JVM). By distributing the program code as bytecode and compiling it only at runtime, Java's JVM translates from the Java IL to machine code specific to the machine it's running on. While this approach can negatively impact file size and performance, it pays off in portability.

JIT compilation also makes reverse engineering these applications much easier. These intermediate languages are similar enough to the original source code that they can be decompiled or converted back into usable source code. Source code is designed to be human-readable, making it far easier to understand the application's logic and identify software protections or other embedded secrets.

Decompiling JIT Programming Languages

For JIT languages like .NET, several free decompilers are available. One widely used .NET decompiler is JetBrains dotPeek, which is available from www.jet brains.com/decompiler. Figure 1.1 shows an example of .NET code decompiled in dotPeek.

As shown in the figure, the .NET code is easily readable after decompilation because the intermediate language encodes a wealth of information as metadata, enabling more accurate reconstruction of the source code. Any sensitive information or trade secrets contained within the code are easily accessible to a reverse engineer.

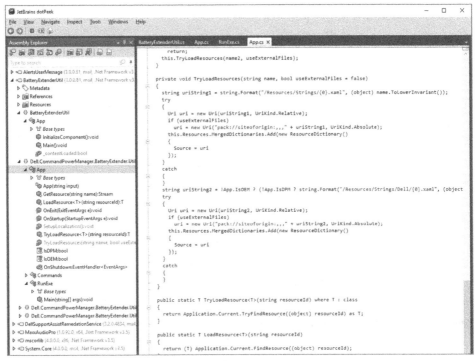

Figure 1.1: JetBrains dotPeek .NET decompiler

Defending JIT Languages

Unlike true machine code programs, JIT-compiled programs can often be converted to source code. Lowering the bar for reverse engineering the code makes many of the x86 anti-reverse engineering defenses discussed in later chapters unnecessary and overkill.

For decompilable languages, a commonly used defense against reverse engineering is obfuscation. Figure 1.2 shows an example of a .NET application before and after obfuscation.

The top half of the figure contains code before obfuscation occurs, where the function and variable names and strings are easily readable. The information in these variable names makes it easier for a reverse engineer to understand the purpose of each function and how the application works as a whole.

In the bottom half of the image, we see the obfuscated version of the same code. Now, function names, variable names, and strings are all mangled, making it much harder to understand the purpose of the function shown, let alone the application as a whole.

Another important security best practice is to avoid writing security or privacy-critical code in JIT languages where reverse engineering is easy. Instead, write

Figure 1.2: Obfuscation in JetBrains dotPeek

this code in an assembled language, such as C/C++, where reverse engineering is significantly more difficult. This code can be included in DLLs that are linked to the executable containing the nonsensitive code written in a JIT language.

Lab 1: Decompiling

This is the first hands-on lab for this book. Labs and all associated instructions can be found in their corresponding folder here:

```
https://github.com/DazzleCatDuo/X86-SOFTWARE-REVERSE-ENGINEERING-
CRACKING-AND-COUNTER-MEASURES
```

For this lab, please locate Lab Decompiling and follow the provided instructions.

Skills to Practice

Every lab in this book is designed to teach and provide hands-on experience with certain skills. This lab's skills to practice include the following:

- Decompiling
- Performing introductory reverse engineering

To learn these skills, you'll be using JetBrains dotPeek to reverse engineer and modify a .NET application.

Takeaways

Decompiling is a powerful and easy approach to understanding and modifying a program. However, it doesn't work on every program. While programs written in languages such as C/C++ can be decompiled using tools such as IDA's Hex-Rays Decompiler or Ghidra, the result is often low-quality and difficult to use.

When developing applications that contain sensitive information or that you don't want modified, it's better to use a language that isn't easily decompiled. For example, C/C++ is a better choice for sensitive functionality than a .NET language such as C#.

Architecture

Decompilation is the easy approach to reverse engineering because it gets you back to higher-level languages and logic structures. However, this easy path is not often available. For languages that build to machine code, we need to go deeper and understand how computer architectures and machine and assembly code work.

Computer Architecture

It's generally thought that the average programmer doesn't need an in-depth understanding of how computers work. When writing a program in a procedural language, the operating system handles all of the low-level operations. A program is displayed as a process that has access to the processor, memory, and file system whenever it needs them. Processes appear to have their own contiguous memory spaces, and files are just a sequence of bytes to read and write.

However, none of this is actually true, and your operating system has been abstracting the truth from you (to make it easier to program). A solid understanding of how computer architecture actually works is essential for a reverse engineer. Figure 1.3 shows the main components that make up a computer, including the central processing unit, bridge, memory, and peripherals.

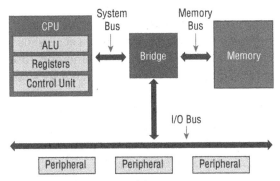

Figure 1.3: Computer architecture

The Central Processing Unit

The *central processing unit (CPU)* is where processing occurs on a computer. Inside the CPU are the following components:

- **Arithmetic logic unit (ALU):** The ALU performs mathematical operations within the computer, such as addition and multiplication.

- **Registers:** Registers perform temporary data storage and are used as the primary inputs and outputs of x86 instructions. Registers provide extremely fast access to a single word of data and are typically accessed by name.

- **Control units:** Control units execute code. This includes reading instructions and orchestrating the operations of other elements within a computer.

Bridges and Peripherals

The CPU is connected via a *bus* to a *bridge*. The purpose of the bridge is to connect the CPU to other components of the system, including memory and the *I/O bus*, which is where peripherals such as the keyboard, mouse, and speakers are connected to the system. While information flows over a bus, the bridge is responsible for controlling this traffic and ensuring that traffic flowing in over one bus is routed out over the appropriate bus.

Peripherals, connected via the I/O bus, allow the computer to communicate with the outside world. This includes sending and receiving data from the graphics card, keyboard, mouse, speakers, and other systems.

Memory and Registers

As its name suggests, *memory* is where data is stored on the computer. Data is stored as a linear series of bytes that are accessed via their address. This design allows moderately fast access to data stored on the system.

When a program wants to access data in memory, the CPU sends a request via a bus to the bridge, which forwards it to the memory, where the data at the indicated address is accessed. The requested data then needs to retrace that route and return to the CPU before it can be used by the program. In contrast, a register is physically located within the CPU, making it far more accessible.

Registers are storage that lives inside of the CPU and, unlike memory, are not a linear series of bytes. Registers are specifically named and have set sizes associated with each.

Registers and memory both serve the same purpose: they store data. However, they have different specializations (quality versus quantity). Registers are few in number and expensive, but they provide extremely fast access to data. Memory is cheap and plentiful but offers slower access speeds.

The bulk of the data associated with a program, the code itself and its data, will be stored in memory. While the program is running, small chunks of data will be copied to the registers for processing.

Assembly

Computers run on binary, digital logic. Everything is either on (1) or off (0). This includes programs running on a computer. All high-level languages are eventually converted into a series of bits called *machine code*. This machine code defines the set of instructions that the computer executes to perform a desired function.

Introduction to Machine Code

Every programmer begins learning a language with a "hello world" program. In x86, the machine code for "hello world" is as follows:

```
55 89 e5 83 e4 f0 83 ec 10 b8 b0 84 04 08 89 04 24 e8 1a ff ff ff b8 00
00 00 00 c9 c3 90
```

This machine code is written in hexadecimal for readability and compactness, but its true value is a binary string of 1s and 0s. This binary string contains instructions to flip transistors to calculate information, fetch data from memory, send signals over the system buses, interact with the graphics card, and, finally, print out the "hello world" text. If this string of characters seems a bit short to accomplish all this, it's because these instructions trigger the operating system (in this example Linux) to help out.

Machine code controls the processor at the most detailed possible level. Some of the functions that machine code performs include the following:

- Moving data in and out of memory
- Moving data to and out of registers
- Controlling the system bus
- Controlling the ALU, control unit, and other components

This low-level control means that applications written in machine code can be incredibly powerful and efficient. However, while memorizing and inputting various series of bits to perform certain tasks is pretty awesome, it is inefficient and prone to error.

From Machine Code to Assembly

In machine code, a series of bits represents a particular action. For example, 0x81 or 10000001 is an instruction that adds two values together and stores the result at a particular location.

Assembly code is designed to be a human-readable version of machine code. Instead of memorizing a binary or hexadecimal string like 0x81 or 10000001, a programmer can use add. The add mnemonic is mapped to 0x81, so this shorthand makes programming easier without losing any of the benefits of writing in machine code.

Translating machine code to assembly code makes it much easier to understand. For example, the previous "hello world" example code can be converted into a series of comprehensible instructions.

MACHINE CODE	ASSEMBLY
55	push ebp
89 e5	mov ebp,esp
83 e4 f0	and esp, 0xfffffff0
83 ec 10	sub esp, 0x10
b8 b0 84 04 08	mov eax
89 04 24	mov [esp], eax
e8 1a ff ff ff	call 80482f4
b8 00 00 00 00	mov eax, 0x0
c9	leave
c3	ret
90	nop

If you understand machine code, writing directly in it can be fun, and there are cases where it may make sense. However, the majority of the time, it is inefficient and impractical. Writing in assembly provides the same benefits as writing in machine code but is much more practical.

After code has been written in assembly, it can be translated to machine code by an *assembler* in a process called *assembling*. A program already in machine code can be disassembled into assembly code by a disassembler.

DEFINITION

Assemblers convert assembly code to machine code. Disassemblers convert machine code to assembly.

Many programmers don't write in machine code or assembly. Instead, they use higher-level languages that abstract away more of the details. For example, the following pseudocode is similar to many high-level procedural languages.

```
int x=1, y=2, z=x+y;
```

During the compiling process, these higher-level languages are converted into assembly code similar to the following:

```
mov    [ebp-4], 0x1
mov    [ebp-8], 0x2
mov    eax, [ebp-8]
mov    edx, [ebp-4]
lea    eax, [edx+1*eax]
mov    [ebp-0xc], eax
```

An assembler can then be used to convert the assembly code into the following machine code that a computer can use:

```
c7 45 fc 01 00 00 00 c7 45 f8 02 00 00 00 8b 45 f8 8b 55 fc 8d 04 02
89 45 f4
```

Instruction Set Architectures and Microarchitectures

The word *computer* covers a wide range of systems. A smartwatch and a desktop computer both work in similar ways. However, their internal components can differ significantly.

An *instruction set architecture (ISA)* describes the ecosystems where programs run. Some of the factors that an ISA defines include the following:

- **Registers:** The ISA specifies whether a processor has a single register or hundreds. It also defines the size of these registers, whether they contain 8 bits or 128 bits.

- **Addresses and data formats:** The ISA specifies the format for addresses used to access data in memory. It also defines how many bytes the system can grab from memory at a time.

- **Machine instructions:** Different ISAs may support different sets of instructions. The ISA defines whether addition, subtraction, equality, halt, and other instructions are supported.

By defining the capabilities of the physical system, the ISA also indirectly defines the assembly language. The ISA specifies which low-level instructions are available and what those instructions do.

A microarchitecture describes how a particular ISA is implemented on a processor. Figure 1.4 shows an example of the Intel Core 2 architecture.

Together, an ISA and microarchitecture define the *computer architecture*. The existence of thousands of ISA and thousands of microarchitectures means that there are thousands of computer architectures as well.

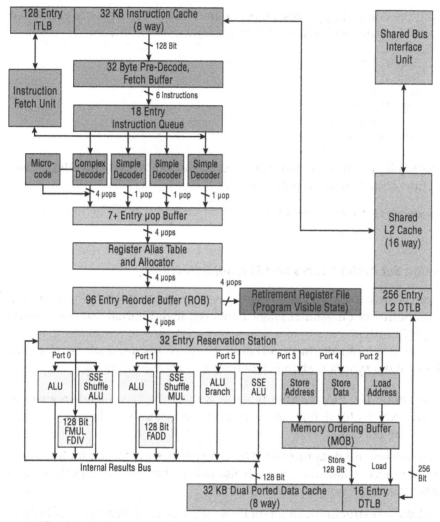

Intel Core 2 Architecture

Figure 1.4: Intel Core 2 architecture

DEFINITION

An instruction set architecture defines how registers, addresses, data formats, and machine instructions work. Microarchitectures implement ISAs on a processor. Together, an ISA and microarchitecture define a computer architecture.

RISC vs. CISC Computer Architectures

While thousands of computer architectures exist, they can be broadly divided into two main categories. Reduced instruction set computing (RISC) architectures define a small number of simpler instructions. In general, RISC architectures are cheaper and easier to create, and the hardware is physically smaller and consumes less power.

In contrast, a complex instruction set computing (CISC) architecture defines a larger number of more powerful instructions. CISC processors are more expensive and difficult to create and are typically larger and consume more power.

While CISC architectures may seem objectively worse than RISC ones, their main benefit lies in the ease and efficiency of programming. For example, consider a hypothetical example where a program wants to multiply a value by 5 in a RISC versus CISC system.

CISC	RISC
mul [100], 5	load r0, 100
	mov r1, r0
	add r1, r0
	add r1, r0
	add r1, r0
	add r1, r0
	mov [100], r1

In this example, a CISC processor can perform the calculation in a single instruction if it has a multiplication operation that can load a value from memory, multiply it, and store the result at the same memory location. However, a RISC processor may lack a multiplication operator because it is a complex operation. Instead, the RISC loads the value from memory, adds it to itself four times, and stores the result in the same memory location across seven steps.

RISC and CISC architectures both have their advantages, disadvantages, and use cases. For example, a RISC operator may take 100 instructions to perform the same operation that a CISC operator can perform in one. However, that single CISC operation may take 100× as long to run or 100× the power.

Both RISC and CISC instruction sets are in common use today. Some examples of widely used RISC architectures include the following:

- ARM (used by phones, tablets)
- MIPS (used by embedded systems and networking equipment)
- PowerPC (used by original Macs and Xbox360)

In this book, we focus on the x86 assembly language, which is a CISC architecture. This architecture is in use on all modern PCs and servers and is supported by all the main operating systems (Windows, Mac, Linux) and even some gaming systems, such as the Xbox One. Making it one of the most powerful to learn for software cracking.

Summary

The machine code that actually runs on computers isn't designed for humans to read and understand. To be usable, it needs to be converted into a different form.

One option for this is decompilation, which produces a result that is similar or identical to the original source code. However, decompilation is not always possible.

For fully compiled languages, such as C/C++ , and many other languages, it is necessary to disassemble a compiled executable and analyze it in assembly. However, this requires a much deeper understanding of the computer's architecture and how it actually works than writing and reading code in a higher-level language. Now that we know the role decompilation can play and the need for disassembly, in the next few chapters we'll look at how computers work, so we can learn to disassemble like a pro.

x86 Assembly: Data, Modes, Registers, and Memory Access

Most software reverse engineering requires disassembling a compiled executable and analyzing the result. This disassembly results in assembly code, not a higher-level language.

While a few assembly languages exist, x86 is one of the most widely used. This chapter introduces some of the key concepts of x86 assembly, providing a foundation for later chapters.

Introduction to x86

Thousands of computer architectures exist. While they all work similarly, a computer is a computer—but there are minor or major differences between each.

To study reverse engineering, we need to select an architecture to focus on. In this book, we'll be using x86, which was selected for a few different reasons:

- **Ubiquity:** x86 is the most widely used assembly language, making it widely applicable for reverse engineering.

- **Computer support:** x86 applications can be built, run, and reverse engineered on any desktop, laptop, or server.

- **Market share:** x86 is the core of the major operating systems (Windows, Linux, and macOS), so it is used in billions of systems.

The x86 architecture has been around for decades and has evolved significantly over the years. It was first introduced in 1974 by Intel, and some of the main milestones in the history of x86 include the following:

- **Intel 8080:** 8-bit microprocessor, introduced in 1974
- **Intel 8086:** 16-bit microprocessor, introduced in 1978
- **Intel 80386:** 32-bit microprocessor, introduced in 1985
- **Intel Prescott, AMD Opteron, and Athlon 64:** 64-bit microprocessor, introduced in 2003/2004

Over its nearly 50-year history, the x86 architecture has regularly added new features while maintaining backward compatibility. Even if a feature was determined to be unused, it was never removed from the system. As a result, programs written for the Intel 8086 processor released in 1978 can still run on the latest x86 chips with no modifications.

This focus on backward compatibility has created an immense, complex, and interesting architecture. The latest Intel Software Developer's manual (www .intel.com/content/www/us/en/developer/articles/technical/intel-sdm .html) is more than 5,000 pages long and only begins to scratch the surface of what this architecture can do. This book focuses on understanding the basics of x86, which is all that is needed to read, write, and manipulate most x86 code.

As the x86 architecture has changed, the term *x86* has become an umbrella term for all of the architectures that have evolved from the Intel 8086 16-bit architecture. This includes the Intel 80286 architecture, which contains both 16-bit and 32-bit architectures, and the Intel 80886 architecture, which adds a 64-bit architecture. The term *x64* specifically refers to the 64-bit version of x86.

This book will show examples in 32-bit x86 architecture. All of the concepts from 32-bit x86 translate exactly to x64. It is substantially easier to work on examples in 32 bits versus 64 as you're learning. After studying 32-bit x86 throughout this book, you will be immediately able to look at x64-bit assembly and understand it. However, your eyeballs will be thanking you for not having to look at 64 bits all the time, as even 32 bits are a bit painful to stare at. So, do not let the examples being in 32-bit give you pause that this is outdated or that you should focus on 64-bit out of the gate. Both of us learned 32-bit first, and we've taught software cracking a lot and can confidently say that if you give yourself the solid 32-bit foundation first, 64-bit becomes just another few register names and longer values.

Assembly Syntax

Selecting x86 from the thousands of possible computer architectures is important, but it isn't enough. While an instruction set architecture (ISA) defines factors such as the registers, data format, and machine instructions, it doesn't specify the syntax.

As long as an assembly language follows all of the rules for registers, addressing, etc., and defines the right set of instructions, it's a valid x86 language. For example, an x86 language must have a multiply operation. However, its mnemonic could be mul, MUL, multiply, or any other variation across any language.

The syntax of an assembly language is entirely defined by the assembler. There is no standard syntax for assembly language in general or for x86 assembly in particular. As a result, there are hundreds of different variations.

However, there are two prevalent x86 syntax options that you will find most x86 assembly tools use: AT&T syntax and Intel syntax. Under each of these main branches are hundreds of assembler-specific variations.

While Intel and AT&T assembly are both x86, they look very different. For example, consider a statement designed to move the memory at address ebx+4*ecx+2020 into register eax.

This instruction looks very different in the Intel and AT&T syntaxes:

INTEL SYNTAX	AT&T SYNTAX
mov eax, [ebx+4*ecx+2020]	mov 0x7e4(%ebx,%ecx,4),%eax

In the Intel syntax, after the instruction mov comes the location where the result will be stored. Memory access is indicated by square brackets, and the calculation of the memory address [ebx+4*ecx+2020] is performed within these brackets.

AT&T syntax differs from Intel syntax in a few ways:

- **Ordering:** The arguments are swapped, so the destination location is listed second.

- **Registers:** AT&T indicates registers using a percent sign (%), while Intel does not.

- **Memory Access:** AT&T uses parentheses to indicate memory access, while Intel uses brackets.

- **Calculation:** The calculation of the desired memory address looks very different in AT&T and Intel syntax.

- **Instructions:** While not shown here, AT&T often uses different, longer instruction mnemonics than Intel.

For clarity and consistency, the Intel syntax was chosen for the examples in this book. These are some of the reasons for selecting Intel over AT&T:

- **Intel support:** Intel is the dominant processor developer, and they use Intel syntax.

- **Tool usage:** Most major reverse engineering tools, such as IDA, use the Intel syntax.

- **Readability:** Intel syntax is widely considered cleaner and easier to read and write than AT&T syntax.

Data Representation

Unlike humans, computers run on binary, so most reverse engineering tools don't display numbers in a base-10 system. To understand what an application is doing, it's necessary to understand the data it's processing and how that data may be represented.

Number System Bases

A *base* within a numbering system defines the number of symbols used to represent the value of a digit. Most humans perform math in base 10, which uses the symbols 0, 1, 2, 3, 4, 5, 6, 7, 8, and 9.

However, this is not the only option. It's possible to use any base as long as you have enough symbols to represent the values. For example, base 5 uses the symbols 0–5, and base 8, also known as *octal*, uses the symbols 0–7.

> **TIP**   The base that a number is written in may be indicated by a subscript. For example, 10_{10} is written in base 10, while 10_2 is a binary (base 2) number.

For bases greater than 10, letters are also used as symbols. For example, base 11 would add the letter a and use the symbols 0, 1, 2, 3, 4, 5, 6, 7, 8, 9, and a. Base 16, also known as *hexadecimal*, uses the symbols 0, 1, 2, 3, 4, 5, 6, 7, 8, 9, a, b, c, d, e, and f.

> **TIP**   In base 16 or hexadecimal, case is irrelevant, so a and A are both equivalent to the value 10 in base 10.

In every base, we need the ability to represent values larger than the base number. To do this, we use multiple digits. For example, counting in base 10 goes . . . 8, 9, 10, 11, . . ., 98, 99, 100, 101, ... In base 16, counting goes . . . 8, 9, a, b, c, d, e, f, 10, 11, . . . 19, 1a, . . . 1f, 20, ...

Computers are binary systems and perform all of their data storage and processing using 1s and 0s. However, these are inefficient and quickly become cumbersome to write. For example, the value 2014_{10} is equal to 11111011110_2.

While computers work with binary, values will often be displayed by tools in hexadecimal or "hex" for readability. Values written in hex may be indicated by a subscript ($1d_{16}$), prefixed with 0x (0x1d), or suffixed with h (1dh).

One advantage of hexadecimal (base 16) is that hexadecimal is a power of 2. This means that values can be converted easily between binary and hexadecimal via character substitution. Figure 2.1 shows how each hexadecimal symbol maps to base 10 and base 2 (binary).

$$0_{10} = 0000_2 = 0_{16} \qquad 8_{10} = 1000_2 = 8_{16}$$
$$1_{10} = 0001_2 = 1_{16} \qquad 9_{10} = 1001_2 = 9_{16}$$
$$2_{10} = 0010_2 = 2_{16} \qquad 10_{10} = 1010_2 = A_{16}$$
$$3_{10} = 0011_2 = 3_{16} \qquad 11_{10} = 1011_2 = B_{16}$$
$$4_{10} = 0100_2 = 4_{16} \qquad 12_{10} = 1100_2 = C_{16}$$
$$5_{10} = 0101_2 = 5_{16} \qquad 13_{10} = 1101_2 = D_{16}$$
$$6_{10} = 0110_2 = 6_{16} \qquad 14_{10} = 1110_2 = E_{16}$$
$$7_{10} = 0111_2 = 7_{16} \qquad 15_{10} = 1111_2 = F_{16}$$

Figure 2.1: Hexadecimal

For example, consider the binary value 11111011110_2. Each hexadecimal digit represents four binary digits, so this value can be broken up into three chunks starting from the right: 111, 1101, and 1110. From the figure, we see that these chunks are equal to the hex digits 7, d, and e, and the entire value can be represented as 0x7de.

111110111102	Binary number
111 1101 11102	Broken up into 4-bit nibbles from right to left
7 d e	Each nibble is translated to hex
0x7de	The resulting hex value

While these conversions can be performed by hand, it's often faster and more accurate to use a tool. Figure 2.2 shows an example of performing base conversions using the Windows calculator.

Bits, Bytes, and Words

Bits are the base unit used by computers. However, they are too small to provide much utility. Instead of accessing and processing individual bits, computers use bytes as their smallest unit of memory. A *byte* contains 8 bits on all modern systems.

While bytes are larger than bits, they're also too small for many operations. Computers are designed to optimally access a certain number of bytes at a time. This number of bytes is referred to as a *word*, is usually a power of 2, and can vary across computers. For example, microcontrollers have small word sizes, often using words containing 1 or 2 bytes (8 or 16 bits). On general-purpose computers, the word size is usually 4 or 8 bytes (32 or 64 bits).

Bits, bytes, and words are the most important terms to know when working with memory, but they aren't the only ones. A complete list of common terms is as follows:

- **Bit:** Binary digit, a 0 or 1
- **Byte:** 8 bits

- **Nibble:** 4 bits
- **Double-byte:** 16 bits
- **Quad-byte:** 32 bits
- **Word:** Architecture-dependent, some number of bytes
- **Halfword:** Half a word
- **Doubleword (DWORD):** Two words
- **Quadword (QWORD):** Four words
- **Octoword, double quadword (DQWORD):** Eight words

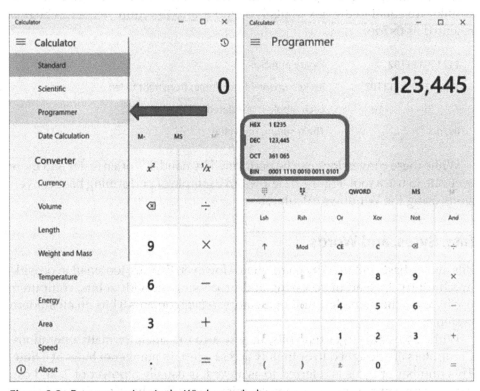

Figure 2.2: Base conversions in the Windows calculator

This book focuses on 32-bit architecture. In a traditional 32-bit architecture, that would dictate that a word is 32 bits. But this is a quirk of the x86 architecture. Because x86 has maintained its backward compatibility with the original 16-bit architecture, a word on x86 is 16 bits, and a double word is 32 bits.

> **TIP**   In 32-bit x86, a byte is 8 bits, and a doubleword is 32 bits.

Working with Binary Values

Reverse engineering commonly involves working with large binary numbers that span multiple different bytes. When working with these numbers, understanding concepts such as zero-extension, bit and byte significance, and endianness is necessary to correctly interpret the number that a binary string represents.

Zero-Extension and Readability

Binary values are commonly *zero-padded* or *zero-extended* to the word size of the architecture. On a 32-bit architecture, this means adding 0s to the left of the value until it is 32 bits long. For example, the value 11001_2 would be zero-padded to 00000000 00000000 00000000 00011001_2.

Note that the bits are also broken into groups of four or eight to improve readability. This is just like commas are sometimes added every three digits in base 10 (i.e., 1,000 instead of 1000). When values are written in hexadecimal, they are also grouped by bytes with two characters per byte. For example, the value $4D2_{16}$ (equivalent to 1234_{10}) can be written as 04_{16} $D2_{16}$.

Bit and Byte Significance

The bits and bytes within a binary number may be labeled based on their relative weight in a number. Figure 2.3 illustrates some of these common labels.

Figure 2.3: Bit and byte significance labels

In the value 00000000 00000000 00000000 00011001_2, the least significant bit (LSB) is the one at the far right, which has a value of 1. The most significant bit (MSB) is at the far left and has a value of 0. When converting from binary to base 10, the MSB will be multiplied by 2^{31}, while the LSB will be multiplied by 2^0.

In addition to MSBs and LSB, there are also the concepts of the least and most significant bytes. In the value 00000000 00000000 00000000 00011001_2, the least significant byte has a value of 00011001_2, while the most significant byte has a value of 00000000_2.

Bits and bytes may also be labeled based on their proximity to the ends of the value. For example, bits and bytes near the LSB are said to be low-order, while bits and bytes near the MSB are high-order.

Endianness

In memory, data is stored in bytes. However, many data types use multiple bytes. For example, an int is 32 bits or 4 bytes.

Endianness describes the order that these bytes are stored in memory. In a *little-endian* system, the least significant byte is stored first (at the lowest address). In a *big-endian* system, the most significant byte is stored first (at the lowest address).

For example, consider the value 1337_{10}, which is 0000 0000 0000 0000 0000 0101 0011 1001$_2$ in binary or 0x00000539 in hex. Figure 2.4 shows how these values would be stored in memory.

Address	1828	1829	1830	1831
Little Endian	0x39	0x05	0x00	0x00
Big Endian	0x00	0x00	0x05	0x39

Figure 2.4: Endianness

DEFINITION

In a *little-endian* system, the least significant byte is located at the smallest address. In a *big-endian* system, the most significant byte is at the smallest address.

Regardless of the endianness of the system, the address associated with a variable is the lowest address used or *base address*. In both a little and big-endian system, this would be address 1828 in this example.

This book focuses on the x86 architecture, which is little endian. As a result, the least significant byte of a chunk of data will be located at offset 0 from the base address. You'll notice that this looks "backwards" to humans, as we read and write in big endian.

TIP   x86 is a little-endian architecture, so the lowest address contains the least significant bit.

Registers

Registers provide the processor with high-speed access to data. Since registers are physically located within the CPU, they have much lower latency than memory, where requests must traverse buses and bridges to access data.

In a 32-bit architecture, a register contains 32-bits of data and can be treated like a variable in a program. Each register has a unique name, and the data within a register can be modified based on computations or loading new values from memory.

The main limitation of registers is that they are limited in number and must be shared by the whole program. If a program runs out of registers, it needs to start storing information in memory, which negatively impacts performance. With a limited number of registers, the normal execution cycle is as follows:

- Fetch data from memory and store it in registers
- Work with data
- Save data back to memory
- Repeat

Registers in x86

As we've mentioned before in the architecture overview, registers are special names and places in the CPU that allow for very fast operations. All registers can be thought of in two distinct categories.

- **General-purpose registers (GPRs):** Used for general storing data, addresses, etc., and are directly manipulable
- **Special-purpose registers (SPRs):** Used to store the program state

The x86 architecture defines numerous registers, which are shown in Figure 2.5. However, many of those are reserved for use by the CPU itself, making it necessary to know only a subset of them.

Figure 2.5 x86 registers

Source: Liam McSherry/ wikimedia Commons /CC BY-SA 3.0.

x86 General-Purpose Registers

GPRs perform most of the heavy lifting within an application, storing values fetched from memory, doing data manipulations, and storing the results of calculations. The following GPRs are the most significant ones in x86, and each can store 32 bits of data. Each accumulator has a role that it is traditionally used for and that it is named after; however, GPRs can be used for any purpose, and you can put a counter in any register, not just the ecx register.

eax

eax is the "accumulator" register. Its name comes from the fact that it is commonly used to hold the result of an arithmetic operation. For example, a program may perform the calculation eax += ebx.

ebx

ebx is the "base" register. It is commonly used to hold the base address of the chunk of memory used to store a variable. For example, the expression [ebx + 5] can be used to access the fifth element of an array.

ecx

ecx is the "counter" register and is traditionally used to count. For example, ecx might be used to track the current iteration of a loop. In the command for (i=0; i<10; i++), the variable i is likely to be stored in the ecx register.

edx

edx is the "data" register. Its name comes from the fact that it is commonly used to hold data. For example, an application may include the instruction sub edx, 7.

esi

esi is the "source index" register. It is traditionally used to store an index into a source array. For example, in the command array[i] = array[k], the value of k would likely be stored in esi.

edi

edi is the "destination index" register. It is used to store an index into a destination array. For example, in the command array[i] = array[k], the value of i would likely be stored in edi.

ebp

ebp is the "base pointer" register. Its purpose is to store the address of the base of the current stack frame. The concepts of the program stack and stack frames will be explored in later chapters.

esp

esp is the "stack pointer" register. It stores the address at the top of the current stack frame.

Special-Purpose Registers

SPRs are designed for specific tasks and are not allowed to be directly modified. For example, the instruction mov eip, 1, which uses an SPR, will not assemble, while mov eax, 1, which uses a GPR, will.

eip

eip is the "instruction pointer" register. It stores the address of the next instruction to execute.

eflags

eflags is the "flags" register. It stores "flags," which have a value of true or false and hold information about the system state and the results of previously executed instructions.

> **TIP** GPRs are both readable and writable, but SPRs are read-only.

Working with Registers

In assembly, GPRs can be treated just like variables and accessed by name. For example, the instruction mov eax, 1 stores the value 1 in *eax*, while add eax, ebx adds the contents of *eax* to *ebx*.

Note that all of these register names begin with the letter e. This is because these 32-bit registers were "extended" from the original 16-bit registers.

The lower half of a register's contents can be accessed by removing this e from the name. For example, the register *ax* contains the low 16 bits of the *eax* register.

If a register's name ends with x (*eax*, *ebx*, *ecx*, and *edx*), this 16-bit register can be further divided into two 8-bit registers, which are identified by l and h. *al* contains the low-order 8 bits of the register *ax*, while *ah* contains the high-order 8 bits. This is illustrated in Figure 2.6, where eax=0x01234567, ax=0x4567, ah=0x45, and al=0x67.

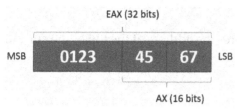

Figure 2.6: Pieces of the eax register

64-Bit Registers

In 64-bit x86, all of the instructions and behavior are the same as 32-bit x86. However, 64-bit architectures have more and larger registers.

Figure 2.7 shows the commonly used registers in 64-bit x86. In addition to the 32-bit registers described differently, 64-bit architectures include eight more registers labeled r8-r15.

All 64-bit registers are also larger than their 32-bit counterparts. For the registers that exist in 32-bit x86, such as *eax*, the full 64-bit counterpart replaces the e with an r, which makes the register *rax*. The lower 32 bits of the register are then accessible using the 32-bit name, and the uses of names such as *ax*, *al*, and *ah* remain unchanged.

For new registers like *r8*, 64-bit x86 allows access to the lower 32, 16, and 8 bits. These are labeled as d (*r8d*), w (*r8w*), and b (*r8b*) respectively, as shown in Figure 2.8.

Memory Access

A 32-bit (or 64-bit) system has only a limited number of registers available. When ignoring the SPRs and GPRs used to track the stack (*esp* and *ebp*), you're left with only six registers available for general computation (*eax, ebx, ecx, edx, esi,* and *edi*). This isn't enough to do much, which is why a program also needs to be able to read and write data to memory.

In Intel x86 assembly syntax, memory access is indicated using [] notation. For example, the data stored at address 0x12345678 can be accessed using [0x12345678]. Memory addresses can also be stored in registers, such as the instruction [eax].

Specifying Data Lengths

When accessing data from memory, it's necessary to not only know the address where the data is located but also how much memory to access. For example, the instruction [0x12345678] doesn't specify whether the program wants a byte, a word, a double word, or more.

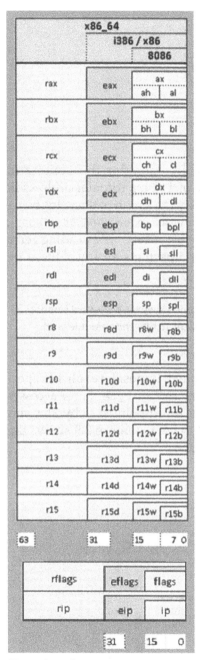

Figure 2.7: Common x64 registers

In some cases, the length of the data being accessed can be inferred from context. For example, in the instruction mov eax, [0x12345678], the data being fetched from memory will be stored in eax. Since eax is a 32-bit register, the program must be requesting 32 bits of data.

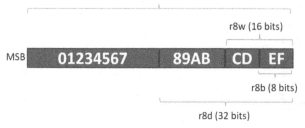

Figure 2.8: Pieces of the r8 register

This is not always the case. For example, consider the command mov [0x12345678], 1, which places a value of 1 at a particular address in memory. However, this instruction doesn't specify the length of the value being set. Should 1 be considered a byte (0000 0001), a word (0000 0000 0000 0001), or a doubleword (0000 0000 0000 0000 0000 0000 0000 0001)? Leading zeros are often trimmed from values for clarity and compactness, so any of these are potentially valid interpretations of moving a 1.

TIP Traditionally, 32-bit x86 should have 32-bit words. However, backward compatibility with 16-bit x86 architectures means that words are 16 bits and a doubleword (dword) is 32 bits.

When the size of a memory access is not implied, it must be explicitly specified within the instruction. For example, the instruction byte [100] accesses the byte at address 100, word[ebx] accesses the word pointed to by *ebx*, and dword[ax] accesses the doubleword pointed to by *ax*. Figure 2.9 shows the difference between the following three instructions.

```
mov byte[100], 1
mov word[100], 1
mov dword[100], 1
```

Address	Value	Address	Value	Address	Value
98	0x00	98	0x00	98	0x00
99	0xff	99	0xff	99	0xff
100	0x01	100	0x01	100	0x01
101	0xfd	101	0x00	101	0x00
102	0x92	102	0x92	102	0x00
103	0xe8	103	0xe8	103	0x00
104	0x42	104	0x42	104	0x42
105	0x13	105	0x13	105	0x13
mov byte [100], 1		mov word [100], 1		mov dword [100], 1	

Figure 2.9: Comparing differently sized mov instructions

Addressing Modes

In Intel x86 syntax, memory addresses are indicated by square brackets. For example, [0x1234] indicates that the program should access the memory located at address 0x1234.

However, memory addressing is not limited to specifying addresses with immediate values like 0x1234. The x86 language supports a few different *addressing modes*. Different addressing modes are used to access different types of variables.

Absolute Addressing

Absolute addressing uses a constant value to specify an address. This constant value can be specified in any base, such as [1] or [0x1234]. It also can be the result of an arithmetic operation, [0x1337 + 0777], or indicated by a label [label].

Example: Global Variables

In C/C++, global variables are intended to be accessible from anywhere within a program. To achieve this, they are stored in memory at a fixed address and do not move as the application moves through various stack frames.

This means that, in assembly, the exact address of the variable will always be known. Therefore, global variables will be accessed using absolute addressing such as mov eax, [0x1000].

Indirect Addressing

Indirect addressing uses registers to specify the address. This includes both 16-bit GPRs, such as [ax], and 32-bit GPRs, such as [eax]. However, 8-bit GPRs (al, bh, etc.) and SPRs can't be used for addressing.

Example: Pointers

Many programming languages use the concept of pointers, some more directly and others hidden behind the scenes. Direct usages and manipulation of pointers are an example of a C/C++ data type that commonly uses indirect addressing. A C program may contain the line int x = 1; int* p = &x; where the pointer *p* is set to point to *x*. If you aren't familiar with C, don't worry; just know that *p* holds the address of where *x* is in memory.

However, the value of *p* may be changed to point to other things, so the address of its target is not fixed. To access the value indicated by *p* in assembly, *p* will first be loaded into a register, and then this register will be used to find the desired value. This is shown in the following x86 instructions:

```
mov ebx, [p]      ; Load the address indicated by p into ebx
mov eax, [ebx]    ; Move the value indicated by p into eax
```

Base + Displacement Addressing

Some variables, such as arrays, are stored in memory using a base address and offsets. Individual values within the array can be accessed using the base address and a displacement.

Base + displacement addressing or *based addressing* uses the combination of a register value and a displacement to indicate an address. This type of mode is often used for access into arrays. So in a language where you might have had *myList[8]*, you're accessing eight elements from the base of *myList*. In assembly, for example, [eax + 8] indicates the eight bytes from the base address of the array, which is stored in eax.

Indexed Addressing

Base + displacement addressing works well if the elements in an array are always a single byte long. For arrays with larger elements, the offset must be computed by hand, which is tedious and prone to error.

In these cases, *indexed addressing* can be a better choice. Indexed addressing uses an index register, a scale factor, and a displacement to specify the address. The scale factor must always be 1, 2, 4, or 8.

Example: Arrays

Let's define an array of integers, int x[100] ;, which declares an array containing 100 ints. In memory, each value in the array is stored at a particular offset from the base address. This offset is determined by the size of the values in the array, such as a 32-bit or 4-byte int.

Assume that the int array was created at offset 0x1000. The following instruction would move the *n*th element of the array into eax if *n* is stored in ebx:

```
mov eax, [ ebx * 4 + 0x1000]
```

Based-Index Addressing

Based-index addressing combines elements of indexed addressing and base + displacement addressing. It uses a base register, an index register, a scale factor (1, 2, 4, or 8), and a displacement for the address.

For example, consider [ebx + edi * 4 + 0x1000]. This address has a base stored in *ebx*, an index stored in *edi*, and a displacement of 0x1000.

Example: Structs

Based-index addressing is ideal for accessing elements of nested data types. For example, consider the C command struct { int i; short a[4]; } s;. This creates a struct containing multiple fields, including an array.

Each element within this struct is located at a particular offset, which means that the array *a* has a certain displacement or base address. However, the elements contained within *a* are also located at different offsets from this base address.

Assume that base address of the struct *s* is stored in *ebx*, and the array *a* is stored 4 bytes from this base address. The following instruction will access the *n*th element within *a* if *n* is stored in *ecx*:

```
mov eax, [ebx + 2 * ecx + 4]
```

Don't get too tripped up if the more advanced addressing is hard to grasp. Your operating system has been hiding memory from you, so it's natural that thinking about how arrays are stored in memory is new territory. These addressing modes need to be introduced as theory first, but they can be hard to grasp before you start to see them in use later in real assembly code. And don't worry, you will.

Summary

x86 is a commonly used assembly language. Understanding how it works is essential to becoming a successful software reverse engineer and cracker.

This chapter explored some of the key concepts of x86 assembly. These include data representation, assembly syntax, and the use of registers and memory addresses for data access and storage.

x86 Assembly: Instructions

Cracking and reverse engineering involve reading, writing, and modifying assembly code. In this book, the focus is on the x86 assembly language.

It isn't necessary to understand every detail of x86 assembly to be a reverse engineer or even to write programs in assembly. This chapter explores the fundamentals of x86 and the main instructions that make up more than 90 percent of assembly code for software.

x86 Instruction Format

Mnemonics are used in x86 assembly to make human-readable assembly code. Each of these mnemonic instructions is assembled into the machine code that controls the processor. So, the processor has no notion of mnemonics, only the machine code. For example, the mnemonic add assembles to the machine code value 0x04.

In x86, instructions are written in a particular format. An example of a simple x86 instruction is:

```
add eax, 1
```

In this instruction, add is the mnemonic used to instruct the processor on what to do. This instruction also includes a couple of operands that indicate the data to be used in this operation. In this case, the operands are the register eax and the value 1. An x86 instruction under normal conditions can have up to three operands if it has any at all. There are special extensions to the language that allow extensions up to four operations (VEX prefix), but we won't be delving into this corner of assembly.

The operands to x86 instructions can be registers, immediates, or memory addresses. Registers are usually the general-purpose registers (GPRs), and memory locations are specified by address. Immediates are numbers or constants like 12345.

While an x86 instruction can include any of these, it can contain a maximum of one memory location. For example, the instructions add eax, ebx and add eax, [0x12345678] are valid because they access two registers and a register and a memory location, respectively. However, the instruction add [0x12345678], [0x87654321] is invalid because it uses two memory addresses at once. This is because the processor pipeline is a delicate design that can perform only one memory fetch per instruction.

x86 Instructions

The x86 assembly language includes hundreds of different instructions. Some of the most commonly used include the following:

- Arithmetic
  - add
  - sub
  - mul
  - inc
  - dec
- Bit Manipulation
  - and
  - or
  - xor
  - not
- Stack
  - call
  - return
  - push
  - pop

- Data movement:
  - `mov`
- Execution flow
  - `jmp`
  - Conditional jumps
- Comparison
  - `test`
  - `cmp`
- Other
  - `lea`
  - `nop`

While this may seem like a lot, consider the common operators used in programming languages (`+`, `-`, `*`, `/`, `%`, `&&`, `||`, `&`, `|`, `^`, `!`, `~`, `<`, `>`, `>=`, `<=`, `==`, `.`, `->`, etc.) and the main keywords (`if`, `else`, `switch`, `while`, `do`, `case`, `break`, `continue`, `for`, etc.). It takes a lot of capability to achieve these behaviors in assembly.

Truthfully, no one knows all of the x86 instructions or has a need to (unless they really want to impress their friends). A complete list of x86 instructions can be found at `http://ref.x86asm.net/coder32.html`, and the details of any instruction can be looked up when needed.

However, a clear understanding of how the most common x86 assembly works is essential to success as a reverse engineer. If you understand this important subset of x86 instructions, you will be able to read and understand most x86 programs.

mov

As its name suggests, the `mov` instruction is designed to move data from one location to another. This includes copying data between registers and memory locations or placing an immediate at a particular location. Note that despite its name being move, it copies data; it does not move it (meaning it is not removed from source; it is rather copied from source to destination).

The syntax of the `mov` instruction is `mov destination, source`. For example, the command `mov eax, 5` places the value 5 in the register `eax`. Similarly, the instruction `mov eax, [1]` moves the value at address `0x1` into `eax`.

When working with `mov` and similar instructions, it is important to recall that the names of the variables used impact the length of the value being moved. For example, the instruction `mov eax, [0x100]` moves a 32-bit value into `eax`, while the instruction `mov dx, [0x100]` moves a 16-bit value into `dx`.

> **NOTE**   An x86 operand can use a register value to indicate a memory address. For
> example, the instruction mov [eax], ebx moves the value stored in ebx into the
> memory location whose address is stored in eax. So, if eax has a value of 0x7777,
> memory address 0x7777 is where the value of ebx is stored.

mov is an extremely versatile operator and a great example of the power of mnemonics versus machine code. mov can be used in a variety of different ways as shown in Figure 3.1, and each of those translates to a different machine code depending which two operands are used. However, all of these different variations are represented as mov at the mnemonic level. It's the assembler's job to translate the mnemonic to the correct machine code.

MOV—Move

Opcode	Instruction	Op/En	64-Bit Mode	Compat/Leg Mode	Description
88 /r	MOV r/m8, r8	MR	Valid	Valid	Move r8 to r/m8.
REX + 88 /r	MOV r/m8[1], r8[1]	MR	Valid	N.E.	Move r8 to r/m8.
89 /r	MOV r/m16, r16	MR	Valid	Valid	Move r16 to r/m16.
89 /r	MOV r/m32, r32	MR	Valid	Valid	Move r32 to r/m32.
REX.W + 89 /r	MOV r/m64, r64	MR	Valid	N.E.	Move r64 to r/m64.
8A /r	MOV r8, r/m8	RM	Valid	Valid	Move r/m8 to r8.
REX + 8A /r	MOV r8[1], r/m8[1]	RM	Valid	N.E.	Move r/m8 to r8.
8B /r	MOV r16, r/m16	RM	Valid	Valid	Move r/m16 to r16.
8B /r	MOV r32, r/m32	RM	Valid	Valid	Move r/m32 to r32.
REX.W + 8B /r	MOV r64, r/m64	RM	Valid	N.E.	Move r/m64 to r64.
8C /r	MOV r/m16, Sreg[2]	MR	Valid	Valid	Move segment register to r/m16.
8C /r	MOV r16/r32/m16, Sreg[2]	MR	Valid	Valid	Move zero extended 16-bit segment register to r16/r32/m16.
REX.W + 8C /r	MOV r64/m16, Sreg[2]	MR	Valid	Valid	Move zero extended 16-bit segment register to r64/m16.
8E /r	MOV Sreg, r/m16[2]	RM	Valid	Valid	Move r/m16 to segment register.
REX.W + 8E /r	MOV Sreg, r/m64[2]	RM	Valid	Valid	Move lower 16 bits of r/m64 to segment register.
A0	MOV AL, moffs8[3]	FD	Valid	Valid	Move byte at (seg:offset) to AL.
REX.W + A0	MOV AL, moffs8[3]	FD	Valid	N.E.	Move byte at (offset) to AL.
A1	MOV AX, moffs16[3]	FD	Valid	Valid	Move word at (seg:offset) to AX.
A1	MOV EAX, moffs32[3]	FD	Valid	Valid	Move doubleword at (seg:offset) to EAX.
REX.W + A1	MOV RAX, moffs64[3]	FD	Valid	N.E.	Move quadword at (offset) to RAX.
A2	MOV moffs8, AL	TD	Valid	Valid	Move AL to (seg:offset).
REX.W + A2	MOV moffs8[1], AL	TD	Valid	N.E.	Move AL to (offset).
A3	MOV moffs16[3], AX	TD	Valid	Valid	Move AX to (seg:offset).
A3	MOV moffs32[3], EAX	TD	Valid	Valid	Move EAX to (seg:offset).
REX.W + A3	MOV moffs64[3], RAX	TD	Valid	N.E.	Move RAX to (offset).
B0+ rb ib	MOV r8, imm8	OI	Valid	Valid	Move imm8 to r8.
REX + B0+ rb ib	MOV r8[1], imm8	OI	Valid	N.E.	Move imm8 to r8.
B8+ rw iw	MOV r16, imm16	OI	Valid	Valid	Move imm16 to r16.
B8+ rd id	MOV r32, imm32	OI	Valid	Valid	Move imm32 to r32.
REX.W + B8+ rd io	MOV r64, imm64	OI	Valid	N.E.	Move imm64 to r64.
C6 /0 ib	MOV r/m8, imm8	MI	Valid	Valid	Move imm8 to r/m8.
REX + C6 /0 ib	MOV r/m8[1], imm8	MI	Valid	N.E.	Move imm8 to r/m8.
C7 /0 iw	MOV r/m16, imm16	MI	Valid	Valid	Move imm16 to r/m16.
C7 /0 id	MOV r/m32, imm32	MI	Valid	Valid	Move imm32 to r/m32.
REX.W + C7 /0 id	MOV r/m64, imm32	MI	Valid	N.E.	Move imm32 sign extended to 64-bits to r/m64.

Figure 3.1: mov instructions

Hands-on Example

How would the following pseudocode be written in assembly? Assume that variable *i* is located at address 100, and *j* is located at address 200.

```
int i = 42, j = i;
```

This single line of pseudocode could be assembled into three x86 instructions.

```
mov [100], 42
mov eax, [100]
mov [200], eax
```

Note that the register eax is used to store the value being copied from memory address 100 to memory address 200. The reason for this is that a single instruction can't perform two different memory accesses. A register, such as eax, must be used for temporary storage.

When looking at the code, it might seem like it would make more sense to load address 200 with the immediate 42 rather than taking two operations to load it from memory address 100. However, a compiler won't and shouldn't do this.

The reason for this is the potential for multithreaded applications. If another thread is running on the system, the value at location 100 may have been updated between the step assigning it a value of 42 and the step assigning its value to location 200. Copying the value from location 100 rather than using an immediate helps to ensure that the variable *j* at location 200 receives the most up-to-date version of the value stored in *i*.

inc, dec

The inc and dec x86 instructions increment or decrement the indicated value by 1, respectively. This is the equivalent of the instructions i++ or i-- in traditional code.

These instructions take a single operand, which can be a register or memory address. For example, the instruction inc eax increases the value stored in eax by 1, while dec [0x12345678] decreases the value stored at memory address 0x12345678 by 1.

add, sub

The add and sub instructions add or subtract value from a specific value, respectively. These instructions accept two operands. For example, an add instruction would be specified as add destination, value.

The *destination* in an add instruction can be a register or memory location, while the *value* can be a register, memory location, or immediate. The operation takes *destination* + *value* and stores the result in *destination*. This means destination's incoming value is relevant to the mathematical expression but is overwritten to save the result. Note that the size of the two operands must be the same. For example, add eax, ebx is a valid instruction (32-bit plus 32-bit), while sub eax, bx is not (32-bit minus 16-bit).

When using add and sub, it is important to consider the sizes of the values being used. For example, the instruction sub ecx, [100] implies a 32-bit value by its use of ecx as the destination. However, the instruction add dword [edx], 100 requires the dword size specifier because the 32-bit value edx indicates that the memory address is 32 bits long but doesn't specify the size of the data being modified at that location.

mul

The mul operation performs unsigned integer multiplication. However, it is a bit unusual because it takes only a single operand but implicitly uses two additional registers. The syntax of a mul operation is mul operand, where operand can be a register or memory address. The operation multiplies the value stored in eax with the value specified in the operand.

The result of a mul operation is stored in edx:eax with edx containing the high 32 bits of the result. The values stored in edx and eax are always modified by mul even if the result is less than 32 bits long and edx is not needed. mul is interesting because you can get a 64-bit output (edx:eax) on 32-bit math.

An example of the mul operation is mul eax, which squares the 32-bit value stored in eax. When operand contains a memory address, the length of the value can vary. For example, mul dword [0x555] multiplies eax by a 32-bit value stored at 0x555, while mul byte [0x123] uses an 8-bit value stored at 0x123 in the multiplication.

div

The div operation performs unsigned division. Like mul, it takes a single operand and modifies the eax and edx registers implicitly. In this case, the quotient is stored in eax, and the remainder is stored in edx. For those in need of a quick math lingo reminder (don't be embarrassed, math buzzwords hurt my brain too) 5 divided by 2 would have a quotient of 2, and a remainder of 1.

The div operation uses both eax and edx for its input and formats them in the same way as mul's output with the high 32 bits contained within edx. As with mul, the output always modifies eax and edx even if edx is not needed (i.e., the remainder is zero).

An example of the div operation is div eax. This is equivalent to the calculation eax, edx = edx:eax / eax. In this case, the operand is a 32-bit register, but memory addresses can indicate and use divisors of different lengths.

Hands-on Example

Assume that you wanted to calculate the remainder of 123/4. This can be accomplished via four assembly instructions.

```
mov eax, 123   ; Load the lower 32 bits of the dividend into eax
mov edx, 0     ; Clear the edx register, which holds the higher 32 bits of
                 the dividend
mov ecx, 4     ; Load the divisor into ecx since div can't take an
                 immediate operand
div ecx        ; Perform the division
```

At the end of this process, the quotient is stored in eax, and the remainder is stored in edx.

and, or, xor

The x86 standard includes support for a few different Boolean operations. The and, or, and xor operations all take two operands. Truth tables for these three operations are shown here. The input options are shown on the top and left edges of the table. For example, to find 1 AND 1, we find the intersection of the 1 column and 1 row, and the result is a 1. So, 1 AND 1 is 1.

AND	1	0	OR	1	0	XOR	1	0
1	1	0	1	1	1	1	0	1
0	0	0	0	1	0	0	1	0

All three operations use the same syntax: mnemonic destination, source. For example, the and operation syntax is and destination, source. Like the add operation, the *destination* must be a register or memory address, while the *source* can be a register, memory address, or immediate. And also like the add operation, the *destination* is used in the calculation but also overwritten to save the result.

Boolean operations can be used for a variety of different purposes. For example, the operation or eax, 0xffffffff is a quick way to set the value of eax to all 1s. The operation and dword [0xdeadbeef], 0x1 masks off everything but the low bit of the 32-bit value at location 0xdeadbeef. The operation xor eax, eax is a common method for clearing the value of eax.

not

The not operation is a Boolean operation that computes the one's complement of a value. For those not familiar with the term *one's complement*, you can essentially think of it as taking all 0s and making them 1s and vice versa. It inverts the number. It takes a single operand with the syntax not operand.

The not operator can work on values of various lengths. For example, the operation not ch computes the one's complement of the 8-bit register ch. The command not dword [2020] computes the one's complement of a 32-bit value located at address 2020.

shr, shl

shr and shl are two of the shift operations available in x86, with shr being shift right, and shl being shift left. They take two operands: the location of the value to be shifted and the amount by which they should be shifted. An example shift operation is shr register, immediate.

shr and shl are logical shift operators. This means that when shifting the value by the indicated immediate value, they will zero-extend the value to the left or right. So, any new digits that appear as a result of the shift will be automatically 0.

For example, the operation shr al, 3 will shift the value stored in al to the right by three bits. If al contains the value 00010000, then the resulting value will be 00000010.

> **TIP**   Zero-extending a right-shifted value will fill empty bits with zeros and is called a *logical shift*. Sign-extending a right-shifted value will fill empty bits with the same value as the most significant bit and is called an *arithmetic shift*.

sar, sal

sar and sal are arithmetic shift operators. Their syntax is identical to that of the logical shifts, but they differ in implementation. sar does an arithmetic shift to the right and sal an arithmetic shift left.

When performing a left shift, sal operates the same as shl, zero-extending the value. For example, the instructions shl al, 3 and sal al, 3 with the value 00000100 stored in al will both produce the value 00100000. All new positions that were opened in the number were filled with 0s.

However, a sar operation will sign-extend the value, while shl will zero-extend it. A sign-extend means it will replicate whatever bit was the most significant. For example, if al contains the value 10000000, then the command shr al, 3 will produce the value 00010000, as shown here:

```
10000000      Initial value
01000000      1-bit shift
00100000      2-bit shift
00010000      3-bit shift
```

However, the instruction sar al, 3 will result in 11110000. Because the most significant bit is a 1, a 1 is replicated in all new positions.

nop

The nop operator stands for "no operation." It is a one-byte operator (0x90) that does nothing.

While nop technically does nothing, it is used for a variety of legitimate purposes, including the following:

- Timing
- Memory alignment
- Hazard prevention
- Branch delay slot (RISC architectures)
- A placeholder to be replaced later by a future patch

And in the security world it is used for the following:

- Hacking (nop sleds)
- Cracking (nop outs)

lea

The lea operator stands for *load effective address*. It takes two operators, including the *destination* (a register or memory address) and the *source*, which must be a memory address. The lea instruction computes the address of the indicated source operand and places it in the destination. For those familiar with pointers, it is similar to the & operator.

While lea is designed to work with addresses, it is also commonly used for simple mathematical operations. For example, the operation lea eax, [ebx + ecx + 5] asks what address ebx+ecx+5 points to and then stores that into eax. This essentially computes ebx + ecx + 5 and stores the result in eax. A more standard use of the lea operator, lea eax, [100], would place the value 100 in eax.

While on the surface this can look a little silly or pointless, lea is a useful operator because it makes working with arrays in assembly more efficient. In arrays, values are stored at a particular offset from a base address. (Remember our base + displacement addressing modes?) With lea, it is possible to efficiently calculate the address of a particular element in an array. For example, assume that eax contains the base address of a character array. In that case, the instruction lea ebx, [eax + 2] would place the address of the second element in the array in ebx. This single instruction is more efficient than the series of instructions mov ebx, eax and add ebx, 2, which accomplishes the same result.

Hands-on Example

How would the following pseudocode be written in assembly? Assume that *i* is at address 100, *j* is at address 200, and *k* is at address 300.

```
int i = 7;
char j = 5;
int k = i + j;
```

This pseudocode would be assembled into the following x86 instructions:

```
mov dword [ 100 ], 7   ; set i
mov byte [ 200 ], 5    ; set j

mov eax, [ 100 ]       ; load i into eax
xor ebx, ebx           ; zero ebx
mov bl, [ 200 ]        ; load j into ebx

add eax, ebx           ; add ebx to eax, store in eax

mov [ 300 ], eax       ; save result to k
```

In this example, note the use of both ebx and bl. The value that was to be stored in this register fits in bl. However, when performing the add operation, the entire ebx register is used. This is because of class promotion, if you add a 1 byte value to a 4 byte value the 1 byte values promoted to 4 bytes, and the additional bytes must be 0. So in this case what was 0x05 in bl, is promoted to 0x00000005 in ebx. The XOR operation to clear ebx was necessary to ensure that the previous value stored in the ebx register was completely purged and did not affect the result of the add.

Putting It All Together

So far, many of the examples have been simple operations using only a couple of x86 operators. Now, try to write assembly code for the following pseudocode, assuming that *i* is at address 100, *j* is at address 200, and *k* is at address 300.

```
int i = 7;
char j = 5;
int k = i * i + j * j;
```

This pseudocode assembles into the following x86 instructions:

```
mov dword [ 100 ], 7   ; set i
mov byte [ 200 ], 5    ; set j

mov ecx, [ 100 ]       ; load i into ecx
xor ebx, ebx           ; zero ebx
```

```
mov bl, [ 200 ]          ; load j into ebx

mov eax, ecx             ; copy ecx into eax (eax = ecx = i)
mul ecx                  ; multiply ecx by eax, store result in eax
mov ecx, eax             ; save result back to ecx to free up eax

mov eax, ebx             ; copy ebx into eax (eax = ebx = j)
mul ebx                  ; multiply ebx by eax, store result in eax

add eax, ecx             ; add ecx to eax, store result in eax
mov [ 300 ], eax         ; save final value to k
```

Common x86 Instruction Mistakes

x86 is a powerful assembly language, and most instructions follow a consistent set of rules. However, it does have its inconsistencies that can trip people up.

Here are some examples of common mistakes that people make when trying to write their own x86 that result in code that will not assemble:

- `mov [bl]` , `0xf`: x86 supports indirect addressing using 16 and 32-bit GPRs. Since `bl` is only 8 bits long, it can't be used for addressing.

- `mov [0xabcd]`, `1337`: This instruction doesn't specify the size of the value to be moved since 1337 may be recorded as `0x0539` or `0x00000539`.

- `mov word [0xabcd]`, `eax`: This instruction has an incorrect memory size specified since a `word` is 16 bits but `eax` holds 32 bits.

- `mov byte [1]`, `byte [2]`: Two memory locations can't be used in the same instruction.

- `mov sl, al`: While `eax` has an `al` register, no `sl` register exists.

- `mov 0x1234`, `eax`: The value `0x1234` is an immediate, not a memory address, and can't be the destination of a command.

- `mov eax, dx`: This instruction has a size mismatch between the 16-bit source `dx` and the 32-bit destination `eax`.

When In Doubt, Look It Up

Remember, nobody (not even me, though that's hard for me to admit) knows all of the x86 instructions by heart. Whether you're writing x86 or reading it, if you encounter something you don't understand, knowing how to look it up quickly is key. We always have this tab open for quick lookups: http://ref
.x86asm.net/coder32.html.

Summary

x86 is a complex, powerful assembly language. However, it isn't necessary to understand every bit of it to be an effective software cracker and reverse engineer.

This chapter covered the x86 instructions that make up the vast majority of assembly code. Learning these instructions is essential and provides a strong foundation for reverse engineering.

Building and Running Assembly Programs

Software reverse engineering is about taking a compiled executable and turning it into human-readable code. However, understanding how to do the opposite, building and running an assembly program, can be invaluable to understanding this process.

This chapter explores some of the key concepts needed to understand how assembly programs are built and run. This includes how these programs interact with the outside world, how to actually build and run them, and how they manage strings.

Output

ANECDOTE

In college, I found out it's pretty fun to go to a thrift store and buy a bunch of broken electronics, tear them apart, and rebuild the pieces into something else. Figure 4.1 is one of the first things I ever built. I really like working with impractical things because thinking and designing and building and learning is fun, but as soon as you start to worry about actual applications and usability, it takes away from the enjoyment. So, I go out of my way to try to work on impractical things.

Figure 4.1: Binary wristwatch

I was trying to think of the most impractical thing that I could make here. This is a binary wristwatch that has to be plugged into a power outlet. I never did find a wristband for it, but I was trying to think of the nerdiest thing I could make, and this seemed pretty nerdy.

Assembly and machine code are great, but at some point your code will want to communicate with the outside world. For that we need a way to output information.

If you've ever looked at a processor, they are covered in little pins. A processor's pins enable the processor to communicate with the outside world. Using assembly, it is possible to control these pins by toggling them on and off, causing effects such as turning LEDs on and off. A modern x86 processor has between 400 and 1,000 pins, making it possible to control a lot of things.

Pins are organized into groups called *ports*. With ports, instead of controlling individual pins, which would be tedious and time-consuming, it is possible to control several at the same time. Setting a value on the pins is equivalent to writing to the port, and getting a value from the pins is reading from the port.

A number of different ports are defined for x86. Table 4.1 shows some examples of a small subset.

Table 4.1: x86 Ports

PORT RANGE	SUMMARY
0x0000-0x001F	The first legacy DMA controller, often used for transfers to floppies
0x0020-0x0021	The first programmable interrupt controller

PORT RANGE	SUMMARY
0x0022-0x0023	Access to the model-specific registers of Cyrix processors.
0x0040-0x0047	The programmable interval timer (PIT)
0x0060-0x0064	The "8042" PS/2 controller or its predecessors
0x0070-0x0071	The CMOS and RTC registers
0x0080-0x008F	The DMA (page registers)
0x0092	The location of the fast A20 gate register
0x00A0-0x00A1	The second PIC
0x00C0-0x00DF	The second DMA controller, often used for sound blasters
0x00E9	Home of the Port E9 hack
0x0170-0x0177	The secondary ATA hard disk controller
0x01F0-0x01F7	The primary ATA hard disk controller
0x0278-0x027A	Parallel port
0x02F8-0x02FF	Second serial port
0x03B0-0x03DF	The range used for the IBM VGA, its direct predecessors
0x03F0-0x03F7	Floppy disk controller
0x03F8-0x03FF	First serial port

Controlling Pins

In x86, pins can be controlled via the in and out instructions, which take a register and a port as parameters.

The syntax of the in instruction is in register, port. For example, in al, 0x64 gets the status of the keyboard.

The out instruction reverses the order of the parameters, with the syntax out port, register. For example, out 0x3c0, eax sets the value of a pixel.

In actuality, you are often not directly hardwired to the destination or source ports, and things are a little more complicated. Pins are attached to a shared bus, and the work of sending reads/writes to the correct destination is offloaded to a separate card or bridge. The in and out instructions access predefined addresses on the bus that the bridge translates. However, the idea is the same.

Tedium

Let's get back to this notion of output: through in and out instructions it is possible to set and unset individual pixels. However, a single display screen can contain thousands or millions of pixels. Setting them individually would be tedious and inefficient.

Instead, these details are abstracted away. When displaying images, the graphics card handles the details of setting each of the individual pixels. However, learning exactly how to communicate with the graphics card can be tedious.

This is where the operating system steps in. It can handle the complexity of interfacing with the graphics card, which sets the pixel values and displays the image. Interacting with the operating system requires a system call. So if you want to play x86 on epic hard mode, you can go down the route of directly interfacing with the graphics card, but for the purposes of this book, we like to play on hard-with-help mode, and we'll leverage the OS to do this heavy lifting for us.

System Calls

System calls are available in x86 to provide limited I/O functionality invoking behavior through the operating system (OS). The sets of available system calls vary depending on the operating system.

Since system calls are a notion of the OS, they are OS-dependent; we will go through some of the more useful system calls in Linux. System calls are invoked by loading a function number into the eax register. In Linux, a system call is then made by invoking an interrupt through the instruction int 0x80.

sys_write

In a higher-level programming language, the sys_write function would have the syntax ssize_t sys_write(unsigned int fd, const char * buf, size_t count). This function will return a size indicating the amount of data written.

The sys_write function takes three arguments. The first, fd, is a file descriptor that indicates where the data should be written. A value of 1 would indicate writing data to the Linux console. The buf argument contains the data to be written as output, and count tells the function the number of characters to print.

In x86 assembly, functions can't be called using this function description. Instead, the arguments would be loaded into registers, as shown in Table 4.2. After loading these registers, the system call can be performed with the int 0x80 instruction.

Table 4.2: sys_write

REGISTER	VALUE	DESCRIPTION
eax	4	sys_write identifier
ebx	1 (console out)	File descriptor
ecx	const char* buf	String to write
edx	size_t count	Length of string

The registers used in the `sys_write` function must be loaded over a series of assembly instructions. The following example shows how `sys_write` could be used:

```
mov    edx,len        ; message length
mov    ecx,buff       ; message to write
mov    ebx,1          ; file descriptor (stdout)
mov    eax,4          ; system function(sys_write)
int    0x80           ; call kernel
```

sys_exit

The `sys_exit` system call is equivalent to your `main` doing a `return status;` in higher-level programming languages. This will cause the program to exit. It takes a single argument, the status code, that is stored in `ebx`, as shown in Table 4.3.

Table 4.3: `sys_exit`

REGISTER	VALUE	DESCRIPTION
eax	1	`sys_exit` identifier
ebx	int	Status code

A call to `sys_exit` begins by loading values into the registers `eax` and `ebx`, as shown in the following example:

```
mov eax, 1            ; system function (sys_exit)
mov ebx, 0            ; return 0;
int 0x80              ; call kernel
```

Printing a String

Printing a string requires turning certain pins on and off on the processor. By making a system call, an assembly program can offload the work of determining which pins to turn on and off to the operating system. The OS informs the graphics card, which selects its bits to turn on and off. This sends information to the monitor microcontroller, causing it to turn its pins on and off, which draws on the screen. Along the way, dozens of other controllers may be involved in the process as well.

An assembly program that prints a string and then exits would use both the `sys_write` and `sys_exit` system calls. We'll get into the overall file syntax in the next section. For now, as a way to get you excited and on the edge of your seat as you read the next section, here's a sneak peek. The following example prints the message "Hello, world!" to the console:

```
global _start

section .text
_start:
    mov eax, 4 ; write
    mov ebx, 1 ; stdout
    mov ecx, msg
    mov edx, msg.len
    int 0x80

    mov eax, 1 ; exit
    mov ebx, 0
    int 0x80

section .data
msg:    db  "Hello, world!", 10
.len:   equ $ - msg
```

Building and Linking

Reverse engineering and cracking are about understanding someone else's existing assembly code. However, you will find that if you do any type of patching/cracking, writing your own assembly and reverse engineering is much easier if you understand how the process works in the other direction, writing, building, and assembling your own assembly code. Building and linking is a crucial step in this process of moving from assembly code to a functional application.

Building and Linking in Linux

The process of building and linking assembly code varies based on the operating system, so this section focuses on Linux. In a Linux environment, we traditionally name assembly files with an .asm extension like program.asm. The program can then be assembled, linked, and executed using the following three commands:

```
nasm -f elf program.asm
ld -melf_i386 program.o -o program.out
./program.out
```

The first of these commands uses the Netwide Assembler, nasm, to assemble the code into an object file. The -f flag specifies the format, which is ELF, a Linux executable file. The output will be an object file named program.o.

The next step in the process is linking, which will use `ld`, the GNU linker. The `-melf_i386` specifies the architecture that should be used for linking and specifies that this should be an ELF binary using i386 (x86). The `-o` flag specifies the output filename, which will be `program.out`.

After linking is complete, the file `program.out` is a fully functional Linux executable. This executable can be run using the command `./program.out`.

Writing an Assembly Program

The previous example demonstrates how to build and link an assembly program in Linux. However, before this can occur, you need to have written a program in assembly! This section covers the core concepts needed to do so.

Sections and Stat

The following example shows the overall structure of an assembly file:

```
section .text ; section for code
global _start ; exports start method
_start:       ; execution starts here

; code here

section .data ; section for data

; variables here
```

An assembly source file is broken up into a couple of main sections. The `.text` section contains the actual assembly code. This section will begin with the command `global _start`, which exports the `_start` label, telling external programs where to begin running your code. After that comes the `_start` label, which indicates the memory address of the first instruction in the program. The remaining code would follow this first instruction.

After the `.text` section is the `.data` section, which contains data that the assembly program will need to run. A common example of data within an assembly program is the variables defined within that program.

Labels

The `_start` label is vital to the function of an assembly program, but it is also possible to define other labels. Including the text `label:` in the code would create a label named `label`, which is a constant value synonymous with that location in memory.

After a label has been defined, it can be used in lieu of a traditional memory address. Labels can be used anywhere a constant or immediate value could be used. The following examples show equivalent instructions with and without labels:

```
mov eax, [ label ]        ; access the dword stored at the label
mov eax, [ 0x1000 ]       ; if the label was on data at address 0x1000,
; this is equivalent to the previous instruction

jmp label2                ; jump to the code at the label2
jmp 1337h                 ; if the label2 was on code at address 1337h,
; this is equivalent to the previous instruction
```

Labels are used only to make assembly code easier to read and write. After the code has been built, the word `label` will be replaced with the equivalent memory address by the assembler and linker.

Constants

Constants make it easier to work with data. So, for example, instead of recalling that the maximum size of a buffer is 1000, it is much easier to define a constant named *MAX_SIZE* with a value of 1000.

Constants can be defined in x86 assembly using the EQU directive. For example, the constant *MAX_SIZE* can be defined with a value of 1000 with the command `MAX_SIZE EQU 1000`.

Global Data

`nasm` makes it possible to declare space for global data of various sizes. Some commands include the following:

- db: Reserve space for one `byte`.
- dw: Reserve space for one `word` (two bytes).
- dd: Reserve space for one `dword` (four bytes).
- dq: Reserve space for one `qword` (eight bytes).

The following example shows some instructions that use these commands to allocate various types of data:

```
db 0x01       ; store the value "1" in a single byte
db 1, 2, 3    ; store the array 1, 2, 3 as 1 byte elements
db 'a'        ; store the ascii value of 'a' in one byte
db "hello", 0 ; store the nul terminated string "hello"
dw 0x1234     ; store 0x1234 as a two byte value
dd 0xdeadbeef ; store 0xdeadbeef as a four byte value
dq 1          ; store 1 as an 8 byte value
```

Storing data in memory provides no benefit unless that data can be accessed later. Typically, when defining global data, a label is assigned to it as well to enable it to be referenced in the code.

The following example shows a simple assembly program that defines space for a dword with value 0, labels it as *i*, and places the value 1 in it.

```
section .text
mov dword [ i ], 1
section .data
i: dd 0
```

In this example, it's important to note that *i* is not a variable, it's a symbol created with a label. The use of *i* in the code is the same as using the memory address of the allocated data.

Strings

A string is defined in assembly as a sequence of bytes, with each character taking up a single byte. For example, the word "hello" can be stored in memory using the command label: db "hello" and referenced in the code as *label*.

When working with strings in assembly, it is important to note that they are not null-terminated by default. To explicitly null terminate the string, add a null (0x0) byte to the end as in label: db "hello", 0. Null termination is used in almost all programming languages to store strings; however, the compiler has been doing this for you. Now that you wield the assembly power, you will need to do it manually, so any functions that use strings will correctly execute. Without a null terminator at the end of a string, string-based functions will continue to grab memory after the intended string and try to use or print it as a character. This has an unpredictable outcome, as benign as printing some unprintable characters, to as severe as crashing a program by trying to pull from memory it doesn't have permission to use.

times

The times prefix can be used to specify that a particular instruction or prefix should be repeated a certain number of times. This can be helpful for creating fixed-length buffers and other applications, as shown in the following examples:

```
times 100 db 0    ; create 100 bytes, initialized to 0

times 64 db 0x55 ; create 64 bytes, each initialized to 55h

; pad "hello world" to a length of 64
buffer: db     'hello, world' times 64-$+buffer db ' '
```

$

$ is shorthand for the address of the current line. It can be used similarly to a label, as shown in the following examples:

```
jmp $                    ; Infinite loop

string: db "hello"
length EQU $-string   ; Calculate length of string on previous line
```

In this example, *length* is an example of a variable name. The value of *length* is set to the current address ($) minus the address indicated by the label *string*. Since *length* sits right after the string, that effectively takes the address after "hello" and subtracts the address at the start, giving you a length of the string "hello".

> **NOTE**   Prefixes like *times* and *$* are specific to *nasm* and will not show up in the built code. Different assemblers may have different shortcuts.

objdump

Tools like nasm and ld are used to create an executable from assembly code. Object Dump (objdump) is a Linux tool that reverses this process, taking an executable and dumping its assembly code. While we will introduce increasingly stronger tools as we progress through the book, we're starting with objdump because it's on every Linux-based system and provides a good foundation.

objdump can dump the assembly code of any application running on Linux. As a result, it has a number of possible configuration options. But the two most important when getting started with reverse engineering include the following:

- ▪ -d: Instructs objdump to disassemble the content of all sections
- ▪ -Mintel: Specifies that the assembly output should be shown in Intel syntax (sadly, it uses AT&T by default)

Taking this into account, the syntax for disassembling a program named *appname* is objdump -d -Mintel appname. Some sample output for this is shown here:

804a030	<test_key>:		
804a030	55	push	ebp
804a031	89 5e	mov	ebp, esp
804a033	53	push	ebx
804a034	83 ec 14	sub	esp, 0x14

`objdump`'s output is organized into three columns. The first column contains memory addresses, which are the virtual addresses where the instructions will be located when the code is run. The second contains the x86 machine code at that location, and the third holds the x86 assembly code equivalents of that machine code.

The main exceptions to this layout are labels, as shown at the top of the preceding table. This label contains a name. Note that the address associated with the label is the same as that of the first instruction in the code; a label doesn't consume any memory space.

Lab: Hello World

It's now time for the second lab exercise. Please navigate to the book's GitHub at `https://github.com/DazzleCatDuo/X86-SOFTWARE-REVERSE-ENGINEERING-CRACKING-AND-COUNTER-MEASURES` and find the "hello world" lab.

Skills

This lab provides an opportunity to learn to write and build x86 code applications. Some of the key skills that will be tested include the following:

- Registers
- Memory
- Instructions
- Systems calls
- Building and linking x86 assembly

This lab also provides hands-on experience with a few different tools, including the following:

- `nasm`
- `ld`
- Makefiles
- `objdump`

Takeaways

Applications are fundamentally composed of some form of assembly instructions. Usually, on a PC, this is x86, but sometimes it might be a JIT language or intermediate language (IL).

Understanding how to create programs in this low-level language provides insight into how to take them apart as well. When cracking programs, the ability to write x86 can be invaluable for developing patches to circumvent software protections.

ASCII

The American Standard Code for Information Interchange (ASCII) and Unicode Transformation Format (UTF) are both standards that define how computers represent text. In fact, ASCII is a subset of UTF-8.

ASCII was developed in 1960 and uses seven bits to represent each character. Figure 4.2 shows a full ASCII table.

Dec	Hx	Oct	Char	Dec	Hx	Oct	Html	Chr	Dec	Hx	Oct	Html	Chr	Dec	Hx	Oct	Html	Chr
0	0	000	NUL (null)	32	20	040	&#32;	Space	64	40	100	&#64;	@	96	60	140	&#96;	`
1	1	001	SOH (start of heading)	33	21	041	&#33;	!	65	41	101	&#65;	A	97	61	141	&#97;	a
2	2	002	STX (start of text)	34	22	042	"	"	66	42	102	&#66;	B	98	62	142	&#98;	b
3	3	003	ETX (end of text)	35	23	043	&#35;	#	67	43	103	&#67;	C	99	63	143	&#99;	c
4	4	004	EOT (end of transmission)	36	24	044	&#36;	$	68	44	104	&#68;	D	100	64	144	&#100;	d
5	5	005	ENQ (enquiry)	37	25	045	&#37;	%	69	45	105	&#69;	E	101	65	145	&#101;	e
6	6	006	ACK (acknowledge)	38	26	046	&	&	70	46	106	&#70;	F	102	66	146	&#102;	f
7	7	007	BEL (bell)	39	27	047	'	'	71	47	107	&#71;	G	103	67	147	&#103;	g
8	8	010	BS (backspace)	40	28	050	&#40;	(	72	48	110	&#72;	H	104	68	150	&#104;	h
9	9	011	TAB (horizontal tab)	41	29	051	&#41;	)	73	49	111	&#73;	I	105	69	151	&#105;	i
10	A	012	LF (NL line feed, new line)	42	2A	052	&#42;	*	74	4A	112	&#74;	J	106	6A	152	&#106;	j
11	B	013	VT (vertical tab)	43	2B	053	&#43;	+	75	4B	113	&#75;	K	107	6B	153	&#107;	k
12	C	014	FF (NP form feed, new page)	44	2C	054	&#44;	,	76	4C	114	&#76;	L	108	6C	154	&#108;	l
13	D	015	CR (carriage return)	45	2D	055	&#45;	-	77	4D	115	&#77;	M	109	6D	155	&#109;	m
14	E	016	SO (shift out)	46	2E	056	&#46;	.	78	4E	116	&#78;	N	110	6E	156	&#110;	n
15	F	017	SI (shift in)	47	2F	057	&#47;	/	79	4F	117	&#79;	O	111	6F	157	&#111;	o
16	10	020	DLE (data link escape)	48	30	060	&#48;	0	80	50	120	&#80;	P	112	70	160	&#112;	p
17	11	021	DC1 (device control 1)	49	31	061	&#49;	1	81	51	121	&#81;	Q	113	71	161	&#113;	q
18	12	022	DC2 (device control 2)	50	32	062	&#50;	2	82	52	122	&#82;	R	114	72	162	&#114;	r
19	13	023	DC3 (device control 3)	51	33	063	&#51;	3	83	53	123	&#83;	S	115	73	163	&#115;	s
20	14	024	DC4 (device control 4)	52	34	064	&#52;	4	84	54	124	&#84;	T	116	74	164	&#116;	t
21	15	025	NAK (negative acknowledge)	53	35	065	&#53;	5	85	55	125	&#85;	U	117	75	165	&#117;	u
22	16	026	SYN (synchronous idle)	54	36	066	&#54;	6	86	56	126	&#86;	V	118	76	166	&#118;	v
23	17	027	ETB (end of trans. block)	55	37	067	&#55;	7	87	57	127	&#87;	W	119	77	167	&#119;	w
24	18	030	CAN (cancel)	56	38	070	&#56;	8	88	58	130	&#88;	X	120	78	170	&#120;	x
25	19	031	EM (end of medium)	57	39	071	&#57;	9	89	59	131	&#89;	Y	121	79	171	&#121;	y
26	1A	032	SUB (substitute)	58	3A	072	&#58;	:	90	5A	132	&#90;	Z	122	7A	172	&#122;	z
27	1B	033	ESC (escape)	59	3B	073	&#59;	;	91	5B	133	&#91;	[	123	7B	173	&#123;	{
28	1C	034	FS (file separator)	60	3C	074	&#60;	<	92	5C	134	&#92;	\	124	7C	174	&#124;		
29	1D	035	GS (group separator)	61	3D	075	&#61;	=	93	5D	135	&#93;	]	125	7D	175	&#125;	}
30	1E	036	RS (record separator)	62	3E	076	&#62;	>	94	5E	136	&#94;	^	126	7E	176	&#126;	~
31	1F	037	US (unit separator)	63	3F	077	&#63;	?	95	5F	137	&#95;	_	127	7F	177	&#127;	DEL

Source: www.LookupTables.com

Figure 4.2: ASCII table

The ASCII standard can support the following types of characters:

- Digits (0–9)
- Lowercase letters (a–z)
- Uppercase letters (A–Z)
- Common punctuation

An understanding of ASCII is useful for reverse engineering because it is how strings are likely to be represented within assembly code and memory. For example, the string "Hello, world" is stored in memory as 0x48, 0x65, 0x6C, 0x6C, 0x6F, 0x2C, 0x20, 0x77, 0x6F, 0x72, 0x6C, 0x64.

Identifying ASCII Strings

One of the challenges when reverse engineering is identifying if a series of bytes is an ASCII string, a number, or something else. For example, the series of bytes 0x48, 0x65, 0x6C, 0x6C, 0x6F, 0x2C, 0x20, 0x77, 0x6F, 0x72, 0x6C, and 0x64 could be the string "Hello, world"; the values 1,819,043,144; or any of many more possibilities.

TIP The difficulty of identifying ASCII strings is why tools like *strings* often return a lot of garbage. They just look for a series of bytes that *could* be interpreted as a string of printable characters.

The only way to know for certain that a series of bytes is a string is to look at how it is used by the program. If the bytes are passed to a function that interprets them as a string, then they are likely a string.

In many languages, a helpful sign of a string is a series of printable bytes terminated by a NULL character. In fact, because there is nothing to tell the processor where a string starts or stops, if a string forgets its null terminator, the process will just keep reading characters until it reaches a problem!

For example, the following program will print "hello" followed by the 16 Bs and then continue reading and printing memory until it reaches a NULL byte.

```
#include <stdio.h>
int main()
{
        char mybuffer[16];
        for (int i = 0; i < 16; i++)
        {
                mybuffer[i] = 'B';
        }
        Printf("hello %s\n", mybuffer);
}
```

Figure 4.3 shows the output of this code.

Figure 4.3: Program output

ASCII Manipulation Tip

The ASCII standard is designed so that capital and lowercase letters are always separated by 0x20, as shown in Figure 4.4. In higher-level programming languages, a `toUpper` function will simply add `0x20` to the value of a lowercase letter, and a `toLower` function will simply subtract `0x20`.

Dec	Hx	Oct	Html	Chr	Dec	Hx	Oct	Html	Chr
64	40	100	@	@	96	60	140	`	`
65	41	101	A	A	97	61	141	a	a
66	42	102	B	B	98	62	142	b	b
67	43	103	C	C	99	63	143	c	c
68	44	104	D	D	100	64	144	d	d
69	45	105	E	E	101	65	145	e	e
70	46	106	F	F	102	66	146	f	f
71	47	107	G	G	103	67	147	g	g
72	48	110	H	H	104	68	150	h	h
73	49	111	I	I	105	69	151	i	i

Figure 4.4: ASCII uppercase and lowercase values

Summary

This chapter explores how assembly programs are put together in a forward direction. This includes how they interact with the outside world, the process of building and linking them, and how they manage strings.

Understanding these processes in the forward direction can be invaluable to understanding how it works in reverse. If you know how assembly code moves from code to executable, you have a better understanding of how to take it apart and put it back together again.

Understanding Condition Codes

Assembly instructions commonly include destination registers where the result of an operation will be stored. However, some instructions can have effects beyond those recorded in this destination register.

x86 uses *condition codes* to track these effects. This chapter explores these condition codes and describes the main ones you need to understand to effectively reverse engineer x86 applications.

Condition Codes

Most architectures, including x86, need a means of tracking the basic properties of previous operations. For example, when evaluating an if statement, the program needs to evaluate the condition and then act on its result. The ability to track state information across instructions is essential to the ability to perform this and similar operations.

To store this state information, the computer has a special-purpose register (SPR) called flags. On a 32-bit system, this is called the eflags register, while the 16-bit and 64-bit versions are called flags and rflags, respectively.

eflags

The `eflags` register is composed of a set of flags, each of which is represented by a single bit. Each bit can be set to true (1) or false (0).

The `eflags` register is broken up into three types of flags.

- **Status flags:** Status flags represent the status of some operation such as whether the previous operation evaluated to zero.

- **Control flags:** Control flags affect how the processor operates, such as enabling and disabling interrupts.

- **System flags:** System flags reflect the state of the processor, such as whether the system is virtualized.

With 32 bits in the `eflags` register, a significant amount of state information can be stored in these bits. For reverse engineering, only some of the status flags are significant.

Of the status flags, four are significant to reverse engineering; these include the carry, zero, sign, and overflow flags.

Carry Flag

The carry flag (CF) is bit 0 of the `eflags` register. It specifies whether the last arithmetic operation resulted in a carry.

A carry indicated that an addition carried a 1 out of the highest bit or a subtraction borrowed a 1 into the highest bit. For example, consider the following calculation, which would cause the carry bit to be set:

```
                    unsigned        signed
  0011 0000               48            48
+ 1110 0000            + 224          + -32
1 0001 0000               16            16
```

Recall that there is nothing inherent about binary to indicate what the value is; it's all in how it's used or interpreted. So, the binary representation in this example could be interpreted as an unsigned value or signed. Signed, as you can see, means the option of negative or positive, whereas unsigned means always positive.

In this example, if you trace the addition, you can see the left-most column, carried out a 1. Looking at the signed versus unsigned values, you can see that for unsigned, the carry flag represents an overflow, meaning the result was too big to store in the size (in this case we're looking at 1 byte). And this is how it is traditionally used, to identify overflows/underflows in unsigned math. If the carry condition is met, then the CF is set to 1.

Zero Flag

The zero flag (ZF) is bit 6 of the `eflags` register and indicates whether the last arithmetic operation ended in a zero. For example, the following calculation would set the zero flag:

```
  0100 0000        64
- 0100 0000       - 64
  0000 0000        00
```

The zero flag is easier to reason about, in that the answer is simply all zeros. There is no interpretation difference between signed or unsigned. If the result is a 0, then the zero flag is set to 1.

Sign Flag

The seventh bit of the `eflags` register, the sign flag (SF), specifies whether a sign bit was set as a result of the previous arithmetic operation. In signed numbers, the sign bit is the high bit of the register used.

For example, in the instruction `add ax, bx`, the sign bit is bit 15 of `ax`. In the instruction `sub bl, dl`, the sign bit is bit 7 of `bl`. If the bit is set, it's considered negative, and if it's not, it's positive. In the case of the sign bit being set, the SF will be set to 1. If the top bit of the result is set, we know it's a negative number, but it's not as simple as then using our normal translation to decimal on the remaining bits to get the value. If a number is negative, it's stored in "two's complement" format, which requires some more massaging to get back to its true value.

Overflow Flag

The overflow flag (OF) is the eleventh bit of the `eflags` register and states whether the previous arithmetic operation resulted in an overflow. An overflow happens when the carry into the highest bit doesn't match the carry out. Just like the carry flag is useful for unsigned math, the overflow flag is used for signed math to detect when something didn't go right.

Often, this indicates one of two cases:

■ Positive + Positive = Negative

■ Negative + Negative = Positive

For the first case, consider the following calculation:

```
  0101 0000         80
+ 0101 0000       + 80
0 1010 0000        -96
```

In this calculation, two positive values are added together. However, the result sets the sign bit, indicating a negative number. Tracing this column by column in its binary form, you will see that a 1 is carried into the left-most column, but nothing is carried out (i.e., a 0 is carried out). This means the carry in did not match the carry out, and as you can see in its decimal format, we got an incorrect negative value as the result.

For an example of the second case, consider the following:

```
  1000 0000            -128
+ 1011 0000          + -80
1 0011 0000            48
```

In this case, two negative numbers are being summed. However, the overflow causes the result to be a positive value. Again, tracing this at a binary level, we can see that there is no carry into the left-most column, but there is a carry out, so the carry in does not match the carry out. When looking at this in the decimal form we see we get an incorrect positive value.

Other Status Flags

While these four are the most important status flags, they are not the only ones. Some of the other, less important flags that are still worth knowing include the following:

- **Adjust (AF):** Indicates that the last arithmetic results in a carry out of the lowest 4 bits (used for BCD arithmetic)
- **Trap (TF):** Enables CPU single-step mode, which is used for debugging
- **Interrupt Enable (IF):** Enables the CPU to handle system interrupts
- **Direction (DF):** Sets the direction of string processing from right to left
- **Parity (PF):** Indicates that the last arithmetic/logical operation results in even parity (even number of 1s in lowest byte)

Operations Affecting Status Flags

Status flags can be affected by various operations. Four examples include add, sub, cmp, and test.

add

The add instruction has the potential to modify the carry, zero, sign, and overflow flags. For example, the instruction add al, bl can trigger different combinations of flags dependent on the values stored in al and bl. Figure 5.1 shows the results of five different add operations.

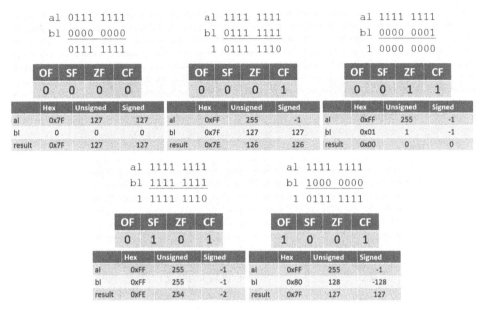

Figure 5.1: Effects of add al, bl with various inputs

Note the effect that the use of signed or unsigned integers has on the interpretation of the values and their correctness. For example, the second add operation has a correct result for signed values but an incorrect one for unsigned values.

sub

The sub instruction also has the potential to modify the same flags as add, which is all four significant status flags. Figure 5.2 shows the various results of sub al, bl with different values of al and bl.

As with the add operation, the correctness of the result of sub depends on the values stored in al and bl. For example, both versions of the first example are correct, but only the signed version of the second has a correct result.

cmp

The cmp instruction is designed to compare two values, which can be memory, constants, or register. It works by subtracting the second operand from the first operand. However, the result of the subtraction is discarded, but the flags are adjusted.

The goal of cmp is to determine whether one value is greater than, less than, or equal to another. Consider the following example where eax < ebx:

```
mov eax, 0x100
mov ebx, 0x200
cmp eax, ebx  ; evaluates eax-ebx
```

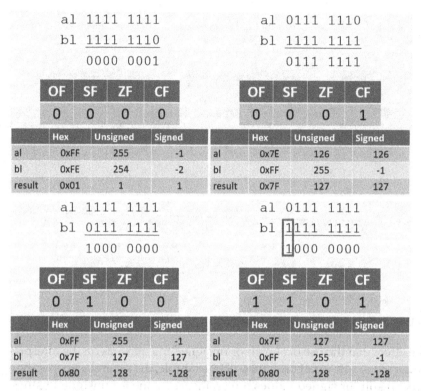

Figure 5.2: Effects of sub al, bl with various inputs

The final instruction here is a subtraction, which would result in a negative value since ebx is greater than eax. As a result, the sign flag would be set to 1 (indicating a negative result), while the zero flag would be set to 0 (i.e., the result is not zero).

In another example, the value of the first operand, eax, may be greater than that of the second operand, ebx.

```
mov eax, 0x300
mov ebx, 0x200
cmp eax, ebx   ; evaluates eax-ebx
```

In this case, the result of the subtraction would be a positive value. As a result, both the sign and zero flags would be zero.

The final potential case for cmp is if the two operands are equal, as shown here:

```
mov eax, 0x500
mov ebx, 0x500
cmp eax, ebx   ; evaluates eax-ebx
```

If the operands are equal, the result of the subtraction is zero, which would set the zero flag but not the sign flag. Figure 5.3 shows a truth table summarizing the impacts of cmp operations on the sign and zero flags.

If...	SF	ZF
eax > ebx	0	0
eax = ebx	0	1
eax < ebx	1	0

Figure 5.3: cmp truth table

test

The test instruction performs a bitwise and between the two operands, which can be memory, constants, or registers. Like cmp, the result of the operation is discarded, but the values of flags are adjusted.

The test instruction is commonly used to check if one or more specific bits are set within a value by checking the zero flag. For example, the following instructions check if bits 0 or 2 are set:

```
mov ax, 0x1450
test ax, 0x05 ; check if bit 0 or 2 is set (0x5 is 0000 0101 in binary)
```

These instructions are equivalent to performing the following mathematical operation:

```
  0001 0100 0101 0000      (0x1450)
& 0000 0000 0000 0101      (0x0005)
  0000 0000 0000 0000
```

The result of this and operation is zero, which would cause the zero flag to be set. This indicates that neither bit 0 nor bit 2 was set.

The following instructions perform the same test when the value 0x1451 is placed in ax:

```
mov ax, 0x1451
test ax, 0x05 ; check if bit 0 or 2 is set
```

These instructions are equivalent to the following calculation:

```
  0001 0100 0101 0001      (0x1451)
& 0000 0000 0000 0101      (0x0005)
  0000 0000 0000 0001
```

In this case, the result of the and operation is nonzero, so the zero flag is not set. This indicates that at least one of the two bits was set.

TIP The test instruction can be used to determine whether a number is even or odd.

Summary

Condition codes are used to record some of the effects of an operation that might not show up in a destination register. For example, a condition code may indicate if an operation resulted in a zero or caused an overflow. Tracking these condition codes is essential to understanding the current state of an application when reverse engineering it.

Analyzing and Debugging Assembly Code

Earlier chapters focused on the theory and fundamentals of reverse engineering. Learning how x86 works and common instruction formats is essential to success.

This chapter takes a hands-on approach to reverse engineering and software cracking. It introduces gdb, a powerful debugger, and explores some important tips and tricks for software reverse engineering and cracking.

Binary Analysis

Analyzing existing executables makes up a great deal of reverse engineering. Binary analysis can be accomplished in a few different ways, including static and dynamic analysis and debugging.

Static and Dynamic Analysis

A program's functionality can be analyzed in a few different ways. Two of the main techniques are static and dynamic analysis.

Static analysis involves analyzing the source code without ever running it. Static analysis has a few advantages, including the following:

- Good starting point for further analysis
- Risk-free method of analyzing potential malware
- No need for access to specialized architectures

Static analysis has its advantages, one of the biggest being it's always an option. But it can be time-consuming and won't catch everything. There will always be pieces of code that are meaningful only at runtime. When analyzing complex code, without watching the code run, it can be difficult or impossible to anticipate where something like a jump might go. Also, many code flows are dictated by the input given to the program, so static analysis isn't enough to reason about where code execution will go, making it harder to analyze.

Dynamic analysis is a complementary technique that involves running the program and analyzing its behavior while it's running. Some of the benefits of dynamic analysis include the following:

- More rapid analysis
- Wider detection of potential issues

Dynamic analysis can take a variety of different forms. For reverse engineering, one of the most common is debugging. By watching an application running, many of the unknowns during static analysis can be solidified (such as where code is most likely to jump to). However, dynamic analysis means running the code in question, and depending on the code, this might not always be feasible. It could be an excerpt from a larger application, it could require a unique execution environment that you don't have access to, or, in the case of malware, it could be potentially malicious if executed.

Debugging

Recall that the goal of software reverse engineering and cracking is to understand and modify existing software. *Debugging* is one of the fastest and most effective ways of accomplishing this. By dynamically analyzing a program's functionality and modifying its behavior on the fly, it's possible to collect the information necessary for cracking and to test potential cracks of the software.

Debugging is commonly a multistage process. The typical debug flow includes the following:

1. Set *breakpoints* on points of interest.
2. Run the code.
3. The execution pauses ("breaks") at the breakpoint.
4. Examine the program state.
5. Optionally make modifications.
6. Repeat.

Breakpoints

Breakpoints instruct the processor to stop a program's execution at a particular point. Breakpoints come in one of two forms:

- **Software:** Software breakpoints are set on assembly instructions and are unlimited in number.

- **Hardware:** A limited number of hardware breakpoints (four in x86) can be set on assembly instructions or memory accesses.

In this book, early labs focus on the use of software breakpoints, with hardware breakpoints appearing in later labs. This book will demonstrate the use of a variety of debuggers, and configuring breakpoints will be different in each of them.

Software Breakpoints

Software breakpoints are the default option for most debuggers. When setting a software breakpoint, what actually happens behind the scenes is the debugger actually modifies the instruction, replacing it with a breakpoint instruction. In x86, this is the int3 instruction (0xcc). A software breakpoint is limited to execution, meaning the int3 instruction must be executed for the breakpoint to execute.

When the processor reaches the breakpoint instruction, it halts execution and hands control back over to the debugger. This allows a reverse engineer to inspect the program state and potentially make modifications.

The main limitation of software breakpoints is that they can be easily detected by a program that reads its own memory. Through anti-debugging, the program can remove the breakpoint or take other defensive actions in response to it.

Hardware Breakpoints

Most debuggers support hardware breakpoints. However, they generally must be manually selected and configured.

A hardware breakpoint doesn't modify a program's code like a software breakpoint does. Instead, the addresses of the breakpoints are stored in hardware registers.

In x86, the debug registers DR_{0-7} are used for hardware breakpoints. Registers DR_{0-4} hold the breakpoint addresses, while $DR_{6,7}$ store configuration information.

Hardware breakpoints can be configured to break on executing, reading, or writing a specific address. When the processor detects a condition matching the breakpoint registers, it hands control over to the debugger.

Hardware breakpoints are useful because they can detect memory access. For example, a hardware breakpoint can be used to identify where in the code a particular byte is set or a string is used.

Hardware breakpoints are also useful to evade a program's defenses against software breakpoints. If a program is scanning its own code looking for int3 instructions, it will overlook hardware breakpoints, which don't modify the code. It's not anti-debugger proof; with advanced system knowledge, an application could dig deep enough to watch hardware breakpoints, but it raises the bar a lot over software breakpoints.

gdb

The GNU Debugger (gdb) is the de facto standard for debugging on Linux. It comes installed on many Linux distros and can be installed on any of them. Some of the key features that gdb provides include the following:

- Command-line debugger (no GUI)
- Scriptable
- Remote debugging support

gdb is such a ubiquitous debugger that many systems and processors include a *gdb stub* to support gdb debugging. While many debuggers are constrained to a few architectures and platforms, gdb works on hundreds. This book will explore many different debuggers and will introduce graphical user interface (GUI)–based debuggers later. However, it's important to foundationally understand how to use GDB, which is command line. Many "prettier" debuggers use GDB and its protocol under the hood; they've simply wrapped a pretty interface over it.

Debugging with gdb

As a command-line program, gdb is controlled by entering commands at the prompt, which displays as (gdb). While the gdb interface may seem archaic, it is an extremely powerful and hugely popular debugger.

One useful feature of gdb is that commands can be entered as the shortest nonambiguous form of the command. For example, run can be shortened to r, info registers to info reg, and disassemble to disas. You'll get a feel for some of these as you go.

Launching gdb

gdb can be launched using the gdb command. For example, the executable printreg-shift.out can be launched with gdb printreg-shift.out, as shown in Figure 6.1.

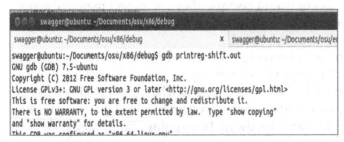

Figure 6.1: The gdb command

Disassembly with gdb

Recall that x86 has a few different syntaxes, including Intel and AT&T. The instruction to specify Intel syntax in gdb is (gdb) set disassembly-flavor intel.

After setting the disassembly flavor, there are a few different options for starting debugging, including the following:

- disassemble starts disassembly from the current instruction pointer.
- disassemble address starts disassembly at the specified address.
- disassemble label starts disassembly at the specified label (*loop*, *main*, etc.).

Figure 6.2 shows an example of disassembly using a label, where the desired code segment begins with the *loop* label. The image on the left is the original assembly source code, and the right half of the image shows the equivalent disassembly in gdb.

```
20 loop:
21     mov edx, eax     ;copy the value into edx for us to do manipulations on
22     mov ecx, ebx
23     shl ecx, 2  ;multiply by 4
24     shr edx, cl
25     and edx, 0xf     ;get rid of all but the bottom nibble
26
27     cmp dl, 10       ;check if the remainder is less than 10
28     jge _ascii_to_hex   ;if it was greater or equal to 10 then we know its A-F
29     add dl, '0'      ; its a numeric digit, add '0' to conver to ascii
30     jmp _ascii_to_end
31 _ascii_to_hex:
32     add dl,'7'       ;its A-F, add 0x55 which how to convert to a letter
33 _ascii_to_end:
34     dec ebx
35     mov [byteToPrint], dl; store the result into memory
36     ;save our values
37     push eax
38     push ebx
39     ;print it
40     mov eax, 4                ; system call #4 = sys_write
41     mov ebx, 1                ; file descriptor 1 = stdout
                                                                   37,1-4
```
```
(gdb) disassemble loop
Dump of assembler code for function loop:
   0x080483f1 <+0>:     mov     edx,eax
   0x080483f3 <+2>:     mov     ecx,ebx
   0x080483f5 <+4>:     shl     ecx,0x2
   0x080483f8 <+7>:     shr     edx,cl
   0x080483fa <+9>:     and     edx,0xf
   0x080483fd <+12>:    cmp     dl,0xa
   0x08048400 <+15>:    jge     0x8048407 <_ascii_to_hex>
   0x08048402 <+17>:    add     dl,0x30
   0x08048405 <+20>:    jmp     0x804840a <_ascii_to_end>
```

Figure 6.2: Disassembly in gdb

After specifying a starting point, it's possible to specify a certain number of instructions to disassemble. For example, the command disassemble main +50 will start disassembly at the *main* label and print 50 instructions.

Starting and Stopping Code in gdb

The run command is used to execute the program from the very beginning. This will discard any state information from running the program to this point.

The continue command is used to resume execution after pausing. For example, a breakpoint could be used to stop execution to view the program stack, followed by a continue command to resume.

Program execution can be terminated with the quit and kill commands. kill terminates the running process, while quit does so and leaves gdb.

gdb Breakpoints

Breakpoints halt code execution to allow analysis of the program state. In gdb, the break address command specifies a breakpoint at a particular address, while `break label` uses a label to indicate the desired breakpoint location, as shown in Figure 6.3.

```
(gdb) disassemble loop
Dump of assembler code for function loop:
   0x080483f1 <+0>:     mov     edx,eax
   0x080483f3 <+2>:     mov     ecx,ebx
   0x080483f5 <+4>:     shl     ecx,0x2
   0x080483f8 <+7>:     shr     edx,cl
   0x080483fa <+9>:     and     edx,0xf
   0x080483fd <+12>:    cmp     dl,0xa
   0x08048400 <+15>:    jge     0x8048407 <_ascii_to_hex>
   0x08048402 <+17>:    add     dl,0x30
   0x08048405 <+20>:    jmp     0x804840a <_ascii_to_end>
End of assembler dump.
(gdb) break loop
Breakpoint 1 at 0x80483f1: file printreg-shift.asm, line 21.
(gdb) ▌
```

Figure 6.3: Setting a breakpoint in gdb

gdb info Commands

The `info` command in `gdb` can be used to access various types of information. Some common `info` commands include the following:

- `info files`: Shows the various parts of the disassembled file. Figure 6.4 shows an example for a simple executable named `a.out`.

```
(gdb) info files
Symbols from "/home/swagger/Documents/osu/x86/a.out".
Unix child process:
        Using the running image of child process 61165.
        While running this, GDB does not access memory from...
Local exec file:
        '/home/swagger/Documents/osu/x86/a.out', file type elf32-i386.
        Entry point: 0x80480d1
        0x08048080 - 0x080480dd is .text
        0x080490e0 - 0x080490e5 is .data
(gdb) ▌
```

Figure 6.4: gdb `info files` command

- `info breakpoints`: Lists the currently defined breakpoints for the disassembled program.

- `info register`: Displays the current values of the x86 registers as shown in Figure 6.5.

- `info variables`: Shows all defined variables in the application as shown in Figure 6.6.

In addition to the `info register` command, it is also possible to print the values of individual registers with the `print $reg` command, as shown here:

```
(gdb) print $esp
$1 = (void *) 0xffffd260
(gdb)
```

```
Starting program: /home/swagger/Documents/osu/x86/debug/printreg-shift.out

Breakpoint 1, loop () at printreg-shift.asm:21
21              mov edx, eax    ;copy the value into edx for us to do manipulations on
(gdb) info register
eax             0xabcdef12      -1412567278
ecx             0xffffd304      -11516
edx             0xffffd294      -11628
ebx             0x7             7
esp             0xffffd268      0xffffd268
ebp             0x0             0x0
esi             0x0             0
edi             0x0             0
eip             0x80483f1       0x80483f1 <loop>
eflags          0x246           [ PF ZF IF ]◄── Flags currently set
cs              0x23            35
ss              0x2b            43
ds              0x2b            43◄── Decimal Value
es              0x2b            43
fs              0x0             0
gs              0x63            99  HexValue
(gdb)
```

Figure 6.5: `gdb info register` command

```
(gdb) info variables
All defined variables:

Non-debugging symbols:
0x080490e0  loop_index
0x080490e4  byteToPrint
0x080490e5  __bss_start
0x080490e5  _edata
0x080490e8  _end
(gdb)
```

Figure 6.6: `gdb info variable` command

Stepping Through Instructions

The run and continue commands simply start the program running again until something forces execution to stop such as a breakpoint. This makes it more difficult to watch what the program is doing or how variables change over time.

The stepi command steps one instruction at a time, as shown in Figure 6.7, allowing more in-depth analysis. Note that comments are shown because the application was built in debug mode.

```
(gdb) stepi
34          dec ebx
(gdb) stepi
35          mov [byteToPrint], dl; store the result into memory
(gdb) stepi
37          push eax
(gdb) stepi
38          push ebx
(gdb) stepi
40          mov eax, 4              ; system call #4 = sys_write
(gdb) stepi
41          mov ebx, 1              ; file descriptor 1 = stdout
(gdb)
```

Figure 6.7: `gdb stepi` command

> **NOTE**   Debug information, such as function/variable names, comments, etc., can be enabled when compiling using a debug flag, which is supported by most compilers. For example, in gcc/g++, this is the -g flag. However, this is rarely found when reverse engineering a commercial executable.

If the next instruction to execute is a function call, stepi will follow the call into the called function. In many cases, this is undesirable, especially if the function is well-understood. For example, knowing that an instruction will print a string is enough information, and there is no need to inspect each instruction within the printf function.

The nexti command makes it possible to step over a function call. This will execute the function call and advance to the next visible instruction.

Examining Memory

In gdb, the x command (for "eXamine memory") can be used to examine memory. The syntax of the command is x/nfu addr.

In this command, n, f, and u are optional parameters with the following meanings:

- n: Specifies the number of units (u) of memory that should be displayed
- f: Specifies the display format
  - s: Null-terminated string
  - i: Machine instruction
  - x: Hexadecimal (default)
- u: Specifies the unit size
  - b: Bytes
  - h: Halfwords (two bytes)
  - w: Words (default)
  - g: Giant words (eight bytes)

Figure 6.6 showed a variable named byteToPrint, which was located at the address 0x080490e4. To display 16 bytes of memory at this location, the command would be x/16x 0x80490e4, as shown in Figure 6.8. The output of the command shows that the byte of interest has a value of 0x41, which is A in ASCII.

```
(gdb) x/16x 0x80490e4
0x80490e4 <byteToPrint>:     0x00000041     0x00000001     0x00210000
0x00000014
0x80490f4:        0x00000001     0x00000064     0x08048080     0x00000000
0x8049104:        0x000a0044     0x08048080     0x00000000     0x000b0044
0x8049114:        0x08048085     0x00000000     0x000c0044     0x0804808a
(gdb) ▌
```

Figure 6.8: gdb x command

In addition to using memory addresses, the x command can also use registers to specify the dump location. For example, Figure 6.9 shows an example of dumping 10 bytes in hex format at the location specified by *esp*.

```
(gdb) x/10x $esp
0xffffd260:     0x00000006      0xabcdef12      0x0804843b      0xf7e324d3
0xffffd270:     0x00000001      0xffffd304      0xffffd30c      0xf7fda858
0xffffd280:     0x00000000      0xffffd31c
(gdb)
```

Figure 6.9: Printing 10 bytes with the gdb x command

Segmentation Faults

Segmentation faults, or *segfaults*, occur when the CPU attempts to read or write an inaccessible memory location. This could happen because the indicated location doesn't exist or the CPU lacks the permissions necessary to access or modify that memory location.

For example, the command mov eax, [0x00000000] will always result in a segfault. The reason for this is that address 0x0 is typically not mapped or accessible by an application, so a read from memory address 0x0. gdb will cause a segfault to occur.

Segfaults can occur for a variety of different reasons. When exploiting software, a buffer overflow can cause a segfault. When cracking software, segfaults can happen if a program is incorrectly patched or errors are made when modifying execution during debugging. As you start to get into writing and manipulating assembly code, you will become good friends with segfault. Keeping a stress ball nearby that you use every time you see a segfault can be therapeutic when cracking. As a silver lining, when hooked to GDB, as a segfault occurs, gdb will show the line that caused it, which is helpful for tracking down where the code went haywire.

Lab: Shark Sim 3000

This lab provides a warm-up reverse engineering challenge. The application is intentionally designed so that its behavior is nonobvious. Experience deciphering and analyzing programs like this are the foundation of software cracking.

Head to the book's GitHub page (https://github.com/DazzleCatDuo/X86-SOFTWARE-REVERSE-ENGINEERING-CRACKING-AND-COUNTER-MEASURES) and locate the Shark Sim 3000 lab.

Skills

This lab is designed to test foundational skills in reverse engineering, including the ability to take apart and understand an unknown program. Some of the skills being tested include the following:

- ASCII
- Condition codes
- Debugging compiled programs
- Deciphering unknown assembly instructions and programs

Takeaways

Debugging is an invaluable tool in reverse engineering an application. A fundamental part of reverse engineering is deciphering new instructions—there's not always enough time to understand everything!

One of the secrets to success in reverse engineering is to not get caught up on unknown assembly instructions. Try to quickly understand the basics of what they are doing, so you can proceed. In future chapters, you'll keep working with gdb and other more powerful debuggers. Now that you've started to modify assembly, you can progress to doing it without any source at all.

Tuning Out the Noise

Effective reverse engineering and software cracking requires proficiency in a few different skill sets. However, one of the most important is the ability to tune out the noise and focus on what matters.

Even small programs contain too much code to analyze everything. The vast majority of the instructions have no relevance to the core application features and are a waste of time to reverse engineer. Often, knowing what to focus on is less important than knowing what *not* to focus on.

When determining what to focus on and not focus on, understanding the basics is essential. Some extremely common code that should be immediately recognizable includes the following:

- Control flow constructs
- Stack layout (local variables, incoming parameters, and outgoing parameters)
- Compiler boilerplate (prologues/epilogues, canaries, stack allocation, and register management)

These will all be explored in detail in the upcoming chapters to make you a pro at recognizing them quickly.

There is an order of operations to follow when prioritizing reverse engineering efforts: function calls ⇨ control flow ⇨ instructions ⇨ boilerplate.

- **Function calls:** Focus on determining what functions are called. Often, knowing that a function calls `CreateDialog` is enough to understand its purpose.

- **Control flow:** If necessary, explore the control flow, such as determining that `CreateDialog` is called in a loop within that function.

- **Individual instructions:** If that is not enough, examine individual instructions.

- **Compiler boilerplate:** Examining boilerplate is almost never useful to software RE or cracking. However, it's important to understand typical boilerplate so that it can be quickly identified and ignored.

Summary

This chapter introduced `gdb`, a powerful and widely used debugger for Linux systems. Gaining familiarity and hands-on experience with `gdb` is important for an aspiring reverse engineer or cracker since this tool can be used to analyze software for a wide variety of different systems.

Functions and Control Flow

A program is a series of instructions, and an application may not move linearly from one instruction to the next. When reversing and cracking an application, it's vital to understand control flows and the various factors that can affect them, such as if statements and loops in higher-level languages.

When reversing a function in x86 or a higher-level language, you'll likely run into functions as well. This chapter also explores how functions work in x86 and their effects on the program stack.

Control Flow

So far, the assembly code that has been explored in this book has followed a sequential stream of instructions. Execution simply continues from top to bottom. However, most applications are not completely sequential. Consider the following code block:

```
if (x) {
    // Do something
}
```

When executing this code, the processor will evaluate the condition, x, and determine whether it is true. If so, it moves on to the instructions within the if block.

However, if the condition, *x*, is not true, then the instructions within the `if` block are skipped. This requires the ability to tell the processor to execute some instructions and not others, changing the flow of execution.

The Instruction Pointer

The `eip` register is known as the *instruction pointer* and holds the address of the next instruction to execute. The processor will automatically increment the value stored in `eip` after an instruction is executed.

Allowing `eip` to be incremented after each instruction makes it possible to run a sequential series of instructions. However, in some cases, we want to conditionally execute code. This requires a different updating of `eip`. However, `eip` can't be manipulated directly (recall it's a special-purpose register [SPR]). Instead, control flow instructions are used to adjust `eip`.

Control Flow Instructions

The most common deviations from the normal execution flow that force changes to `eip` are known as *jumps* or *branches*. For example, the following code block has a branch at the `if` statement:

```
int x = 1;
int y = 2*x;
if (!y) { // branch!
    x = 2;
}
```

When high-level code like this is assembled, jump instructions are used to indicate what the `eip` register should be set to. A jump instruction has the syntax `jmp op`, where *op* can be a memory address or a label.

The `jmp` instruction is a nonconditional jump that is always followed (conditional jumps are covered later in this chapter).

jmp

The `jmp` instruction has the syntax `jmp op`. Its purpose is to transfer the program's control flow to the memory location *op* by setting `eip` to the value stored in *op*.

Some examples of `jmp` instructions include the following:

```
jmp eax        ; Copies eax into eip (branches to eax)
jmp label      ; Branches to the instruction at label
jmp $          ; An infinite loop in nasm (valuable
               ;debugging tool in assembly)
```

`jmp` instructions can be used to implement various functions. For example, the following instructions count up from zero in an infinite loop:

```
      mov eax, 0
loop: add eax, 1
      jmp loop
```

Conditional Jumps

Conditional jumps are a way to tie whether or not a jump is taken to a condition being either true or false. This determines whether a jump should be performed based on the values stored in the status flags. For example, consider the following instructions:

```
cmp eax, ebx
jle done
```

The `jle` (jump less than or equal to) instruction will jump to the specified address or label if the flags register indicates that a previous comparison resulted in a less than or equal to. In this case, the instruction right before it (`cmp`) is being used to compare `eax` and `ebx` and set the flags. Recall that `cmp` takes operand 1 minus operand 2 and throws away the result. So, to get a less than or equal to condition, `eax` would need to be less than or equal to `ebx`. In this case, the processor will jump to the label *done*. Otherwise, the jump will be skipped, and execution will continue to the next instruction after `jle`.

Numerous conditional jump instructions exist in the x86 language. Table 7.1 lists these instructions and the conditions that determine whether the jump is performed.

Table 7.1: x86 conditional jump instructions

INSTRUCTION	MEANING	CONDITIONS
`je`	Jump if equal.	ZF = 1
`jz`	Jump if last result is zero.	ZF = 1
`jne`	Jump if not equal.	ZF = 0
`jge`	Jump if greater than or equal to.	SF = OF
`jl`	Jump if less than.	SF != OF
`jle`	Jump if less than or equal to.	ZF = 1 OR SF != OF
`jg`	Jump if greater than.	ZF = 0 AND SF == OF

Looking at the table, you might note that some instructions have identical conditions. For example, jz and je will both jump if the zero flag (ZF) is set to one. This means that the jump is performed if the two indicated values are equal. But logically, they're treated as different things. "Jump if the previous result is zero" might be used after subtracting two numbers, whereas "jump equal" is more likely used after a comparison.

For example, consider the case where eax = ebx = 0x10. The instruction cmp eax, ebx performs subtraction and will set the zero flag if executed. Both the jz and je instructions will perform a jump if they follow this instruction.

These instructions can be used interchangeably, but they are typically chosen based on the instruction used to set the flags that determine the jump. For example, if the instruction sub eax, ebx is used to perform the conditional, then jz will likely be used since you're looking at a zero result to a mathematical operation. If the instruction cmp eax, ebx is used, then je will be used because a comparison tests equivalence.

Remember that cmp performs subtraction behind the scenes, so it has the same effect on flags as the sub operation. jz and je are synonymous instructions designed solely to make assembly code more readable.

Pitfalls of Conditional Jumps

Conditional jumps use the status flags to determine whether a jump should be taken. But every instruction operates in isolation, and the conditional jumps are unaware of which compare or mathematical expression you want to do a conditional jump on. This can cause issues if the status flags are changed between the conditional instruction and the jump. While a compiler would not make this mix up, if you're writing assembly, you will be forced to reason about this.

For example, consider the following set of instructions:

```
cmp eax, ebx
cmp edx, ecx
jle done
```

In this case, your intent may be for the instruction cmp eax, ebx to determine whether the jump is followed. However, cmp edx, ecx sets the flags last before the jump, overwriting the previous settings. Therefore, the jump is performed based on the outcome of the second compare, not the first.

With multiple cmp instructions in a row, it may be obvious that the last cmp instruction sets the flags for the jump. However, with other instructions, this may be less obvious, as in the following instructions:

```
cmp eax, ebx
add ecx, 1
je done
```

In this series of instructions, the intent may have been to use the cmp instruction to set the flags for the jump. However, the add instruction also updates the status flags and overwrites the previous settings. Instead of jumping if eax = ebx, the jump is performed if the add instruction sets the zero flag (i.e., ecx + 1 = 0).

Example

Jump instructions are commonly used to implement if statements and loops. The following assembly code sums the numbers 0–4 using a loop:

```
        mov   eax, 0    ; initialize eax (accumulator) to 0
        mov   ecx, 0    ; initialize ecx (counter) to 0

loop:
        add   eax, ecx  ; add current iteration
        add   ecx, 1    ; increment counter
        cmp   ecx, 5    ; at 5 iterations yet?
        jne   loop      ; loop if not yet 5

done:
```

The iterator in this loop is stored in the ecx register and is initialized before the loop. The eax register is the accumulator register and holds the running sum.

The loop begins by adding the current loop counter to the accumulator and then incrementing the loop counter. This implements the desired logic of summing the values 0–4 as the loop iterates.

The branch occurs at the jne (jump not equal to) instruction in the second-to-last line. The previous instruction is a cmp, which checks if the loop counter is equal to 5 and sets the status flags accordingly. If the loop counter does not equal 5, the jump triggers, and the eip register is set to the address indicated by *loop*, beginning another iteration. If the loop counter does equal 5, the jump is not taken, and the processor continues on to the *done* label.

Logic Constructs in x86

C/C++ and similar high-level languages have multiple logic constructs that cause nonsequential code execution. Some examples include the following:

```
if (...) { ... }
if (...) { ... } else { ... }
if (...) { ... } else if (...) { ... } else { ... }
while (...) { ... }
do { ... } while (...);
for (...; ...; ...) { ... }
switch (...) { ... }
```

In assembly, these logical constructs are written using a combination of comparison (cmp) and jump (jmp, je, jne, jl, jle, jg, and jge) instructions. When code is compiled, the compiler will automatically perform the translation to assembly code.

When writing assembly code, it is necessary to perform the conversion from high-level concepts to assembly manually. Or when reasoning about other people's code, it is essential to be able to understand how these structures look in assembly. To build up this recognition, focus on how you would take these higher-level language concepts and translate them to assembly. Accomplishing this is a two-step process:

1. **Remove code blocks:** Rewrite code replacing logical constructs with goto statements.

2. **Assemble:** Rewrite the program in assembly.

if (. . .) {. . .}

An if statement is one of the simplest high-level logical constructs. With code blocks, it looks like the following:

```
if (condition)
{
        code_if_true;
}
```

The first step is to remove code blocks. Code blocks are code that is nested inside curly braces: {}. When removing these code blocks, use goto statements, which tell code where to jump for execution. Not all higher-level languages have a concept of a goto, but focus on this as pseudocode and leverage the goto. The following code is the same if statement written without code blocks:

```
if (!condition)
        goto skip_block;

code_if_true;

skip_block:
```

Note that, in this version, the condition is inverted. This is because the jump past the if block occurs only if the condition is false, while the if block of an if statement specifies what happens if the condition is true. Removing code blocks will always involve inverting the condition.

Converting this from pseudocode to a functional application requires replacing *condition* and *code_if_true* with actual code.

WITH BLOCKS	WITHOUT BLOCKS
`if (x==5)`	`if (x!=5)`
`{`	`        goto skip_block;`
`    x++;`	
`    y=x;`	`x++;`
`}`	`y=x;`
	`skip_block:`

After removing the code blocks, converting the code to assembly is much easier. Then, this can be directly mapped to their x86 equivalents.

CODE	X86 ASSEMBLY
`if (x!=5)`	`cmp dword [x], 5`
`    goto skip_block;`	`jne skip_block`
`x++;`	`inc dword [x]`
`y=x;`	`mov eax, [x]`
	`mov [y], eax`
`skip_block:`	
	`skip_block:`

if (...) { ... } else { ... }

Adding an `else` statement to an `if` construct increases the complexity and the required number of jumps. In addition to skipping over the `if` block if the condition evaluates as false, an `if (...) { ... } else { ... }` construct jumps over the `else` block after executing the code in the if block.

The following samples show how this logical construct appears with and without blocks:

WITH BLOCKS	WITHOUT BLOCKS
`if (condition)`	`if (!condition)`
`{`	`    goto false_block;`
`    code_if_true;`	
`}`	`code_if_true;`
`else`	`goto skip_block;`
`{`	
`    code_if_false;`	`false_block:`
`}`	`code_if_false;`
	`skip_block:`

Note that the code uses two different labels in its `goto` statements. The label *false_block* is used to skip over the `if` block if the condition is false, while the label *skip_block* is used to jump past the `else` block after executing the `if` block. Just like before, invert the conditional statement when rewriting code without blocks.

Replacing the pseudocode with actual code yields the following with and without code blocks:

WITH BLOCKS	WITHOUT BLOCKS
`if (x)`	`if (!x)`
`{`	`    goto false_block;`
`    x++;`	
`}`	`x++;`
`else`	`goto skip_block;`
`{`	
`    x--;`	`false_block:`
`}`	`x--;`
	`skip_block:`

As before, removing the blocks makes it easier to convert the high-level code into assembly code.

CODE	X86 ASSEMBLY
`if (!x)`	`cmp dword [x], 0`
`    goto false_block;`	`je false_block`
`x++;`	`inc dword [x]`
`goto skip_block;`	`jmp skip_block`
`false_block:`	`false_block:`
`x--;`	`dec dword [x]`
`skip_block:`	`skip_block:`

if (...) {...} else if {...} else {...}

if statements can be made more complex and evaluate multiple different conditions. The following demonstrates an if statement with else if and else with and without blocks. But the process still stays the same. Invert the condition, and add gotos.

WITH BLOCKS	WITHOUT BLOCKS
`if (condition_1)`	`if (!condition_1)`
`{`	`        goto test_2;`
`    code_if_1;`	`code_if_1;`
`}`	`goto skip_block;`
`else if (condition_2)`	
`{`	`test_2:`
`    code_if_2;`	`if (!condition_2)`
`}`	`        goto false_block;`
`else`	`code_if_2;`
`{`	`goto skip_block;`
`    code_if_false;`	
`}`	`false_block:`
	`code_if_false;`
	`skip_block:`

In this version of the code, multiple labels and jumps are necessary to convert the code to a version without blocks. Take a real-world example of this, which implements a grading system with an extremely heavy curve.

WITH BLOCKS	WITHOUT BLOCKS
`if (score>70)`	`if (score<=70)`
`{`	`        goto test_2;`
`    grade='a';`	`grade='a';`
`}`	`goto skip_block;`
`else if (score>50)`	
`{`	`test_2:`
`    grade='b';`	`if (score<=50)`
`}`	`        goto false_block;`
`else`	`grade='b';`
`{`	`goto skip_block;`
`    grade='c';`	
`}`	`false_block:`
	`grade='c';`
	`skip_block:`

Note that, once again, converting to a blockless version requires flipping the conditions. The strictly less than statements become greater than or equal to 1. The following example shows how this code is then easily translated to assembly:

CODE	X86 ASSEMBLY
`if (score<=70)`	`cmp dword [score], 70`
`    goto test_2;`	`jle test_2`
`grade='a';`	`mov byte [grade], 'a'`
`goto skip_block;`	`jmp skip_block`
`test_2:`	`test_2:`
`if (score<=50)`	`cmp dword [score], 50`
`    goto false_block;`	`jle false_block`

CODE	X86 ASSEMBLY
`grade='b';`	`mov byte [grade], 'b'`
`goto skip_block;`	`jmp skip_block`
`false_block:`	`false_block:`
`grade='c';`	`mov byte [grade], 'c'`
`skip_block:`	`skip_block:`

do { ... } while (...);

Higher-level programming languages have a number of different loop structures, each of which works slightly differently. A do...while loop is guaranteed to perform at least one iteration before evaluating the condition that would terminate the loop. The following is an example of a do...while loop with blocks:

```
do
{
    code;
}
while (condition);
```

Unlike if statements, a do...while loop evaluates its condition at the end, so further iterations of the loop require a jump backward. As before, this code needs to be rewritten without code blocks. The following shows the same do...while loop using goto statements instead of blocks:

```
loop:

code;

if (condition)
    goto loop;
```

Unlike an if statement, a do..while loop doesn't invert the condition being tested. This is because the backward jump is performed only if the condition is true and another iteration through the loop is required.

Now, take a look at a version of the code using real conditions and logic.

WITH BLOCKS	WITHOUT BLOCKS
`do`	`loop:`
`{`	`y*=x;`
`    y*=x;`	`x--;`
`    x--;`	
`}`	`if (x)`
`while (x);`	`    goto loop;`

Converting this code to not use blocks is relatively simple because the flow of instructions is largely the same. The main difference is that the `while` statement is replaced by an `if` and a `goto`.

Unlike the previous examples, most of the complexity of converting this to assembly lies in the complexity of the sample code, not the branches.

CODE	X86 ASSEMBLY
`loop:`	`loop:`
`y*=x;`	`mov eax, [y]`
`x--;`	`mul dword [x]`
	`mov [y], eax`
`if (x)`	
`    goto loop;`	`sub dword [x], 1`
	`cmp dword [x], 0`
	`jne loop`

while (...) { ... }

A `do...while` loop guarantees that a single iteration of the loop will occur before the condition is evaluated. A `while` loop evaluates the condition immediately, so the code within the loop may not execute at all. The following code demonstrates a `while` loop with and without code blocks. A `while` loop can be broken down into an `if` statement and thus follows the normal pattern for converting an `if` statement.

WITH BLOCKS	WITHOUT BLOCKS
`while (condition)`	`loop:`
`{`	`if (!condition)`
`    code;`	`        goto done;`
`}`	
	`code;`
	`goto loop;`
	`done:`

Note that since the condition is evaluated at the beginning, it is inverted like with the `if` statements. The following demonstrates how this might look when converted from pseudocode to actual code:

WITH BLOCKS	WITHOUT BLOCKS
`while (tired)`	`loop:`
`{`	`if (!tired)`
`    sleep();`	`        goto done;`
`}`	
	`sleep();`
	`goto loop;`
	`done:`

After the code is converted to remove blocks, it can be translated to x86 assembly as shown in the following:

CODE	X86 ASSEMBLY
`loop:`	`loop:`
`if (!tired)`	`cmp dword [tired], 0`
`    goto done;`	`je done`
`sleep();`	`call sleep`
`goto loop;`	`jmp loop`
`done:`	`done:`

for (...; ...; ...) {...}

A `for` loop operates differently than a `while` or `do...while` loop. Instead of running a variable number of times based on a condition, a `for` loop includes a loop condition plus initializes a value and updates a value.

The `for` statement includes three expressions. The first of these initializes the loop counter. The second defines a condition for terminating the loop's execution, and the third defines how the loop counter will be changed between iterations. The following shows this in pseudocode with and without code blocks:

WITH BLOCKS	WITHOUT BLOCKS
`for (expr_1; expr_2; expr_3)`	`expr_1;`
`{`	
`    code;`	`loop:`
`}`	`if (!expr_2)`
	`    goto done;`
	`code;`
	`expr_3;`
	`goto loop;`
	`done:`

When converting a `for` loop to not use code blocks, the three expressions in the `for` statement are split up across the code. The first expression is a precondition that occurs only one time before the loop, and the second starts out the loop. The final condition, which changes the value of the loop counter, is executed at the end of each loop iteration.

These three expressions in the `for` statement are easier to understand when looking at real code. For example, the following code defines a loop counter, i, and initializes it to zero. This loop counter will be incremented by 1 in each loop iteration (i++), and the loop will stop running when i reaches 100.

WITH BLOCKS	WITHOUT BLOCKS
`for (i=0; i<100; i++)`	`i=0;`
`{`	
`    sum+=i;`	`loop:`
`}`	`if (i>=100)`

WITH BLOCKS	WITHOUT BLOCKS
	`goto done;`
	`sum+=i;`
	`i++;`
	`goto loop;`
	`done:`

Note that, like a `while` loop or `if` statement, a `for` loop inverts the condition. Once again, this is because the condition is evaluated at the beginning of the loop rather than at the end as in a `do..while` loop.

The following shows what a `for` loop looks like in x86 assembly:

CODE	X86 ASSEMBLY
`i=0;`	`mov dword [i], 0`
`loop:`	`loop:`
`if (i>=100)`	`cmp dword [i], 100`
`    goto done;`	`jge done`
`sum+=i;`	`mov eax,[i]`
`i++;`	`add [sum],eax`
`goto loop;`	`inc dword [i]`
`done:`	`jmp loop`
	`done:`

switch (...) {...}

A `switch` statement is a logical structure that exists in some programming languages to simplify conditional logic. The purpose of a `switch` statement is to execute one of several different operations based on the value of a certain variable. The following `switch` statement evaluates the value stored in *op* and prints the character representing that operation:

```
typedef enum {ADD, SUB, MUL, DIV, MOD} op_t;

switch (op) {
    case ADD:
        c='+'; break;
    case SUB:
        c='-'; break;
    case MUL:
        c='*'; break;
    case DIV:
        c='/'; break;
    case MOD:
        c='%'; break;
    default:
        c='?'; break;
}
```

Any `switch` statement can be written using a series of `if` and `else-if` statements. However, this can quickly become both complex to write and inefficient to execute. Because if you're a match for the very last case, you had to execute every single prior comparison to determine that. The following is the equivalent of the previous `switch` statement using `if` and `else-if` statements:

```
if (op==ADD)
    c='+';
else if (op==SUB)
    c='-';
else if (op==MUL)
    c='*';
else if (op==DIV)
    c='/';
else if (op==MOD)
    c='%';
else
    c='?';
```

Building a Jump Table

When evaluating this list of `if` and `else-if` statements, the processor needs to perform five checks to figure out what to do with MOD, which is very inefficient. Imagine a scenario where there were hundreds of options. . .or thousands. Incredibly inefficient to execute. To optimize this process, a compiler may build a jump table instead.

A *jump table* is an assembly data structure that provides a list of target addresses for a `switch` statement, as illustrated in Figure 7.1. Once a `switch` statement has determined which case is correct, it can use that case number as an index into the array of addresses, enabling it to jump directly to the desired code block.

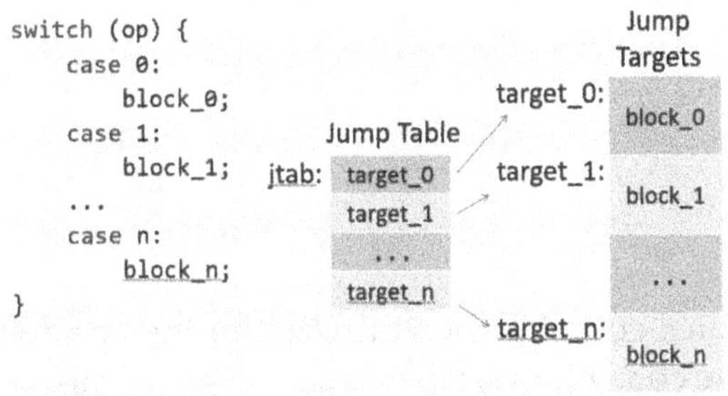
switch (op) {
case 0:
block_0;
case 1:
block_1;
...
case n:
block_n;
}
Jump Table
jtab:
target_0
target_1
...
target_n
Jump Targets
target_0:
block_0
target_1:
block_1
...
target_n:
block_n

Figure 7.1: Example jump table

The following code illustrates what a program using a jump table might look like in assembly:

```
.section data
table:
dd target_0
dd target_1
dd target_2
dd target_3
dd target_4

.section text
mov eax, [op]
cmp eax, 5
jge default
jmp [table+eax*4]

target_0:
mov byte [c], '+'
jmp done

target_1:
mov byte [c], '-'
jmp done

target_2:
mov byte [c], '*'
jmp done

target_3:
mov byte [c], '/'
jmp done

target_4:
mov byte [c], '%'
```

```
jmp done

default:
mov byte [c], '?'
jmp done

done:
```

It begins with the jump table, which contains the addresses of the various code blocks in memory. Each of these code blocks, labeled as `target_x`, moves the appropriate character into `byte [c]` and then jumps to the `done` label.

In between the table and the target code blocks is the code that actually implements the `switch` statement under the `.section text` heading. This code begins by moving *op* into `eax`. It then checks if *op* is greater than or equal to 5. If so, it jumps to the `default` case.

If the value of *op* is less than 5, it maps to one of the targets. By using it as a lookup into the jump table, the processor can retrieve the address of the corresponding code block and jump to that location to execute the code.

In this case, using the jump table, the execution time is the same regardless of which case it is. The last case doesn't take any more instructions or comparisons than the first.

Missing Cases

A jump table assumes that the cases cover a continuous range of values. For example, in the following code sample, a `switch` statement has the cases 1, 2, 4, and 5. In this scenario, the missing 3 can be a problem. Something needs to go in the third spot in the jump table.

```
switch (x) {
    case 0:
        ...
    case 1:
        ...
    case 2:
        ...
    case 4:
        ...
    default:
        ...
}
```

Missing values in a jump table can be filled with the default address or done if there is no default, as shown next. This will cause the processor to jump to the proper location when *op* equals 3, and it attempts to jump to the corresponding location in the jump table.

JUMP TABLE

`target_0`
`target_1`
`target_2`
`default`
`target_4`

Nonzero Bases

A jump table is designed to have a set of cases that start at 0. However, a `switch` statement may have nonzero case values, as shown in the following code sample:

```
switch (x) {
    case 'a':
        ...
    case 'b':
        ...
    case 'c':
        ...
    case 'd':
        ...
}
```

In this case, it's necessary to find a way to zero the cases. With ASCII, it's necessary to find the lowest case in the jump table that, for this example, has a value of a, or 97. When implementing a jump table for this `switch` statement, the code can use an offset, accessing values as `table[x-97]`. In the following jump table, `target_a` will point to case a of the `switch` statement.

JUMP TABLE

`target_a`
`target_b`
`target_c`
`target_d`

Impractical Jump Tables

A compiler will use these tricks to improve code efficiency, and you can too when writing code by hand. However, sometimes a jump table just won't work. For example, consider the following code:

```
switch (x) {
    case 1:
```

```
        printf("this is the beginning."); break;
    case 1000:
        printf("this is the end."); break;
}
```

A jump table for this `switch` statement would need to have 1,000 entries and 998 of them would point to the done label. In this case, an `if/else` statement is the more efficient option.

That's not the only case where it's impractical; a larger jump table with hundreds of cases, or a table that uses an index that can't easily be zeroed or has too many gaps in the table, can be impractical. But as you both write and dissect assembly code, it's important to be able to understand these structures and how they're used.

Continue

Some higher-level languages include the `continue` keyword. `continue` is used inside a loop and instructs the processor to jump to the next iteration of the loop, skipping any instructions that follow.

For example, in the following code sample, the second section labeled *code* would be unreachable. Each time the `continue` statement is evaluated, the processor jumps directly to the `while` statement.

```
do
{
    code;
    continue;
    code;
}
while (condition);
```

A loop with a `continue` statement looks similar to a normal loop of that type when written without code blocks. As shown next, a `continue` can be implemented by using a `goto` that jumps to a label located right before the loop condition.

```
loop:

code;
goto check_condition;
code;

check_condition:
if (condition)
    goto loop;
```

The following examples show an example of a loop with a `continue` statement using actual code:

WITH BLOCKS	WITHOUT BLOCKS
do	loop:
{	
x--;	x--;
continue;	goto check_condition;
x++;	x++;
}	
while (x);	check_condition:
	if (x)
	goto loop;

In this code, the instruction x++; will never execute because the continue always causes it to be skipped. Typically, a continue will be located inside of an if statement because, otherwise, the code following it is pointless. This contrived example is designed to demonstrate how continue works without the complexity of if statements nested within a loop.

Once the code has been converted to remove code blocks, it can be translated to assembly. As before, a goto can be implemented using a nonconditional jump.

CODE	X86 ASSEMBLY
loop:	loop:
x--;	sub dword [x], 1
goto check_condition;	jmp check_condition
x++;	add dword [x], 1
check_condition:	check_condition:
if (x)	cmp dword [x], 0
goto loop;	jne loop

break

The break keyword also exists in some programming languages, and it instructs the processor to exit the current loop. As with continue, the second chunk of code in the following example will never execute, as the break would typically be inside of a conditional statement, but this is an example simply to demonstrate the break mechanism.

```
do
{
    code;
    break;
    code;
}
while (condition);
```

The following example demonstrates how this code would be implemented without code blocks. The break keyword is also replaced with a goto, but this one jumps to a point outside of the loop rather than before the conditional.

```
loop:

code;
goto break;
code;

if (condition)
    goto loop;

break:
```

In the following example, the break statement would terminate the loop after the operation x-- has been evaluated once. In this case, the x++ statement and the loop conditional will never be executed, but again this is sample code. It shows how you'd easily put the break into a conditional.

WITH BLOCKS	WITHOUT BLOCKS
do	loop:
{	
x--;	x--;
break;	goto break;
x++;	x++;
}	
while (x);	if (x)
	goto loop;
	break:

The following example shows how the code can be converted to assembly:

CODE	X86 ASSEMBLY
`loop:`	`loop:`
`x--;`	`sub dword [x], 1`
`goto break;`	`jmp break`
`x++;`	`add dword [x], 1`
`if (x)`	`cmp dword [x], 0`
`    goto loop;`	`jne loop`
`break:`	`break:`

&&

In higher-level languages, a conditional in an `if` statement or a loop has the potential to evaluate multiple different conditions such as a Boolean AND (`&&`). In the following example, the `if` block will be executed only if both *condition_1* and *condition_2* are true.

```
if ( condition_1 && condition_2 ) {
    code;
}
```

When converting this code to remove code blocks, it is necessary to break the multipart `if` statement into two different `if` statements. Each of these negates one of the conditionals that were included in the original `if` statement.

```
if (!condition_1) goto skip_block;
if (!condition_2) goto skip_block;
true:
code;
skip_block:
```

Once rewritten like this (without code blocks), follow the same formula to translate this to assembly.

||

Another option in `if` statements is to combine multiple conditions with a Boolean OR (`||`). An example of this is shown in the following pseudocode:

```
if ( condition_1 || condition_2 ) {
    code;
}
```

A Boolean OR is also broken into two `if` statements when removing code blocks. However, these `if` statements look different than with a Boolean AND.

```
if (condition_1) goto true;
if (!condition_2) goto skip_block;
true:
code;
skip_block:
```

A Boolean OR statement is true if either of the two conditions is true. In the previous example, the first `if` statement uses the original `condition_1` and jumps to the `true` label since, if it is true, there is no need to evaluate the second condition.

However, if this condition is false, the code continues to evaluate `condition_2`. This condition is inverted, and the jump skips to the end of the `if` statement. If `condition_2` is true, the code falls through to the `true` block. Otherwise, it jumps past the `if` statement.

Stack

In assembly, the *stack* is used to store a few different types of data, including the following:

- Local variables
- Scratch space
- Parameters and function calling

The stack gets its name from the fact that it is a last-in-first-out (LIFO) structure like a stack of paper. This conceptually matches programming control flow, and stacks are extremely common in a wide variety of architectures.

The stack will have a *stack pointer* that indicates the top of the stack. A few instructions specifically dedicated to stack manipulation will be explored in depth in this section. A *push* stores a new value at the current top of the stack and updates the stack pointer to indicate the new top of the stack (think of it like adding a new piece of paper to your stack). A *pop* will move the value at the top of the stack into a register or memory address and update the stack pointer to indicate the value below it, which is the new top of the stack (taking the top piece of paper off the stack).

How the Stack Works

The program stack grows up from a base address when new functions are called and shrinks down as functions return. As the stack grows taller, the addresses decrease, and as it shrinks, the addresses increase.

The x86 Stack

The stack is not a fundamentally separate object or memory space on the processor. Instead, it is a region of memory that has been allocated and designated to serve as the stack. It exists in memory alongside the rest of the program, and data is simply space allocated by an application. As an example, the following code would allocate 128 bytes that you could use as stack space:

```
section .data
times 128 db 0
stack equ $-4
```

In x86 there are two registers that are used to manage the stack:

- esp: The stack pointer holds the address of the top of the stack.
- ebp: The base pointer holds the address of the base of the stack frame.

Logically, a stack would grow upward, and in x86 this means decreasing in address as shown in Figure 7.2. Think of it like an upside-down thermometer, where 0 is at the top and the largest number is at the bottom.

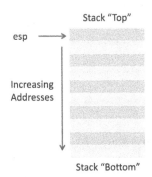

Figure 7.2: Stack address growth

Consider the following fragment of an assembly file:

```
mov esp, stack
...
section .data
times 128 db 0
stack equ $-4
```

The `times 128 db 0` instruction allocates space for a 128-byte stack. Then, the instruction `stack equ $-4` defines a constant *stack*, set to an initial value of the current location ($) minus 4 (i.e., 4 bytes into the end of the stack), that holds the address of the final dword (4-byte chunk) of that stack.

The first instruction in this code sample initializes the stack pointer, *esp*, to this constant value. The stack can then grow up as new data is added via `push` instructions.

Push and Pop

The `push` and `pop` instructions are used to add and remove data from the stack.

Push

The `push` instruction will add 4 bytes or 1 dword to the top of the stack. It takes a single argument that can be a register name, memory address, or constant.

```
push <register>
push <memory>
push <constant>
```

When a `push` is performed, the stack pointer, esp, is automatically decremented by 4 to indicate the new top of the stack. Then, the value being pushed to the stack is placed at this location.

Table 7.2 illustrates how the `push` instruction functions. In this case, the stack pointer, esp, begins with a value of `0x120`, as shown in the left of Table 7.2. Then, the following instructions are executed:

```
; esp = 0x120
mov eax, 0xFEDA8712
push eax
; esp = 0x11C
```

These instructions will place 1 dword or 4 bytes on the stack. To accomplish this, the stack pointer will be decremented to point to address `0x11C`. Then, the value `0xFEDA8712` will be stored on the stack, as shown in the table on the right of Table 7.2.

Table 7.2: Pushing a variable onto the stack

ADDRESS	VALUE
0x11B	
0x11C	
0x11D	
0x11E	
0x11F	
0x120 (**esp**)	0x11
0x121	0x22
0x122	0x33

ADDRESS	VALUE
0x11B	
0x11C (**esp**)	0x12
0x11D	0x87
0x11E	0xDA
0x11F	0xFE
0x120	0x11
0x121	0x22
0x122	0x33

The single `push` instruction wraps a couple of steps into a single instruction. The following code sample is equivalent to the previous:

```
;esp = 0x120
mov eax, 0xFEDA8712
sub esp, 4
mov [esp], eax
; esp = 0x11C
```

In this sample, the value of the stack pointer is explicitly decremented to point to the new top of the stack. Then, the value stored in `eax` is moved to this location. These two approaches are interchangeable, but using `push` is fewer instructions.

Pop

In x86, the `pop` instruction is the inverse of the `push` instruction and removes one dword from the stack. It has the syntax `pop dst`, where *dst* can be a register or memory address.

The `pop` instruction reverses the operations performed by `push`. It starts by moving the value stored at `[esp]` into the indicated register or memory location. Then, it automatically increments `esp` by 4 to point to the new top of the stack.

Table 7.3 illustrates how pop can be used to undo the push from the previous example. At the end of that example, the stack resembled the columns on the left of this table.

```
;esp = 0x11C
pop eax
;esp = 0x120
;eax = 0xfeda8712
```

Table 7.3: Popping a variable from the stack

ADDRESS	VALUE		ADDRESS	VALUE
0x11B			0x11B	
0x11C (esp)	0x12		0x11C	
0x11D	0x87		0x11D	
0x11E	0xDA		0x11E	
0x11F	0xFE		0x11F	
0x120	0x11		0x120 (esp)	0x11
0x121	0x22		0x121	0x22
0x122	0x33		0x122	0x33

Executing the instruction pop eax would update the stack to resemble the image on the right. As part of this process, the eax register would be updated to hold the value 0xFEDA8712. Then, the stack pointer, esp, would be incremented by 4 to a value of 0x120.

As with the push instruction, pop merges a two-step process into a single instruction. The following code is equivalent but explicitly performs each step:

```
;esp = 0x11C
mov eax, [esp]
add esp, 4
;esp = 0x120
;eax = 0xfeda8712
```

The Stack as a Scratch Pad

x86 has a limited number of registers, and it's easy to run out. Often, some kind of swap/scratch area is needed to temporarily store information that you're not done using yet. The stack provides a convenient location to temporarily store values.

For example, consider the following code:

```
mov eax, 0xcafed00d
mov ebx, 0x00c0ffee
add eax, ebx
push eax      ; save to free up eax
...           ; do other things
pop eax       ; retrieve saved eax
```

In this example, the push and pop instructions are used to temporarily store the contents of eax on the stack. This frees up the register to be used in other calculations. When the stored value is needed again, pop can be used to return it to eax.

Using Pop Cautiously

Data is rarely deleted on a computer. For example, when a file is deleted in the file system or a program releases a variable, the memory associated with it is simply marked as available for other uses. The stored data is still present on the disk.

The same is true of the stack in x86. When a value is popped from the stack, it is copied to a register or memory location, but the value remains on the stack. After the stack pointer is adjusted, the popped value is outside the valid range of the stack.

After popping a value, it should be considered deallocated and no longer safe to use. Any attempt to access data outside of the valid range of the stack is dangerous. For example, no legitimate assembly instruction should include [esp-...].

Consider the following example, which shows stack traces of various locations; the relevant stack trace is indicated in the comments (e.g., ; (1)). Each comment location shows the stack after that line has been executed, as shown in Table 7.4.

```
;(1) esp = 0x10C
push 0xbadc0de ; (2)
pop eax  ;(3)  eax = 0xbadc0de
push 0xc0ffee ;(4)
```

Table 7.4: Stack trace examples

(1)	
ADDRESS	VALUE
0x1000	??
0x1004	??
0x1008	??
0x100c (**esp**)	0x11223344
0x1010	0x55667788

(2)	
ADDRESS	VALUE
0x1000	??
0x1004	??
0x1008 (**esp**)	0xbadc0de
0x100c	0x11223344
0x1010	0x55667788

(3)	
ADDRESS	VALUE
0x1000	??
0x1004	??
0x1008	0xbadc0de
0x100c (**esp**)	0x11223344
0x1010	0x55667788

(4)	
ADDRESS	VALUE
0x1000	??
0x1004	??
0x1008 (**esp**)	0xc0ffee
0x100c	0x11223344
0x1010	0x55667788

Notice in stack trace 3, that 0xbadc0de has been popped off the stack, but it is still there, until something else comes to overwrite it, as shown in stack state 4. Again, under legitimate conditions you do not want to rely on/use anything above the currently allocated stack ([esp-..]), but this knowledge can in fact be insightful for other, less legitimate purposes. Later examples either will no longer list the content that is "unallocated" in the stack or will strike through (~~example~~) the value to denote that it's unallocated.

Function Calls and Stack Frames

Higher-level programming languages have the concept of functions, which are chunks of code that can be called from other functions. x86 has the concept of functions as well.

When a function is called, changes are made to the state of the stack. Understanding these changes is essential to understanding how the application works.

Functions in x86

x86's call and ret instructions provide the ability to make functions similar to higher-level programming languages.

call

The call instruction has the syntax call op, where op indicates the address of the function being called. The argument op can be a register, label, or memory address.

```
call eax    ; branch to eax
call label  ; branch to label
call 0x1000 ; branch to 0x1000
```

Like push and pop, call actually bundles multiple steps into a single operation. First, it creates a return address by pushing the address of the next instruction onto the stack. Then, it performs an unconditional jump to the code location indicated by op.

ret

The ret instruction accepts no arguments. Its purpose is to return execution to the calling function.

This is accomplished by a two-step process. First, ret pops the return address saved by call off of the stack. Then, it performs an unconditional jump to that address.

How x86 functions work

With `call` and `ret`, it is possible to build functions directly in x86 or translate them from other languages Consider the following code:

```
void a() {
}

void b() {
    a();
}
```

This code defines two functions, a and b, where b calls a. This code is equivalent to the following in x86:

```
b:
    call a
    ret


a:
    ret
```

Table 7.5 illustrates how running this code would affect the stack. Assume that these instructions are stored at the following locations in memory, with the associated stack traces as marked in comments. Recall the stack shows the state after that instruction has executed.

```
b:
            ; (1)
0x10000   call a   ; (2)
0x10003   ret


a:
0x20012   ret   ; (3)
```

The leftmost image in Table 7.5 shows the initial state of the stack. At this point, `esp` points to address `0x9010`, and `eip` has a value of `0x1000`.

The middle image illustrates what happens when the call to a is executed. At this point, the value of `eip`, which is now `0x10003`, is pushed onto the stack. Now, `eip` points to the first line of code in a, which has an address of `0x20012`.

Once a returns, the original value of `eip` is popped off the stack, causing it to point to the `ret` instruction in b at `0x10003`. The stack pointer is updated as well to point to address `0x9010`. Note that the value `0x10003` remains in memory but is now outside of the stack and should no longer be used or trusted.

Putting together this notion of the stack and functions, take a look at an example. Consider the following set of function definitions:

```
void a() { int x; b(); }
void b() { int x; c(); }
void c() { int x; }
```

Table 7.5: Function calls and the stack

(1)		(2)		(3)	
ADDRESS	VALUE	ADDRESS	VALUE	ADDRESS	VALUE
0x9000	??	0x9000	??	0x9000	??
0x9004	??	0x9004	??	0x9004	??
0x9008	??	0x9008	??	0x9008	??
0x900c	??	0x900c	0x10003	0x900c	~~0x10003~~
0x9010	??	0x9010	??	0x9010	??

REGISTER	VALUE	REGISTER	VALUE	REGISTER	VALUE
esp	0x9010	esp	0x900c	esp	0x9010
eip	0x10000	eip	0x20012	eip	0x10003

This begins with the a() function, which has a single local variable, x, and calls the b function. Table 7.6 illustrates the structure of the stack once a has been called. Note that a's local data is allocated space and added to the stack.

Table 7.6: Program stack after calling a

STACK
a's local data

When a is executed, it declares x and then calls b. This means the flow of execution will switch to run the code contained in b before returning to a.

To ensure that it returns to the correct location in a, the processor stores a *return address* on the stack. This return address is the address of the instruction following the call to b in a.

After a's return address is placed on the stack, the processor stores b's local data there. Table 7.7 shows the state of the stack before the processor executes the first instruction in b.

Table 7.7: Program stack after calling b

STACK
b'local data
a's return address
a's local data

Like a, b will declare its local variables and then make a call to another function, c. When executing this call, a return address for b will be placed on the stack as well as the local variables of the called function. Once this setup for c is complete, the stack will resemble Table 7.8.

Table 7.8: Program stack after calling c

STACK
c' local data
b'sreturn address
b's local data
a's return address
a's local data

In c, the local variable x is declared, and then the function terminates. When the processor is done in c, code flow needs to return to the calling function b.

At this point, c's local data is at the top of the stack but is no longer needed. The processor can pop this data from the stack, changing the stack pointer to indicate b's return address.

The processor can then pop this return address off of the stack, storing it in eip and updating the stack pointer through the ret instruction. This enables the program to return to b and resume executing any code following its call to c. At this point, the stack returns to the state shown in Table 7.7.

The call to c is the last instruction in b, so it will immediately return as well. Like the return from c, this involves popping local variables off of the stack and updating eip by popping a's return address off of the stack and into eip (via ret). Once this is complete, the stack will resemble Table 7.6.

After this return from b, a will also return. a's local data will be popped off of the stack. Then, the eip register will be updated based on the return address of the calling function, which occurred prior to our analysis and is not shown in Table 7.6, and execution will resume within that function.

Stack Analysis

As functions are called and return from calls, they have an impact on the program stack. For example, consider the following code:

```
void a() { }
void b() { }
void c() { a(); b(); }
```

This code defines three functions, a, b, and c, and c calls both of the other two.

When a function is running or is within the call stack of the running function, its return address is in the stack. For example, when a is running, the return addresses for a and c are on the stack. Similarly, when b is running, the return addresses for b and c are on the stack.

Examination of the return addresses stored on the stack provides visibility into how a particular point in the program was reached. Each function in the call stack will have its return address local variables and scratch data visible in the stack.

This practice is called *unwinding* the stack. In gdb, the info stack command will show the current state of the stack.

Calling Conventions

The call and ret instructions make it possible to create functions in assembly. However, with only call and ret, these functions must be self-contained without the ability to pass data between functions.

In higher-level programming languages, functions commonly have parameters or arguments, which are variables that are passed to a function by the calling function. However, machine code doesn't have the concept of parameters; there are only registers and memory.

x86 has all of the tools necessary to create parameters. Higher-level programming languages that use parameters are translated into assembly. It's the responsibility of the programmer or the compiler to choose how to use these tools.

Why Conventions Are Necessary

With registers, the stack, and even memory locations, x86 has the ability to pass values from one function to another. Parameters can be stored in registers or pushed and popped from the stack.

However, communication or agreements between functions is necessary if they plan to use parameters, registers, or the stack in a consistent way. If the calling function is using certain locations to pass parameters, the callee needs to know which locations are used for which values. The same is true if the callee is returning data to the caller.

```
void caller() {   ... callee()} //nomenclature definition
```

Also, if the caller is using a register to store its internal values, the callee needs to know not to overwrite those values. This is especially a concern if the callee uses operations like `mul` that modify registers but are easy to miss.

Within a small program, the developer could design their code to contain that knowledge. If function a takes three parameters, the developer could create a scheme that passes them via registers or the stack. Similarly, the struct needed by function b could be passed by allocating a particular location in memory.

However, while this approach may work on a small scale, it is unscalable and prone to error. An oversight could result in vital data being accidentally clobbered by a `mul` operation. Also, such an ad hoc scheme makes it more difficult to work with teams of developers.

Introduction to Calling Conventions

Calling conventions are designed to make it easier to pass data between functions by defining the rules of engagement between functions. They are part of the application binary interface (ABI), which is the lowest-level definition of how pieces of code interact.

A calling convention must define a few rules, including the following:

- **Parameter location:** Where will parameters be passed from the caller to the callee (stack versus registers)?

- **Parameter ordering:** How will parameters be organized, on the stack or into registers?

- **Stack cleanup:** If the stack is used, which function is responsible for removing values from the stack (caller versus callee cleanup)?

- **Register access:** Which registers can the callee use without needing to back up their previous values and restore them before returning?

■ **Return values:** Where and how will values be returned from the callee to the caller?

Calling conventions can vary based on different factors, including the following:

■ Architecture (x86 versus ARM)

■ Operating system (UN*X versus Windows)

■ Programming language (C versus Java)

■ Even compiler (GCC versus Microsoft)

In the early days of programming, standards didn't really exist. As a result, programs couldn't work together if their developers didn't agree on a calling convention.

Initially, there were many different companies, each with its own conventions. Over time, these have been whittled down to a handful of popular standards, including the following:

■ cdecl

■ syscall

■ optlink

■ pascall

■ register

■ stdcall

■ fastcall

■ safecall

■ thiscall

cdecl

cdecl ("see deckel") is short for "C declaration" and is one of the most common calling conventions on the x86 architecture. While it originated with C, cdecl is used for a variety of different programming languages and architectures. It is also a useful standard when writing assembly by hand.

cdecl defines the following rules:

■ **Stack-based parameters:** Arguments are pushed from right to left onto the stack to be passed to the callee.

■ **Caller cleanup:** The calling function is responsible for removing arguments from the stack once the callee returns.

- **Return value:** The eax register is used to hold a function's return value.

- **Available registers:** The callee is free to modify eax, ecx, and edx. The caller should save any needed values in these registers before making the call. The callee should save the values of other registers before using them and restore them before returning.

Consider the instruction int s = add(1,2). Using the cdecl standard, this would translate to the following x86 assembly code:

```
; Save regs we need to keep according to cdecl.
; Optional if we don't intend to modify these registers.
push    eax
push    ecx
push    edx
; Push parameters from right to left. The original
; code was add(1,2), so left to right is 2, then 1
push    2
push    1

; Call add.
call    add

; Remove parameters from the stack. We pushed 2x 4-byte values
; we can either do 2 pops, or add 8 back to the stack
add esp, 8

; Save the return value into eax (where cdecl says return values go)
mov [s], eax

; Restore the saved registers, remember its last
; in first out, so we pushed edx last, meaning it is the first to pop
pop edx
pop ecx
pop eax
```

Saving Registers

In cdecl, functions are free to modify eax, ecx, and edx without saving their values. Therefore, the following function, f, is valid under the standard.

```
f:  mov ecx, 0xd15ea5e
    mov edx, 0xfee1dead
    lea eax, [ecx + edx]
    ret
```

However, any other registers used by the callee must have their values stored before they are modified and the originals restored before returning.

```
f:   push   ebx
     push   ebp
     push   esi
     mov    ebp, 0xd15ea5e
     mov    ebx, 0xfee1dead
     lea    esi, [ebp + ebx]
     pop    esi
     pop    ebp
     pop    ebx
     ret
```

This function uses ebx, ebp, and esi, so it pushes their previous values onto the stack before using the registers and pops these values back into the registers before returning.

With cdecl, a calling function knows which registers' values it can trust after calling another function. The callee is allowed to modify the values of eax, ecx, and edx at will, so the caller should save these registers' values if it wants to use them later. However, all of the other registers' values should be preserved by the callee, so there is no need to save them before making a call.

For example, consider the following code block:

```
g:
     mov    ebx, 0xd15ea5e
     mov    ecx, 0xfee1dead
     call   f
```

After the call to f, function g can rely on ebx retaining the value 0xd15ea5e. However, it cannot assume that ecx will still have the value 0xfee1dead.

Return Values

In higher-level programming languages, functions commonly use return values to pass information to their callers. For example, a function may be designed to return 0 upon successful completion or an error code if something went wrong. For example, the following function returns a value of 1 upon completion:

```
int f()
{
    return 1;
}
```

When using the cdecl calling convention, this return value is stored in the eax register. The following x86 code is equivalent to the previous function f:

```
f:
     mov   eax, 1
     ret
```

Functions can be of varying types and have different return values that match these types. For example, the following function is designed to return a char* pointer and defaults to a NULL pointer:

```
char* f()
{
    return NULL;
}
```

In x86, a register can be used as a pointer. The following x86 code uses a value of 0 to represent the NULL pointer equivalent; eax could also be used to indicate the location of a char array in memory.

```
f:
    mov  eax, 0
    ret
```

Accessing Parameters

The cdecl standard uses the stack to pass parameters to a function. Some things to keep in mind when attempting to access parameters include the following:

- The top of the stack (last value pushed) is [esp].
- The stack grows down (toward lower addresses).
- The call instruction pushes the return address onto the stack.
- The caller pushed arguments right to left.
- The callee's return value should be stored in *eax*.

Keeping these factors in mind, consider how a call to the following function would be implemented in x86:

```
int add (int x, int y)
{
        return x+y;
}
```

In x86, the equivalent of this would be the following:

```
f:
    push 1   ; y
    push 2   ; x
    call add
    mov  [s], eax   ;save the return value to memory
    pop  eax
    pop  eax
    ret
```

```
; int add(int x, int y) { return x+y; }
add:
    mov eax, [esp+4]      ; retrieve x from stack
    mov edx, [esp+8]      ; retrieve y from stack
    add eax, edx
    ret
```

When a function is called, it has an effect on the current program stack. Table 7.9 shows the state of the stack within the add function.

Table 7.9: Stack in add function

ADDRESS	VALUE
0xeff0	
0xeff4	
0xeff8 (esp)	(Return address)
0xeffc	2
0xf000	1

While it's possible to access parameters from [esp], this approach can run into problems. Consider how the following instructions within add affect the value of esp:

```
; int f(int x);
f:
    mov   eax, [esp+4]     ; x is at [esp+4]
    push ebx               ; save ebx
    mov   ebx, [esp+8]     ; x is now at [esp+8]
    ...
```

As parameters are popped from the stack by the callee, the location of the top of the stack changes. As a result, the locations of parameters relative to esp change as well.

Stack Frames

The value of esp changes too frequently to be a useful frame of reference for the locations of variables within the stack. Each time a value is pushed or popped, the value of esp and the relative locations of the other stack variables change.

This is where the other stack register ebp (also known as the base pointer or frame pointer) comes into play. The ebp register points to the bottom of the current *stack frame*, which is the bottom of a section of memory on the stack used by a particular function.

Prologues and Epilogues

x86 functions commonly start and end with chunks of boilerplate code. The purpose of this code is to set up and tear down the function's stack frame.

Setting Up a Stack Frame

The function *prologue* or preamble sets up the stack frame and is found at the very beginning of the function. The prologue performs two functions.

- Save the previous stack frame with `push ebp`.
- Set the new stack frame with `mov ebp, esp`.

These instructions appear at the very beginning of a function. Table 7.10 shows the effect of each on the stack.

```
; (1)
push ebp ; (2)
move ebp, esp ; (3)
push 0x11223344 ; (4)
```

Table 7.10: Effects of function prologue on stack

(1)		(2)	
ADDRESS	VALUE	ADDRESS	VALUE
0xefe8	??	0xefe8	??
0xeff0	??	0xeff0	??
0xeff4	??	0xeff4 (**esp**)	Old ebp
0xeff8 (**esp**)	(return address)	0xeff8	(return address)
0xeffc	2	0xeffc	2
0xf000	1	0xf000	1

(3)		(4)	
ADDRESS	VALUE	ADDRESS	VALUE
0xefe8	??	0xefe8	??
0xeff0	??	0xeff0 (**esp**)	0x11223344
0xeff4 (**esp, ebp**)	Old ebp	0xeff4 (**ebp**)	Old ebp
0xeff8	(return address)	0xeff8	(return address)
0xeffc	2	0xeffc	2
0xf000	1	0xf000	1

The first table shows the stack before the function begins. At this point, the function parameters are pushed to the stack (from right to left) as well as the caller's return address.

When the `push ebp` instruction executes, the previous function's base pointer is stored on the stack. The resulting stack is shown in the second table.

The third table shows the stack after the `mov ebp, esp` instruction is executed. While the stack itself is not updated, the new `ebp` points to the return address of the calling function, same as `esp`.

After these instructions are executed, the callee can push local variables to the stack. While this will modify the value of `esp`, the value of `ebp` will stay constant (table four). This makes it possible to access parameters and local variables relative to a fixed point, `ebp`, rather than the more mutable `esp`.

Tearing Down a Stack Frame

Creating a new stack frame for the current function means you've lost the calling function's stack frame. Before the function returns, it needs to undo the changes that it's made and restore the caller's stack frame.

The function epilogue appears at the end of the function and accomplishes this process. It consists of the following three instructions:

```
mov esp, ebp
pop ebp
ret
```

The first step of this process is removing any data that has been added to the stack. Since data isn't actually deleted from memory, this simply involves changing the stack pointer with the instruction `mov esp, ebp`. This operation would restore the state of the stack as in Table 7.11.

```
; function body (1)
mov esp, ebp ;(2)
pop ebp ; (3)
```

Next, the value of the base pointer should be restored to that of the calling function. Recall in the preamble this was pushed onto the stack, so this is accomplished via the instruction `pop ebp`, which restores the stack to the original state. At this point, the stack is in the proper state to return to the calling function.

While it's possible to perform this teardown via these two instructions, x86 offers an alternative option. The `leave` instruction is equivalent to the following two instructions:

```
mov esp, ebp
pop ebp
```

Table 7.11: Effects of function epilogue on stack

(1)		(2)	
ADDRESS	**VALUE**	**ADDRESS**	**VALUE**
0xefe8 (**esp**)	0x3325d321	0xefe8	0x3325d321
0xeff0	0x11223344	0xeff0	0x11223344
0xeff4 (**ebp**)	Old ebp	0xeff4 (**ebp**, **esp**)	Old ebp
0xeff8	(return address)	0xeff8	(return address)
0xeffc	2	0xeffc	2
0xf000	1	0xf000	1

(3)	
ADDRESS	**VALUE**
0xefe8	0x3325d321
0xeff0	0x11223344
0xeff4 (**esp**)	Old ebp
0xeff8	(return address)
0xeffc	2
0xf000	1

Accessing Parameters

Stack frames are designed to make it easier to access parameters and other values on the stack from within a function. Using the static ebp as a reference simplifies the process of determining where a particular value is on the stack. For example, Table 7.12 shows the locations of certain values on the stack for

Table 7.12: Stack locations for common values

LOCATION	VALUE
[ebp + 0]	Previous frame pointer
[ebp + 4]	Function return address
[ebp + 8]	First parameter
[ebp + 12]	Second parameter
[ebp + 16]	Third parameter
...	...

any function using the `cdecl` convention. Since `ebp` does not move during a function, these relationships and offsets will always be the same. This means if the caller passed in a variable, the first one will always be at `ebp+8`, the second will always be at `ebp+12`, etc.

The following example shows the build-up and usage of function parameters. As with all of these stack examples, remember that each stack is shown after the instruction has executed.

```
f:
    push  1    ; y
    push  2    ; x    ; (1)
    call  add
    mov   [s], eax
    pop   eax
    pop   eax
    ret


; int add(int x, int y) { return x+y; }
add:
        ; (2)
    push  ebp
    mov   ebp, esp    ; (3)
    mov   eax, [ebp+8]      ; retrieve x from stack
    mov   edx, [ebp+12]     ; retrieve y from stack
    add   eax, edx
    mov   esp, ebp
    pop   ebp
    ret
```

Table 7.13 shows the stack contents for points (1), (2), and (3) in the preceding code.

Table 7.13: Stack content at points 1, 2, and 3 in the program

(1)		(2)		(3)	
ADDRESS	VALUE	ADDRESS	VALUE	ADDRESS	VALUE
0xeff4	??	0xeff4		0xeff4 (**esp, ebp**)	Old ebp
0xeff8	??	0xeff8 (**esp**)	return address	0xeff8	return address
0xeffc (**esp**)	2	0xeffc	2	0xeffc	2
0xf000	1	0xf000	1	0xf000	1

Once location 3 is reached, based on your knowledge of `cdecl` and the stack frame, you know with confidence the first parameter, *x*, will be at location ebp+8 and have a value of 2. The second parameter, *y*, will be at location ebp+12 and have a value of 1.

Local Variables

A function's local variables are stored on the stack above the previous frame pointer (at lower addresses). After the stack frame has been set up, space can be allocated for local variables simply by subtracting the required amount of space from esp. This allocation will automatically be undone in the function epilogue when the stack pointer is reset based on the base pointer.

For example, consider the following function:

```
void one_up(int x)
{
        int y = x + 1;
}
```

In addition to its incoming argument, *x*, it also defines a local variable, *y*, that will be stored on the stack. The following code shows how this function would look after being translated into x86:

```
one_up:
    push ebp
    mov  ebp, esp
    sub  esp, 4          ; allocate space for local y (4 bytes)
    mov  eax, [ebp+8]    ; load parameter x
    inc  eax             ; x + 1
    mov  [ebp-4], eax    ; save local y
      ;stack shown here
    mov  esp, ebp
    pop  ebp
    ret
```

This program's stack frame is shown in Table 7.14. Note that while *esp* now points to 0xeff4, the value of ebp remains the same (pointing to the caller's saved ebp) after local variables are allocated on the stack. Both parameters and local variables can be easily accessed relative to ebp.

Table 7.14: Stack frame of one_up program

ADDRESS	VALUE
0xeff4 (**esp**)	y
0xeff8 (**ebp**)	Old ebp
0xeffc	Ret address
0xf000	x

As with parameters, `cdecl` ensures that local variables are stored at consistent locations across different functions. Table 7.15 shows the locations of local variables relative to `ebp`. In reverse engineering, knowledge of `ebp` becomes incredibly powerful.

> **TIP**   Understanding that `ebp` minus anything is referencing a local variable, something allocated inside of the function, while access to `ebp` plus anything is accessing information provided to the function by the caller, can help you quickly spot interesting pieces of code or identify critical functionality that could be manipulated, say, by input to the program.

Table 7.15: Stack locations for local variables

LOCATION	VALUE
[ebp - 4]	First local variable
[ebp - 8]	Second local variable
[ebp - 12]	Third local variable
. . .	. . .

Shortcuts

It's possible to individually push each parameter or local variable to the stack; each push updates the stack pointer and moves the value into place.

Instead, a common route compilers take is to allocate space all at once before moving values into place. For example, the following instructions are less common to find in compiled code:

```
push 1
push 2
```

Instead, these instructions are more likely to be assembled to the following:

```
sub esp, 8      ; allocate 8 bytes on the stack
mov dword [esp+4], 1 ; put 1 on the stack
mov dword [esp], 2   ; put 2 on the stack
```

Stack Alignment

Some compilers will enforce 32-byte stack alignment when entering a function. This means seeking for the memory address of the stack pointer to be evenly divisible by 32. This was historically more efficient for systems to fetch memory on 32 byte-aligned bounds. This efficiency improvement may not still exist, but you will still see compilers occasionally doing things to maintain stack alignment.

How you might see this manifest is, when allocating space for local variables, they may allocate excess space to maintain this alignment.

This means it is common for unused space to exist within a function's stack frame. When reversing, don't get hung up on excess space because it is completely normal. When writing your own code, this isn't something you need to manually do, but the goal of this book is to equip you to recognize this in code and know it's something you can mostly ignore.

The Big Picture

When a function is called, it makes several changes to the program stack. To see all of these changes in one place, consider the following program:

```
void hack(...)
{
    ...
}

void drink(...)
{
    ...
    hack(...);
    ...
}
```

Each of the two functions in this program may have zero or more parameters and local variables. Figure 7.3 shows the structure of the stack frames for each function.

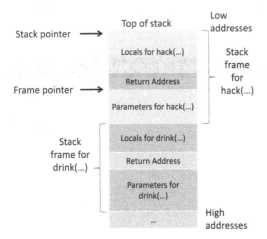

Figure 7.3: Stack frames for hack and drink functions

Things to Memorize

x86 assembly programs can be complex. To be effective at x86 reverse engineering, it is vital that you memorize certain things.

The first of these is the structure of a function's stack frame. Table 7.16 shows the complete stack frame, including parameters, return addresses, local variables, and scratch space.

Table 7.16: Complete function stack frame

STACK	
...	
[ebp–12] or [ebp-0xC]	Third local variable
[ebp-8]	Second local variable
[ebp-4]	First local variable
[ebp]	Previous frame pointer
[ebp+4]	Function return address
[ebp+8]	First parameter
[ebp+12] or [ebp+0xC]	Second parameter
[ebp+16] or [ebp+0xF]	Third parameter
...	

Another important thing to memorize is the difference between boilerplate and complete function prologues and epilogues. Table 7.17 shows how a boilerplate prologue differs from one that includes stack allocations for local variables.

Table 7.17: Two types of prologues

BOILERPLATE PROLOGUE	COMPLETE PROLOGUE

push ebp
  ; save stack frame
	push ebp
	  ; save stack frame

mov ebp, esp ; start new frame	mov ebp, esp ; start new frame
	sub esp, 20 ; allocate 5 4 byte locals
	push ebx ; save modified regs
	push esi
	(etc)

Table 7.18: Two types of epilogues

BOILERPLATE EPILOGUE	COMPLETE EPILOGUE
`mov esp, ebp   ; discard locals`	`(etc)`
`pop ebp        ; restore frame`	`pop esi`
`ret            ; return`	`        ; restore modified regs`
	`pop ebx`
	`mov esp, ebp ; discard locals`
	`pop ebp       ; restore frame`
	`ret           ; return`

The function epilogue reverses the effects of the function prologue. Table 7.18 shows the equivalent epilogues for each of these prologues.

Summary

This chapter explored vital concepts for reversing and cracking applications. Before moving on, be sure that you have a firm grasp of how control flow can work within an applications and the ins and outs of functions and their stack frames.

Compilers and Optimizers

For many higher-level programming languages, compilation is a vital part of the process of converting an application from source code to machine-readable binary code. During this process, a compiler may make minor changes to the code to make it as fast and efficient as possible.

The process of compiling and optimizing an application can make it more difficult to reverse engineer. This chapter describes how to find a starting point for reversing an application and some of the common actions that compilers take that can complicate reverse engineering.

Finding Starting Code

When code is compiled, the compiler introduces a large amount of boilerplate that is executed before the actual application code is ever called. When reverse engineering, one of the art forms you'll need to master is how to skip over this and focus on the target code, not the boilerplate setup. However, identifying the entry point into the target code can be complex.

When reversing someone else's code, it's unlikely that the code will be compiled with debugging symbols. This means function and variable names and other information that could provide a hint regarding the actual code's entry point have been stripped from the application. Figure 8.1 shows what opening a file without debugging symbols looks like in gdb.

```
swagger@ubuntu:~/Documents/osu/ec$ gdb keychecker.out
GNU gdb (GDB) 7.5-ubuntu
Copyright (C) 2012 Free Software Foundation, Inc.
License GPLv3+: GNU GPL version 3 or later <http://gnu.org/licenses/gpl.html>
This is free software: you are free to change and redistribute it.
There is NO WARRANTY, to the extent permitted by law.  Type "show copying"
and "show warranty" for details.
This GDB was configured as "x86_64-linux-gnu".
For bug reporting instructions, please see:
<http://www.gnu.org/software/gdb/bugs/>...
Reading symbols from /home/swagger/Documents/osu/ec/keychecker.out...(no debugging symbols found)...done.
```

Figure 8.1: Application without debugging symbols in gdb

This lack of debugging symbols creates a major challenge because applications written in higher languages rather than pure assembly include much more overhead and compiler-generated symbols. The following is sample output from an info files command in gdb showing the number of different sections that exist in a simple executable:

```
Entry point: 0x80483a0
0x08048154 - 0x08048167 is .interp
0x08048168 - 0x08048188 is .note.ABI-tag
0x08048188 - 0x080481ac is .note.gnu.build-id
0x080481ac - 0x080481cc is .gnu.hash
0x080481cc - 0x0804823c is .dynsym
0x0804823c - 0x080482a6 is .dynstr
0x080482a6 - 0x080482b4 is .gnu.version
0x080482b4 - 0x080482e4 is .gnu.version_r
0x080482e4 - 0x080482ec is .rel.dyn
0x080482ec - 0x08048314 is .rel.plt
0x08048314 - 0x08048338 is .init
0x08048340 - 0x080483a0 is .plt
0x080483a0 - 0x08048648 is .text
0x08048648 - 0x0804865d is .fini
0x08048660 - 0x080486a9 is .rodata
0x080486ac - 0x080486f0 is .eh_frame_hdr
0x080486f0 - 0x080487f4 is .eh_frame
0x08049f08 - 0x08049f0c is .init_array
0x08049f0c - 0x08049f10 is .fini_array
0x08049f10 - 0x08049f14 is .jcr
0x08049f14 - 0x08049ffc is .dynamic
0x08049ffc - 0x0804a000 is .got
0x0804a000 - 0x0804a020 is .got.plt
0x0804a020 - 0x0804a028 is .data
0x0804a028 - 0x0804a02c is .bss
0xf7fdc114 - 0xf7fdc138 is .note.gnu.build-id in /lib/ld-linux.so.2
0xf7fdc138 - 0xf7fdc1f4 is .hash in /lib/ld-linux.so.2
0xf7fdc1f4 - 0xf7fdc2d4 is .gnu.hash in /lib/ld-linux.so.2
0xf7fdc2d4 - 0xf7fdc494 is .dynsym in /lib/ld-linux.so.2
0xf7fdc494 - 0xf7fdc612 is .dynstr in /lib/ld-linux.so.2
0xf7fdc612 - 0xf7fdc64a is .gnu.version in /lib/ld-linux.so.2
0xf7fdc64c - 0xf7fdc714 is .gnu.version_d in /lib/ld-linux.so.2
```

```
0xf7fdc714 - 0xf7fdc77c is .rel.dyn in /lib/ld-linux.so.2
0xf7fdc77c - 0xf7fdc7ac is .rel.plt in /lib/ld-linux.so.2
0xf7fdc7b0 - 0xf7fdc820 is .plt in /lib/ld-linux.so.2
0xf7fdc820 - 0xf7ff4baf is .text in /lib/ld-linux.so.2
0xf7ff4bc0 - 0xf7ff8a60 is .rodata in /lib/ld-linux.so.2
0xf7ff8a60 - 0xf7ff90ec is .eh_frame_hdr in /lib/ld-linux.so.2
0xf7ff90ec - 0xf7ffb654 is .eh_frame in /lib/ld-linux.so.2
0xf7ffccc0 - 0xf7ffcf3c is .data.rel.ro in /lib/ld-linux.so.2
0xf7ffcf3c - 0xf7ffcff4 is .dynamic in /lib/ld-linux.so.2
```

This list can get even longer in more complex binaries, with numerous dependencies and libraries. Looking at this output, you know that the .text section of the executable is located at address 0x080483a0. Disassembling the code at this location can provide a hint to the entry point of the target code. Figure 8.2 shows the result of disassembling the code at this location in gdb.

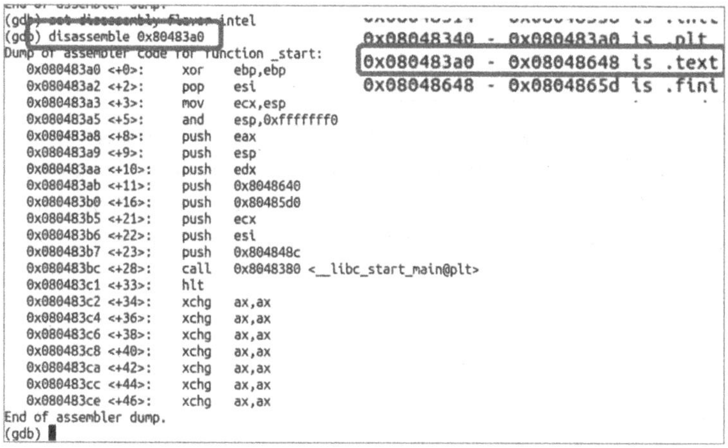

Figure 8.2: .text disassembly in gdb

When searching for the entry point to the target code, this can depend on the exact compiler and language used to build. You'll see an example for finding starting code in a C/C++ application, as that's still one of the most common languages used today. To begin with, look for a call to __libc_start_main. The address of the target code will be passed as a parameter to this function, and given what you know of calling conventions, you know that means we're looking for what's put on the stack before the call.

In Figure 8.2, the address 0x804848c is pushed onto the stack right before the call to __libc_start_main, making it a parameter to the function. Therefore, the target code begins at that address. Figure 8.3 shows a disassembly of the main function, including calls to libc.

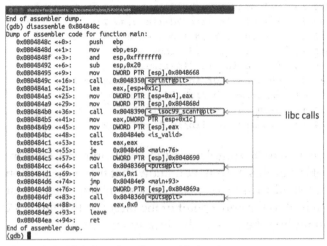

Figure 8.3: Main function disassembly in gdb

Compilers

Compilers take code and translate it to machine code that the processor can read. There are various things that compilers can do to affect reverse engineering, both intentionally and unintentionally. This section focuses on unintentional changes; intentional techniques such as obfuscation will be covered in Chapter 12, "Defense."

Optimization

Compilers can be configured to optimize code based on various metrics, including speed and disk size, or not optimized at all. The code can look very different based on whether optimizations are applied.

Consider the following code sample. This code implements a simple if statement with two conditions.

```
int main(int argc, char* argv[])
{
        if (argc >= 3 && argc <= 8)
        {
                printf("valid number of args\n");
        }
}
```

Figure 8.4 shows what the code looks like in a disassembler (more on this in Chapter 11, "Patching and Advanced Tooling," don't worry) when compiled with no optimizations. Note that the checks for the two conditions comparing the values to 2 and 8 are clearly visible in the code.

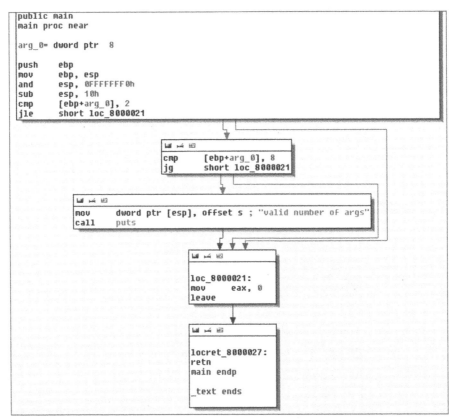

```
public main
main proc near

arg_0= dword ptr   8

push    ebp
mov     ebp, esp
and     esp, 0FFFFFFF0h
sub     esp, 10h
cmp     [ebp+arg_0], 2
jle     short loc_8000021
```

```
cmp     [ebp+arg_0], 8
jg      short loc_8000021
```

```
mov     dword ptr [esp], offset s ; "valid number of args"
call    puts
```

```
loc_8000021:
mov     eax, 0
leave
```

```
locret_8000027:
retn
main endp

_text ends
```

Figure 8.4: Unoptimized code in a disassembler

Figure 8.5 shows the same code when optimized for speed and space. The comparisons with the values 2 and 8 are no longer visible in the code, and the code no longer looks like an `if` statement with two conditions.

Figure 8.6 shows the code optimized solely based on disk space. Again, the two comparisons are missing.

If you examine the code, you'll see that the code checks if $(argc-3) > 5$. If $argc < 3$, then subtracting 3 will cause an underflow and cause the value in eax to be a large positive number. If $argc > 8$, then $argc-3 > 5$. In both of these cases, the result will be greater than 5, so the optimized statement is equivalent to the original test. Compiler optimizations result in equivalent logic, but they can make code much more difficult to read and reason about.

Most compilers have options for setting the level of optimization. While you're learning, if you're having difficulty reversing an application you've written, try disabling optimizations when compiling. On the flip side, if you want to make your code more difficult to reverse engineer, compiler optimizations are an easy and beneficial way to do so.

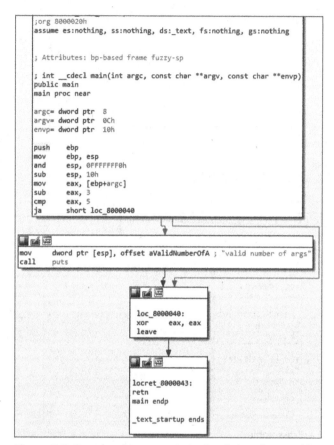

```
;org 8000020h
assume es:nothing, ss:nothing, ds:_text, fs:nothing, gs:nothing


; Attributes: bp-based frame fuzzy-sp

; int __cdecl main(int argc, const char **argv, const char **envp)
public main
main proc near

argc= dword ptr  8
argv= dword ptr  0Ch
envp= dword ptr  10h

push      ebp
mov       ebp, esp
and       esp, 0FFFFFFF0h
sub       esp, 10h
mov       eax, [ebp+argc]
sub       eax, 3
cmp       eax, 5
ja        short loc_8000040
```

```
mov       dword ptr [esp], offset aValidNumberOfA ; "valid number of args"
call      puts
```

```
loc_8000040:
xor       eax, eax
leave
```

```
locret_8000043:
retn
main endp

_text_startup ends
```

Figure 8.5: Speed and space-optimized code in a disassembler

Stripping

Stripping a binary means removing all information that is not necessary for the code to execute, including the symbol table. An unstripped binary retains its symbol table, while a stripped one does not.

Symbols can be extremely useful for debugging an application. For example, consider the following code:

```
// Declare an external function
extern double bar(double x);

// Define a public function
double foo(int count)
{
        double sum = 0.0;

        // Sum all the values bar(1) to bar(count)
        for (int i = 1; i <= count; i++)
```

```
                        sum += bar((double) i);
              return sum;
}
```

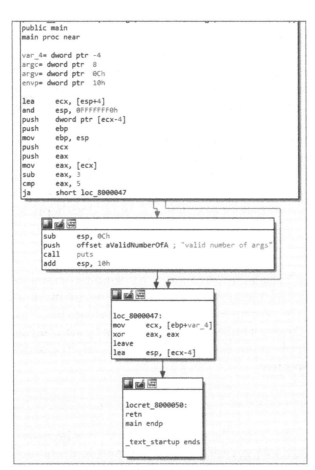

Figure 8.6: Space-optimized code in a disassembler

If this code is parsed by a compiler, it will at least contain the symbol table entries shown in Figure 8.7. Symbols are so useful in debugging that Microsoft allows you to download symbols for their applications in case you need to troubleshoot! This additional information can be invaluable for understanding the intent behind an application.

Symbol name	Type	Scope
bar	function, double	extern
x	double	function parameter
foo	function, double	global
count	int	function parameter
sum	double	block local
i	int	for-loop statement

Figure 8.7: Application debugging symbols

If a file is stripped, it will show that no debugging symbols are found when opened in gdb, as shown in Figure 8.1. These files are much more difficult to reverse engineer.

Symbols can be stripped from an application in a few different ways. One option is to use compiler flags, such as gcc -fno-rtti -s. Another option is to use post-build stripping tools, such as strip in Linux.

Symbols make it easier for an attacker to reverse engineer an application because they can help with locating areas of interest and understanding the intent behind certain variables. However, there are legitimate reasons to leave an application unstripped. For example, symbols help with creating crash reports and error logs and support legitimate debugging to fix client errors. While learning, if you are writing your own code and compiling it to practice with, start by making sure you're building with symbols left in. As you progress in your skills, then remove symbols. When reverse engineering someone else's code, it's highly unlikely you will find symbols have been left in it, but it does happen!

Linking

Applications are rarely written in isolation anymore. What's more common is to include libraries that provide core pieces of capabilities (such as communications, logging, drawing, etc.). When compiling an application that uses libraries, there are two options for how those get built. These libraries can be statically or dynamically linked into the application. Each has its benefits and drawbacks from a software cracking perspective.

Static Linking

With static linking, libraries are built into the application itself. This improves the speed of execution because the target addresses of any calls to the library are built into it at compile time. Also, statically linked applications are more portable because they have fewer dependencies on the environment.

However, static linking also has its downsides. Statically linked applications are larger because the entire library is built into the executable, even if you use only one function from a large library. Additionally, any updates to the library require recompilation of the applications using them.

The file bloat caused by static linking can be significant for programs. For example, as shown in Figure 8.8, even a simple one-line "hello world" program will link dozens of libraries.

Dynamic Linking

Dynamic linking is the other option and the default choice for many compilers. With dynamic linking, the required libraries are located on the system at runtime.

If a library is not already loaded into system memory, the library must be found on the system and loaded into the shared library memory; however, common libraries are likely already loaded and available for use.

```
0xf7fdc114 - 0xf7fdc138 is .note.gnu.build-id in /lib/ld-linux.so.2
0xf7fdc138 - 0xf7fdc1f4 is .hash in /lib/ld-linux.so.2
0xf7fdc1f4 - 0xf7fdc2d4 is .gnu.hash in /lib/ld-linux.so.2
0xf7fdc2d4 - 0xf7fdc494 is .dynsym in /lib/ld-linux.so.2
0xf7fdc494 - 0xf7fdc612 is .dynstr in /lib/ld-linux.so.2
0xf7fdc612 - 0xf7fdc64a is .gnu.version in /lib/ld-linux.so.2
0xf7fdc64c - 0xf7fdc714 is .gnu.version_d in /lib/ld-linux.so.2
0xf7fdc714 - 0xf7fdc77c is .rel.dyn in /lib/ld-linux.so.2
0xf7fdc77c - 0xf7fdc7ac is .rel.plt in /lib/ld-linux.so.2
0xf7fdc7b0 - 0xf7fdc820 is .plt in /lib/ld-linux.so.2

0xf7fdc820 - 0xf7ff4baf is .text in /lib/ld-linux.so.2   96KB!
0xf7ff4bc0 - 0xf7ff8a60 is .rodata in /lib/ld-linux.so.2
0xf7ff8a60 - 0xf7ff90ec is .eh_frame_hdr in /lib/ld-linux.so.2
0xf7ff90ec - 0xf7ffb654 is .eh_frame in /lib/ld-linux.so.2
0xf7ffccc0 - 0xf7ffcf3c is .data.rel.ro in /lib/ld-linux.so.2
0xf7ffcf3c - 0xf7ffcff4 is .dynamic in /lib/ld-linux.so.2

..(many more)...
```

Figure 8.8: Linked libraries in "hello world" program

Dynamic linking reduces application size and eliminates the need to recompile an application after a library update if the update is backward compatible. Additionally, dynamically linked applications can be faster at load time if the libraries that they use are already loaded into memory.

However, dynamically linked applications depend on the libraries that they need being installed on the system and can be slower than statically linked ones (if dependencies are not already loaded and need to be located and loaded). In addition to the need to load any libraries not already in memory, dynamically linked applications need to find the address of called functions at runtime. This involves searching the shared memory space for the library and may require a great deal of memory paging.

Security Impacts of Linking

The choice of whether to use static or dynamic linking depends on the developer or the compiler. But putting your software cracking hats on, both options have their security implications.

Reverse engineers typically prefer that an application be statically linked. Static linking makes it easier to determine the exact load address of shared library functions, which is useful when crafting exploits. It means you can leverage code in the shared libraries to perform your exploitation, and that code will be at a predictable location inside of your binary at runtime. Leveraging a library that is linked dynamically is possible, but it is much more difficult because of the need to search for the desired library in the shared library memory and locate its address every single time, as it will move and be unpredictable.

Crackers, on the other hand, tend to prefer dynamically linked libraries. Dynamic linking results in much less code to sift through, and crackers are interested solely in an application's custom code, not the shared library code.

Summary

The process of compiling and optimizing an application can make it much more difficult to reverse engineer even if the compiler isn't intentionally obfuscating it. However, like any anti-reversing protection, this can only slow down the process since no software is uncrackable.

Reverse Engineering: Tools and Strategies

Up until this point, the focus of this book has been on understanding how the guts of computers work. This is essential to being an effective software cracker.

Now that you have the foundation, the focus shifts to the art of software cracking. To experiment and practice cracking, you'll work with a variety of targets:

- **Real software:** Software taken from the real world. When analyzing real software, you must take into account copyright law to ensure no copyright violations.

- **Manufactured examples:** Applications written for this book to illustrate specific concepts.

- **crackmes:** Small crackable programs written by other software crackers to demonstrate an idea and challenge others.

crackmes like those used in this course are manufactured examples that provide a few benefits to an aspiring cracker. In general, they are designed to be solvable, legal to crack, and safe to run in a debugger.

crackmes are also often labeled based on their focus, level of expertise, etc. As a result, you can specifically seek out challenge problems suited to your interests and skill level (i.e., advanced C cracker versus beginner Java cracker).

Lab: RE Bingo

This lab provides hands-on experience in reversing code that has been built (and obfuscated) by a compiler.

Labs and all associated instructions can be found in their corresponding folder here:

```
https://github.com/DazzleCatDuo/
X86-SOFTWARE-REVERSE-ENGINEERING-CRACKING-AND-COUNTER-MEASURES
```

For this lab, please locate Lab RE Bingo and follow the provided instructions.

Skills

This lab uses `objdump` to practice identifying control flow constructs and compiler settings when reversing. Some of the key skills being tested include the following:

- Reverse engineering x86
- Control flow constructs
- Impact of compiler settings

Takeaways

Quickly identifying control flow constructs can massively speed up reverse engineering. They provide insights into the logic of an application and make it more readable and comprehensible.

However, compiler configuration has a significant impact on the speed of reversing. For example, stripping and optimizing, in general, slow things down.

In larger and more complex programs, automating some reverse engineering is often necessary. It is common to write custom tools for a specific target. Unpacking, deobfuscating, and circumventing anti-debug checks are common tasks for automation.

Basic REconnaissance

As a software cracker, these are the most common situation that you'll face:

- You want to crack a program.
- You have no source code.
- You have an executable.

In this situation, you need a means of quickly assessing the target executable and finding a starting point for your analysis. Some of the most commonly used initial tools for reverse engineers are objdump, strace, ltrace, and strings. You'll see more advanced tools as you progress through the book, but as these are some of the most foundational, they're a good starting point.

objdump

Object Dump (objdump) is a Linux-based tool for dumping the disassembly of any program. As shown in Figure 9.1, it has numerous options. The most important ones for quick reverse engineering include the following:

- -d: Instructs objdump to disassemble the content of all sections
- -Mintel: Tells objdump to display assembly in Intel syntax (as opposed to AT&T)

For example, to disassemble an application named *appname*, use the command objdump -d -Mintel appname.

```
shadowfax@ubuntu:~/Desktop/blackhat5 objdump
Usage: objdump <option(s)> <file(s)>
 Display information from object <file(s)>.
 At least one of the following switches must be given:
  -a, --archive-headers    Display archive header information
  -f, --file-headers       Display the contents of the overall file header
  -p, --private-headers    Display object format specific file header contents
  -P, --private=OPT,OPT... Display object format specific contents
  -h, --[section-]headers  Display the contents of the section headers
  -x, --all-headers        Display the contents of all headers
  -d, --disassemble        Display assembler contents of executable sections
```

Figure 9.1: objdump options

Figure 9.2 shows the output from running objdump on a sample application. Note that objdump will display memory locations, function names, x86 machine code, and x86 assembly.

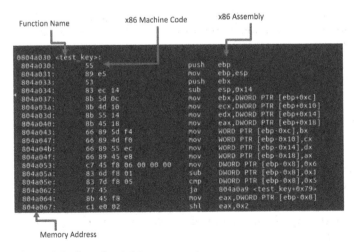

Figure 9.2: Sample objdump output

strace and ltrace

`strace` and `ltrace` provide the ability to monitor library (`ltrace`) and system (`strace`) calls. They make it possible to trace through a program and get a sense of what other programs are doing.

If *any* program in *any* language wants to do *anything* useful, it will have to make system calls. Characterization of what libraries and external functionality it's using can be immensely useful when doing reconnaissance on a system. You'll notice that, with these tools, not only can you see what it's using, but you can also see who is using it (i.e., what address in the application called). So, it can also help you to focus on useful functions. For example, you might see which piece of code calls into cryptography libraries a lot; that's probably interesting from a cracking perspective.

ltrace

`ltrace` (library trace) is a Linux command-line utility that traces library calls. Library calls are calls by your application into dynamically linked libraries. The syntax of the command is `ltrace <command>`.

For example, if you `#include <stdio.h>`, that library gets dynamically linked when your program loads. When you call `printf` or `fopen`, that is calling into the standard C library. This construct holds true for all programming languages, which all include a notion of including external libraries.

strace

`strace` (system trace) is a Linux command-line utility that traces system calls. The syntax of the command is `strace <command>`.

System calls are calls by your application into the operating system, which manages things like files and your console window. Functions like `fopen` and `printf` eventually, in their inner workings, must make calls into the operating system. Just like with `ltrace`, this holds true for all programming languages; it's rare for an application to exist that doesn't utilize OS-level functionality.

strace Example: echo

Monitoring system calls provides a crude way to trace through a program. Suppose you wrote the `echo` utility and wanted to watch how it was running.

`echo` is a Linux command that echoes the input to the output. For example, the command `echo hello!` prints `"hello!"` to the terminal.

But what is it actually doing? Running `strace echo hello!` will produce output similar to Figure 9.3.

```
steph@steph-XPS-9320:-$ strace echo hello!
execve("/usr/bin/echo", ["echo", "hello!"], 0x7ffec41908e8 /* 44 vars */) = 0
brk(NULL)                               = 0x55976ad13000
arch_prctl(0x3001 /* ARCH_??? */, 0x7ffc703b2180) = -1 EINVAL (Invalid argument)
mmap(NULL, 8192, PROT_READ|PROT_WRITE, MAP_PRIVATE|MAP_ANONYMOUS, -1, 0) = 0x7f814463f000
access("/etc/ld.so.preload", R_OK)      = -1 ENOENT (No such file or directory)
openat(AT_FDCWD, "/etc/ld.so.cache", O_RDONLY|O_CLOEXEC) = 3
newfstatat(3, "", {st_mode=S_IFREG|0644, st_size=78555, ...}, AT_EMPTY_PATH) = 0
mmap(NULL, 78555, PROT_READ, MAP_PRIVATE, 3, 0) = 0x7f814462b000
close(3)                                = 0
openat(AT_FDCWD, "/lib/x86_64-linux-gnu/libc.so.6", O_RDONLY|O_CLOEXEC) = 3
read(3, "\177ELF\2\1\1\3\0\0\0\0\0\0\0\0\3\0>\0\1\0\0\0P\237\2\0\0\0\0\0"..., 832) = 832
pread64(3, "\6\0\0\0\4\0\0\0@\0\0\0\0\0\0\0@\0\0\0\0\0\0\0@\0\0\0\0\0\0\0"..., 784, 64) = 784
pread64(3, "\4\0\0\0\0\0\0\5\0\0\0GNU\0\2\0\0\300\4\0\0\0\3\0\0\0\0\0\0\0"..., 48, 848) = 48
pread64(3, "\4\0\0\0\24\0\0\0\3\0\0\0GNU\0\244;\374\204(\337f\315I\214\234\f\256\271\32"..., 68, 896) = 68
newfstatat(3, "", {st_mode=S_IFREG|0755, st_size=2216304, ...}, AT_EMPTY_PATH) = 0
pread64(3, "\6\0\0\0\4\0\0\0@\0\0\0\0\0\0\0@\0\0\0\0\0\0\0@\0\0\0\0\0\0\0"..., 784, 64) = 784
mmap(NULL, 2260560, PROT_READ, MAP_PRIVATE|MAP_DENYWRITE, 3, 0) = 0x7f8144000000
mmap(0x7f8144428000, 1658880, PROT_READ|PROT_EXEC, MAP_PRIVATE|MAP_FIXED|MAP_DENYWRITE, 3, 0x28000) = 0x7f8144428000
mmap(0x7f81445bd000, 360448, PROT_READ, MAP_PRIVATE|MAP_FIXED|MAP_DENYWRITE, 3, 0x1bd000) = 0x7f81445bd000
mmap(0x7f8144615000, 24576, PROT_READ|PROT_WRITE, MAP_PRIVATE|MAP_FIXED|MAP_DENYWRITE, 3, 0x214000) = 0x7f8144615000
mmap(0x7f814461b000, 52816, PROT_READ|PROT_WRITE, MAP_PRIVATE|MAP_FIXED|MAP_ANONYMOUS, -1, 0) = 0x7f814461b000
close(3)                                = 0
mmap(NULL, 12288, PROT_READ|PROT_WRITE, MAP_PRIVATE|MAP_ANONYMOUS, -1, 0) = 0x7f8144628000
arch_prctl(ARCH_SET_FS, 0x7f8144628740) = 0
set_tid_address(0x7f8144628a10)         = 142481
set_robust_list(0x7f8144628a20, 24)     = 0
rseq(0x7f81446290e0, 0x20, 0, 0x53053053) = 0
mprotect(0x7f8144615000, 16384, PROT_READ) = 0
mprotect(0x55976bf6d000, 4096, PROT_READ) = 0
mprotect(0x7f8144679000, 8192, PROT_READ) = 0
prlimit64(0, RLIMIT_STACK, NULL, {rlim_cur=8192*1024, rlim_max=RLIM64_INFINITY}) = 0
munmap(0x7f814462b000, 78555)           = 0
getrandom("\xa1\x77\x9f\xec\xe6\x33\xaa\xf1", 8, GRND_NONBLOCK) = 8
brk(NULL)                               = 0x55976ad13000
brk(0x55976ad34000)                     = 0x55976ad34000
openat(AT_FDCWD, "/usr/lib/locale/locale-archive", O_RDONLY|O_CLOEXEC) = 3
newfstatat(3, "", {st_mode=S_IFREG|0644, st_size=5712208, ...}, AT_EMPTY_PATH) = 0
mmap(NULL, 5712208, PROT_READ, MAP_PRIVATE, 3, 0) = 0x7f8143e00000
close(3)                                = 0
newfstatat(1, "", {st_mode=S_IFCHR|0620, st_rdev=makedev(0x88, 0), ...}, AT_EMPTY_PATH) = 0
write(1, "hello!\n", 7hello!
)                                       = 7
close(1)                                = 0
close(2)                                = 0
exit_group(0)                           = ?
+++ exited with 0 +++
```

Figure 9.3: `strace` output for `echo hello!`

This image is complex and can be a lot to decipher. Looking through the result, you can see some standard system calls at the beginning that are used to get the `echo` program up and running.

The following lines are the interesting output, which are found at the very end:

```
write(1, "hello!\n", 7hello!
)                 = 7
close(1)          = 0
```

This says that `echo` wrote a string to stream 1, which, remember, is *stdout*. The `write` command had a return value of 7 because seven characters were written. Finally, `echo` closed stream 1, which returned 0 for success. While this seems simple, imagine using this to track where an application wrote a piece of configuration data. Say you change a setting and want to see how it stores that on the system.

strace Example: Malicious Kittens

Comet Cursor was an early example of spyware on the Windows OS. It allowed users to change the appearance of the mouse cursor and websites to use customized cursors. The application installed itself without user permission and secretly tracked users.

As shown in Figure 9.4, numerous kitten cursor applications exist in the wild. This example uses an example cursor application that secretly calls out to a Russian IP address.

Running the code shows no signs of the malicious functionality, as shown here:

```
deltaop@deltaleph-ubuntu:~$ ./kittens
Registering kitten cursor!
Done!  Enjoy the kitties!
deltaop@deltaleph-ubuntu:~$
```

Figure 9.4: Kitten cursor applications

However, analyzing the code in `strace` tells a different story, as shown here:

```
deltaop@deltaleph-ubuntu:~$ strace ./kittens
...
poll([{fd=3, events=POLLOUT}], 1, 0)    = 1 ([{fd=3, revents=POLLOUT}])
send(3, "!$\1\0\0\1\0\0\0\0\0\0\7kremlin\2ru\0\0\34\0\1",
     28, MSG_NOSIGNAL) = 28
poll([{fd=3, events=POLLIN}], 1, 5000)  = 1 ([{fd=3, revents=POLLIN}])
ioctl(3, FIONREAD, [28])                = 0
recvfrom(3, "!$\201\200\0\1\0\0\0\0\0\0\7kremlin\2ru\0\0\34\0\1", 1024,
      0, {sa_family=AF_INET, sin_port=htons(53),sin_addr=inet_
         addr("192.168.1.1")}, [16]) = 28
close(3)                                = 0
socket(PF_INET, SOCK_DGRAM|SOCK_NONBLOCK, IPPROTO_IP) = 3
connect(3, {sa_family=AF_INET, sin_port=htons(53),
      sin_addr=inet_addr("192.168.1.1")}, 16) = 0
...
```

This sample output from `strace` shows multiple events. To focus on events of interest, use `grep` (which limits results to lines that match your search string, in this case `connect`).

```
deltaop@deltaleph-ubuntu:~$ strace -f ./kittens 2>&1 | grep connect

connect(3, {sa_family=AF_FILE, path="/var/run/nscd/socket"},
        110) = -1 ENOENT
connect(3, {sa_family=AF_FILE, path="/var/run/nscd/socket"},
        110) = -1 ENOENT
connect(3, {sa_family=AF_INET, sin_port=htons(53),
        sin_addr=inet_addr("192.168.1.1")}, 16) = 0
connect(3, {sa_family=AF_INET, sin_port=htons(53),
        sin_addr=inet_addr("192.168.1.1")}, 16) = 0
connect(3, {sa_family=AF_INET, sin_port=htons(53),
        sin_addr=inet_addr("192.168.1.1")}, 16) = 0
connect(3, {sa_family=AF_INET, sin_port=htons(80),
        sin_addr=inet_addr("195.208.24.91")}, 16) = 0
write(2, "connected.\n", 11) = 11
```

The previous sample output looks for events with the word *connect* in them. This includes multiple Internet connections, including one to 195.208.24.91, which is suspicious as it's an external IP address, and why would your cursor need to do that?

strings

`strings` is a Linux utility designed to extract the printable strings used by an application. It looks for a series of ASCII printable characters with a (configurable) minimum length and prints any that it finds.

`strings` can be very useful in reverse engineering because it provides a high-level understanding of the sorts of things that a program might do. Also, once you find strings of interest, you'll see later how you can use those strings to easily locate the associated piece of code. For example, a string that says `"incorrect password"` can be used to quickly trace where the password handling code is. For example, the following strings provide valuable hints about an application:

- `"Enter password:"`
- `"open_socket"`
- `"YOUR FILES HAVE BEEN ENCRYPTED!"`

The syntax of the command is `strings program`. While it is commonly used with no options, the following flags are sometimes useful when reverse engineering:

- -a: Show all strings in the file, as opposed to only those in the loaded sections of object files. This is often useful when dealing with obfuscated, nested, or otherwise unusual binaries.

- -n: Specify the minimum length of successive printable characters for a sequence of bytes to be considered a string. The default is 4. It is often useful to expand or limit the number of strings found by the tool.

Dependency Walker

Dependency walking is a technique used to quickly understand the imports and exports of an application. Dependency Walker is one example of such a tool. (See the "Tools" section of our repository for links.)

Dependency walking provides a valuable, high-level view into what actions a program will perform and is often a useful first step in cracking. Most applications don't implement all their own functions; they will use functions from the operating system, or external libraries. Each time an application reaches outside of its code, that will show up as an imported function. Also, often applications will share functionality with other applications, and anytime a function is something "available to be shared," it will show up as an export of the application.

Loading a program into a program like Dependency Walker shows the DLLs that it uses and the API calls it is expected to make. Figure 9.5 shows that the program will create several registry keys.

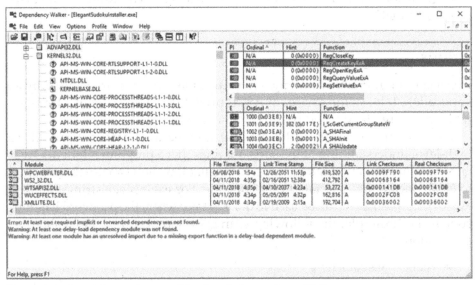

Figure 9.5: Examining registry modifications in Dependency Walker

Reverse Engineering Strategy

Reverse engineering is still more of an art than a science. While great tools and techniques are available to help, effective reversing ultimately relies heavily on intuition and experience.

As such, it is not possible to give a prescriptive solution. However, there are general approaches and best practices that can help.

Find Areas of Interest

Applications contain large volumes of code, and most of it is irrelevant or unnecessary to reverse engineer. An important first step when reversing an application is finding the area of the program you are after.

You'll continue to learn lots of interesting techniques for narrowing this down, but a few are now available to you based on just knowledge of the previous tools:

- **Interesting strings:** Look for program strings that you are interested in (e.g., "Incorrect Key") and find where those strings are used (e.g., identify calls to `printf` using those strings).

- **User input:** Look for where input from the user is received (e.g., `scanf`, dialog boxes, etc.) and find where that input is processed.

- **System input:** Look for where input is read in from the system, such as configuration files and registry settings.

- **Authentication code:** If possible, use a debugger to pause the program after inputting the username/key. Then, scan the memory for the entered values, set HW breakpoints on those locations, and rerun the application to find where the values are read or written.

Iteratively Annotate Code

Even after you identify the code of interest, it may be difficult to understand. One approach to understand complex code is to perform multiple passes, adding information (such as comments) during each pass.

To do so, annotate the target area until you understand how it works using the following process:

- **Identify and mark local variables:** Use calling convention rules to identify locals (e.g., `[ebp-4]` in `cdecl`). These can be labeled using something vague at first (e.g., *local1*).

- **Identify and mark function parameters:** Use calling convention rules to identify parameters (e.g., `[ebp+12]` in `cdecl`). These can also be labeled using something vague at first (e.g., *arg1*).

- **Identify API calls (e.g., `atoi`):** Use knowledge of API parameters to further annotate local variables. For example, API documentation indicates `atoi` is passed a string that will be converted to an integer so can rename our parameter *integer_string*.

- **Add comments to complex control flows:** For example, "this code factors the number."

- **Refine descriptions based on observed data flows:** For example, `local1` may become `loop_counter` if you see it used as the counter in a `for` loop.

A big part of effective reverse engineering is moving quickly. Even small programs have too much code to analyze everything.

The vast majority of an application's code will have no relevance to what you are after. Knowing what to focus on is often less important than knowing what not to focus on. Learning where to make leaps takes time.

Summary

This chapter introduced some of the core tools and techniques that you will use as a software reverse engineer and cracker. Before moving on, take some time to practice and get some hands-on experience using the tools. This practice time will be invaluable later when you move on to more complex software and more advanced RE and cracking techniques.

Cracking: Tools and Strategies

Cracking is the art of reversing software to bypass protections or other undesirable functionality. This chapter explores some of the key tools and strategies used for software cracking, including the use of key generators and patching to defeat key checkers.

Key Checkers

One of the most common practices for licensing software is through license keys. In a goal to defeat piracy, every installation of the software requires a unique key to complete the installation. In the case of software with multiple tiers of features, they may have some features always freely available, while others reside behind a license wall, or the software may not work at all without a license key.

License keys are a common anti-piracy solution, and they have their advantages. These are two of the most significant:

- License keys are easy to generate and verify.
- The ratio of valid to invalid keys is so small that random guessing is unlikely to generate a valid key (assuming a reasonable key length).

However, like all security, if they are implemented poorly, they can be highly susceptible to cracking, and like all security, they are not entirely infallible. A sufficiently knowledgeable and motivated cracker could eventually defeat or bypass them. However, they're still one of the stronger forms of protection; this is just a reminder that there is no such thing as 100 percent secure software.

Back in the day when offline systems were more common, license checking and validation were often done entirely offline, meaning all of the logic to verify the key was resident on the system. Now, with prolific connectivity, we often see license key checks that consist of both an offline and online component, where they reach out to a license server for additional verification. There are a few different ways to implement key checks with varying levels of effectiveness.

The Bad Way

In the past, very popular computer games *StarCraft* and *Half-life* both used a checksum as a license key. Recall checksums are often very simple mathematical expressions performed on a binary blob, some as simple as adding all the numbers together. In the checksum used by these games, the 13th digit verified the first 12.

This meant that a user could enter anything that they wanted for the first 12 digits and then calculate a 13th to create a valid checksum. This lapse in security led to the infamous 1234-56789-1234 key, which was valid for these games and used widely to pirate them.

One of the biggest problems in these cases was that the algorithm used to calculate the checksum was too simple.

```
x = 3;
for(int i = 0; i < 12; i++)
{
    x += (2 * x) ^ digit[i];
}
lastDigit = x % 10;
```

There are two ways to approach cracking this. One is that you run the algorithm and calculate the valid value of the last digit as shown previously.

The other is a brute-force attack. Given it was only one digit you had to figure out, there are only 10 options for the last digit [0-9]. You can randomly select a set of 12 digits and then just guess and check the 10 options for the last one until you find success. The infamous 1234-56789-1234 key was so famous because it was easy to remember, but by following either of these two approaches (calculation or brute force), you could generate any number of new keys.

A Reasonable Way

A brute-force attack against a license key is guaranteed to work. . .eventually. The best that a license key can do is waste enough of a cracker's time that it becomes infeasible or impossible to carry out a brute-force attack.

So, how to protect against brute-force attacks? One common option in other contexts is a cryptographic hash. For example, a license key could be implemented using one of the following options:

- **Username:** SHA(username)
- **Random value:** WXYZ-SHA(WXYZ)

The use of a hash function makes a brute-force attack against this much harder. However, it's trivially easy for a cracker to determine how the algorithm works after a look at the code. Depending on your mindset, if you're an attacker, this means leveraging the reverse engineering skills you've learned to this point to find the algorithm and unravel it, and if you're a defender, it means this is a key piece of code that you need to protect.

An alternative is to use a custom, complex hash rather than a standard one. While this is normally a horrible idea in security, it's not an unheard-of choice for this application. The goal isn't to provide absolute protection, just to slow down reverse engineering. For anyone in the security space whose toes are curling at the suggestion of making your own hash, just note that this suggestion comes with the caveat that you are able to make a decently good one. As a defender, keep in mind there are lots of tools out there to do common hashing techniques, so those will be all the first things an attacker will try to unroll your key.

Also, find ways to add unique complexity so a key can be used only in a unique setting, and not proliferated. Schemes such as concatenating the product name and version and computer name within the hashed value adds a solid level of complexity. This way, a cracked valid key for one installation doesn't unlock other releases.

A Better Way

Hashes are better, and, if implemented correctly, they can be decent. But there are even better options. A great example of this is the approach Microsoft uses when generating license keys for its software.

Instead of hash algorithms, Windows uses public key cryptography. With public key cryptography, a digital signature can be generated using a private key and verified using a public one. This means that a digitally signed license key can be verified by an application without exposing sensitive keys.

When generating its license keys, Windows uses a lot of information about the software, including but not limited to:

- Bitness (32, 64)
- Type (home, professional, enterprise)
- Product ID
- Hardware features

Including all of this information helps to lock a product key to a specific installation of the software. If you're interested in more information on the protocol, there are lots of resources online tearing into Microsoft's key generation.

Digitally Signed Keys

Digital signatures on license keys, like those used by Windows, make it much more difficult to generate fake, valid keys. A valid signature must be generated using the private key but can be validated with a nonsensitive public key.

Digital signatures prevent the straightforward generation of license keys and present attackers with two options. The first is to leak a legitimate key, which could be traced back to a specific user. Alternatively, an attacker can modify the program to remove the key-checking code, which increases the time and complexity of pirating the software.

The Best Way

The examples presented so far have focused predominately on offline verification of license keys, meaning the entirety of the code to verify and unlock the software is resident on the system. However, given the prolific connectedness of systems these days, a way to add more strength is to add an online component.

This can take many forms, but one you see today is each piece of software can be distributed with a license key in the form of a large random number distributed alongside the software. When the product is installed and registered, this value is sent to the license server, which verifies that it is valid and has not been used already. For digital software distribution these days, the key you're sent isn't even valid until after you buy the software, meaning that if you had guessed that key 10 minutes before you bought the software, it wouldn't have worked.

Or you can use hybrid approaches where much of the algorithm to verify through hashing or public key cryptography is resident on the system, but then there is also a step where the license server is checked to see if that key has been used before or if the key has been revoked.

Other Suggestions

The methods introduced align with more of the industry best practices and the most commonly used methods. But there is not a one size fits all to security, and some of the following are techniques you could encounter in a cracking scenario, or you might find them useful in a defensive scenario if you have unique constraints.

Prefer Offline Activation

While the addition of online key servers sounds powerful from a security perspective, and it is, it's worth acknowledging that technique comes with a huge amount of manageability and infrastructure pain. Managing key servers is no small feat, and they become a beacon for cyberattacks. So, you will still often find that many companies aren't able or willing to bite off that level of chaos, so they will still favor going for stronger offline verification. Supporting offline key verification eliminates the complexities of managing a key server and is inclusive to users without Internet access.

Perform Partial Key Verification

In an offline mode, you have no method to perform revocation and have no way to make some keys no longer work. To prevent a single leaked key from working on all future versions of your software, check only some of the key. A simplistic example would be to check only the first character of each group in a license key such as the x, 9, B, and B in X4Z-951-B41-BR0.

If someone releases a key generator for your application, release a new version that checks part of the remaining key. For example, switch to checking the second character of each group (4, 5, 4, and R). This limits the potential damage caused by a single key generator.

Encode Useful Data in the Key

Encoding useful data in the key can help to limit its applicability. For example, a key may specify the maximum version of the application that it applies to, limiting the impact of a compromised key.

Key Generators

If a piece of software uses a key for activation, crackers will want to build a key generator for it. This is true regardless of which type of key activation you did. Key generators are then distributed for people to generate a "free" key for software.

You'll see later how to patch software to simply remove a key check, so for now focus on making a key generator, and assume you can't just bypass the key check. Key generators typically require a more in-depth analysis of the program and a deeper understanding of the key algorithm.

Why Build Key Generators?

If key generators are more difficult to create, why bother building them? There are a few different reasons.

Software can have various defenses that can make patching the more difficult route, such as the following:

- Tamper proofing
- Dynamic checks
- Anti-debugging
- Software guards

Also, patching may require releasing a modified copy of the target software, which may be watermarked. Watermarking is a technique to trace a piece of software back to who originally purchased it. These watermarks can be used to trace a cracked piece of software back to the cracker, which is obviously something they don't want.

The software could implement online checks to look for patched/modified versions of programs. Alternatively, some software may decrypt itself based on the entered key (unpacking, which will be explored in Chapter 13, "Advanced Defensive Techniques"), and removing the key check entirely means it won't be able to decrypt.

Key generators are also more future-proof than patching. An application developer can't easily revoke valid keys.

Finally, crackers may choose key generators *because* they are harder. Patching in some cases is easy, while building a successful keygen is a challenge that carries a certain amount of prestige.

The Philosophy of Key Generation

When cracking key checkers, it is useful to think of the key checker in the form of $f(u) == g(k)$, where:

- u is the username entered by the user.
- f is a transformation function on the username.
- k is the key entered by the user.
- g is a transformation function on the key.

In this model, the key check is a validation that $f(u) == g(k)$. In non-math-speak this means that some transformation/mutation is done on the username and then compared to some type of transformation done on the key. In this example (and the following examples), the username is the input, but keep in mind this can be any combination of things; they could use the version number, computer name, etc. But the idea is something is going into a transformation to come up with a result. And that result is compared to the input key, which has also gone through some type of transformation (note this transformation could be nothing, meaning the result is simply the key, or it could be more hashing or mutation). With this model in mind, there are a few potential variants of key checks.

Going back to the initial *StarCraft*/*Half Life* example, u would actually be the first 12 digits of the key, and k is the last digit. In this setup, there is no username entered; rather, part of the key is used to check the other part.

Another option is that u, and therefore f(u), is a constant (i.e., hard-coded keys). In this setup, there is no username entered; rather, the key is transformed and checked against a fixed value. For example, "the sum of all of the digits in the key is equal to 1337."

Cracking Different Types of Key Checks

By reasoning about key checkers in the formula f(u) == g(k), you can start to build techniques for cracking different permutations.

Key Check Type I: Transform Just the Username

For this case, the username is transformed using some function, and that is then compared to the key that was entered. So, in this case you can consider g() causes no mutation to the key. This allows us to simplify our key check to just f(u) == k. In this setup, the program transforms the username and validates that the transformed value matches the key entered by the user.

To crack this type, locate and extract the transformation function f into a key generation application. For example, multiply ordinals of characters in username together and match against the key. The key generator will prompt the user for the username they desire to use and then perform f(u) and print out the valid key.

Key Check Type II: Transform Both

For Type II, you still have a transformation of the username, but, in addition, g performs a mutation. The very mathematical way to look at this is that g has an inverse. That is, g^{-1} exists, and $g^{-1}(g(k))$ == k. The simple way to think about this is that g will perform a mutation, and every mutation has a way of unmutating it (i.e., do the exact opposite).

In this setup, the program transforms the username, transforms the entered key, and validates that the two produce the same results. However, the function g can be inverted ("reversed" or "backed out").

To crack this type of key check, reverse engineer g and derive g⁻¹. Often, this is as simple as "undoing" each transformation on g in reverse order. Then, generate a key with g-1(f(u)).

For example, assume g(k) = k * 2 + 1000. If so, g⁻¹(h) = (h - 1000) / 2.

In this case, the key generator would prompt for the desired username (as with Type I) and perform the f(u), but then the result now is the mutated key, so you have to do your unrolling with g⁻¹(h). That final result is then the valid key.

Key Check Type III: Brute Forceable

In Type III, a collision on f(u) can be brute forced through g(k). This is a viable approach if the key space is very small or you have a lot of computing power.

In this setup, the program transforms the username, transforms the entered key, and validates that the two produce the same results (same as Type II). But you instead are looking for a solution to f(u) == g(k) by repeatedly testing random or pseudorandom ks.

To crack this type, determine the format of k. Then, extract g into a self-contained key generator. Finally, generate random ks until a solution to f(u) == g(k) is found.

For example, consider the case where g(k) = CRC32(k). If the key mutation is using something so small such as the CRC32 algorithm, then brute force becomes pretty trivial on a standard computer. Since CRC32 has such a small range of possible values, it's possible to brute force.

Defending Against Keygens

Key checks may be a combination of these types. For example, the key transformation g may be both brute forcible and invertible.

Key checks generally must fall into one of these categories. Otherwise, there would be no way to generate keys in the first place.

Key Check Type I is the weakest. The cracker needs only to extract the algorithm from the key checker, with no need to actually RE the algorithm.

Key Check Type III is better. It requires the attacker to extract both algorithms and identify a way to brute force the key transformation, which is not always obvious.

Key Check Type II is likely best but also the hardest to design well. Cracking this requires the attacker to derive the inverse of the key transformation function. This may necessitate a deep analysis of the transformation algorithm, slowing the attack.

As always, there is no silver bullet. Every key checker can be cracked eventually, and the best that a defender can do is slow down the attacker.

Lab: Introductory Keygen

This lab provides experience in creating a keygen for a simple program.

Labs and all associated instructions can be found in their corresponding folder here:

```
https://github.com/DazzleCatDuo/
X86-SOFTWARE-REVERSE-ENGINEERING-CRACKING-AND-COUNTER-MEASURES
```

For this lab, please locate Introductory Keygen and follow the provided instructions.

Skills

This lab practices the use of `objdump` and the `strings` utility to generate a keygen. Some of the key skills it tests include the following:

- Initial reconnaissance
- Reverse engineering x86
- Key generation

Takeaways

In addition to modifying a program, it's often possible to crack a program just by observing how it works. The right approach is often determined by the program constraints, and choosing which to use is an important skill.

Procmon

In reverse engineering, you want to learn as much about how the program works as possible. Before jumping to super-fancy debugging, start easy by just observing software's behavior.

Procmon is a tool distributed as part of the Sysinternals suite of tools (available at `http://technet.microsoft.com/en-us/sysinternals/bb842062`). This repository contains about 60 windows utilities made and freely distributed by Microsoft. Note these tools work only on Windows OSs.

Example: Notepad.exe

Try taking a look at what `notepad.exe` does when you create a new file, change the font, and then save some content. To do so, take the following steps:

1. Open `Procmon.exe`.
2. Launch Notepad.

3. Enter some text into the Notepad document.

4. Click the Format menu and then the Font menu item.

5. In the Font window, change the font to Webdings.

6. In the Font window, change the size to 20.

7. Click the OK button.

8. Save the Notepad document as `Example1.txt`.

9. Close Notepad.

Stop Process Monitor capture activity by clicking the Capture button, as shown in Figure 10.1. The icon should now show an X over the magnifying glass. At this point, Process Monitor has captured all File, Registry, and Process/Thread events.

Figure 10.1: Halting Process Monitor

Process Monitor captures thousands of events a second, which results in too many records to review manually. It's necessary to filter the results down to events of interest. To do so, open the Filter menu by clicking the funnel icon, as shown in Figure 10.2.

Figure 10.2: Filtering events in Procmon

To see only events related to the process `Notepad.exe`, define a filter stating that the `Process Name is Notepad.exe`, as shown in Figure 10.3. You can accomplish this via the following steps:

1. Select Process Name from the Column list box.

2. Select is from the Relation list box.

3. Type **Notepad.exe** in the Value text box.

4. Select Include from the Action list box.

5. Click the Add button.

6. Click Apply and OK.

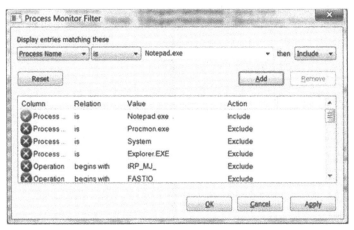

Figure 10.3: Defining a filter in Procmon

Filtering based on the process name dramatically decreases the number of events. However, it's still not enough.

To find events of interest, you need to define additional filters. Procmon has several categories of events that you can filter on, including the following:

- Registry
- File
- Network
- Process thread

To start, try focusing on the Registry values that Notepad modifies. Process Monitor has a handy button for this, as shown in Figure 10.4.

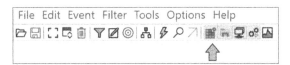

Figure 10.4: Filtering on Registry events in Procmon

If Notepad has saved values to the Registry, it will create an event entry of type `'Operation' 'RegSetValue'`. By right-clicking entries in Procmon's log, you can choose to include or exclude certain types of events, as shown in Figure 10.5. This enables you to further refine your results and focus on events of interest.

Figure 10.6 shows a Procmon entry that seems to be related to the changes to the font in Notepad. To see more information, right-click the entry and select Properties.

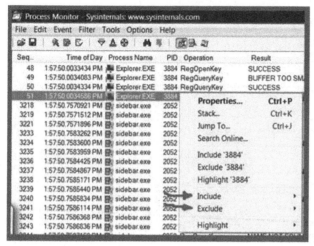

Figure 10.5: Including and excluding event categories in Procmon

8:07:1...	notepad.exe	4460	RegSetValue	HKCU\Software\Microsoft\Notepad\lfClipPrecision
8:07:1...	notepad.exe	4460	RegSetValue	HKCU\Software\Microsoft\Notepad\lfQuality
8:07:1...	notepad.exe	4460	RegSetValue	HKCU\Software\Microsoft\Notepad\lfPitchAndFamily
8:07:1	notepad.exe	4460	RegSetValue	HKCU\Software\Microsoft\Notepad\lfFaceName
8:07:1...	notepad.exe	4460	RegSetValue	HKCU\Software\Microsoft\Notepad\iPointSize

Figure 10.6: Notepad font change registry event

Figure 10.7 shows the properties of the event. In the Data field, you can see the text "Webdings," indicating that this is an event triggered by changing the Notepad font to Webdings.

How Procmon Aids RE and Cracking

Procmon made it possible to see the Registry changes made by Notepad. However, this isn't all that it can do. Further exploration of the tool reveals a great deal of useful information.

Call Stacks

The Properties window for an event has a few different tabs. Clicking over to the Stack tab shows the sequence of calls used to reach this point, as shown in Figure 10.8.

Looking further down this stack trace, it's possible to see the point where the program left notepad.exe, as shown in Figure 10.9. This transition point from application to libraries might be a good starting point for reversing.

File Operations

Procmon also records events for file operations, such as opening, closing, and editing files. Figure 10.10 shows an example of this.

Figure 10.7: Event properties in Procmon

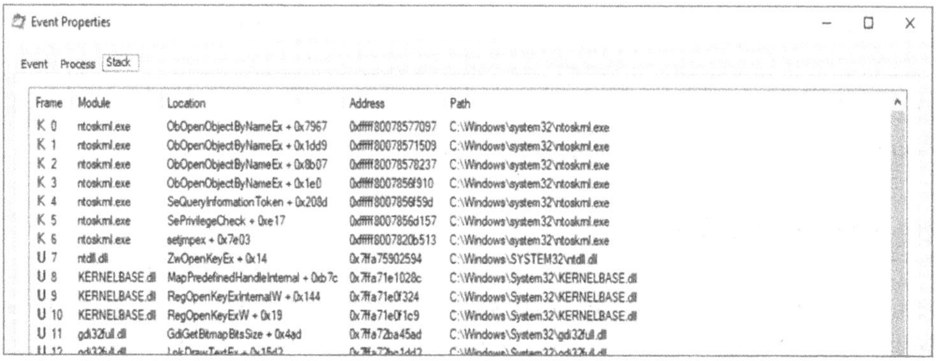

Figure 10.8: Stack view in Procmon's Properties window

These file events can provide useful information for reversing. For example, they can help with identifying and analyzing configuration files, export functions, and proprietary file formats.

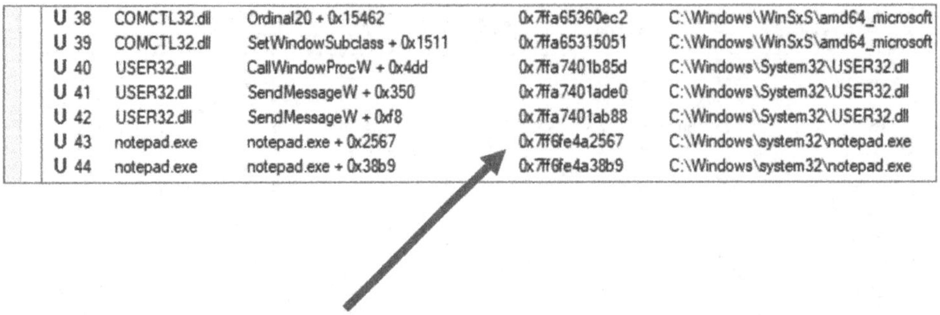

U 38	COMCTL32.dll	Ordinal20 + 0x15462	0x7ffa65360ec2	C:\Windows\WinSxS\amd64_microsoft
U 39	COMCTL32.dll	SetWindowSubclass + 0x1511	0x7ffa65315051	C:\Windows\WinSxS\amd64_microsoft
U 40	USER32.dll	CallWindowProcW + 0x4dd	0x7ffa7401b85d	C:\Windows\System32\USER32.dll
U 41	USER32.dll	SendMessageW + 0x350	0x7ffa7401ade0	C:\Windows\System32\USER32.dll
U 42	USER32.dll	SendMessageW + 0xf8	0x7ffa7401ab88	C:\Windows\System32\USER32.dll
U 43	notepad.exe	notepad.exe + 0x2567	0x7ff6fe4a2567	C:\Windows\system32\notepad.exe
U 44	notepad.exe	notepad.exe + 0x38b9	0x7ff6fe4a38b9	C:\Windows\system32\notepad.exe

Figure 10.9: Stack trace for `notepad.exe`

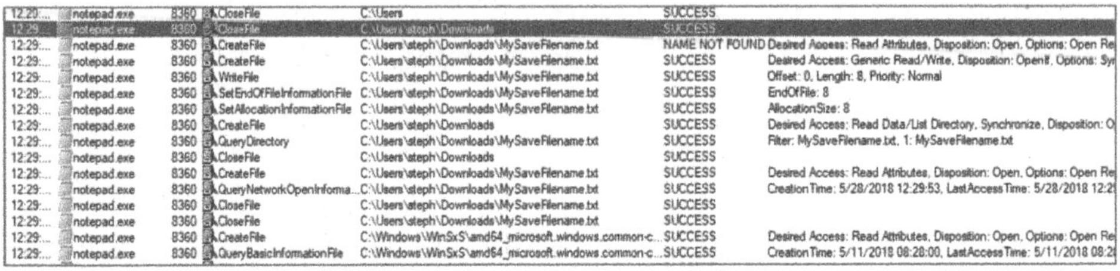

Figure 10.10: File operations in Procmon

Registry Queries

The `Notepad.exe` example showed how to find the Registry operation for changing the font in Notepad. However, this isn't the only possible use for registry queries.

For example, Figure 10.11 shows that Notepad looked for two keys with the word "Security" in them but couldn't find them. You could add these keys to your Registry and place custom values in them to change how Notepad operates.

Figure 10.11: Security Registry queries in Procmon

Resource Hacker

Resource Hacker (also known as ResHacker or ResHack) is a free extraction utility or resource compiler for Windows. Resource Hacker can be used to add, modify, or replace most resources within Windows binaries including strings, images, dialogs, menus, and VersionInfo and Manifest resources. (For tool links, visit the tools section of our GitHub site at `https://github.com/DazzleCatDuo/X86-SOFTWARE-REVERSE-ENGINEERING-CRACKING-AND-COUNTER-MEASURES.`)

Resource Hacker can be a useful tool for exploring the structure of a binary prior to the cracking process. It can be used to find and understand the structure of nag screens, key entry screens, help menus, and more.

Resource Hacker can also be used to add functionality to a program before or after cracking. For example, it's possible to add new icons, menus, and skins to an existing application.

To get started, open an .exe file in ResHack to explore its strings, images, dialogs, menus, etc., as shown in Figure 10.12. Then, click an item in ResHack (left) to show how that item would look in the application (right).

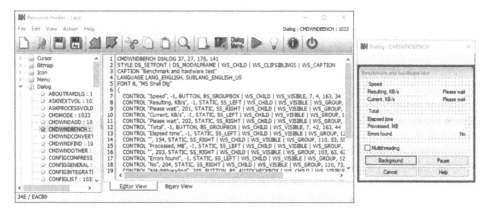

Figure 10.12: Sample application in Resource Hacker

Example

Suppose you see the window shown in Figure 10.13 in a program. As a cracker, you want to understand how that window would be used by the program.

Figure 10.13: Password window

To find out, open the program in ResHack. Then, use Ctrl+F to search for one of the strings used in the dialog box, as shown in Figure 10.14.

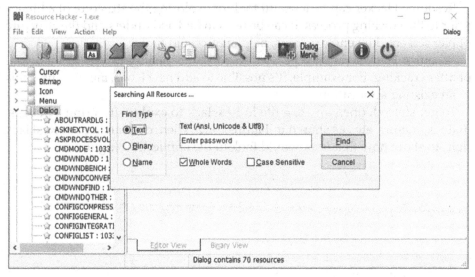

Figure 10.14: String search in Resource Hacker

Resource Hacker identifies this dialog box as the "GETPASSWORD2" dialog box, as shown in Figure 10.15. Knowing this can help to guide the process of reversing the program.

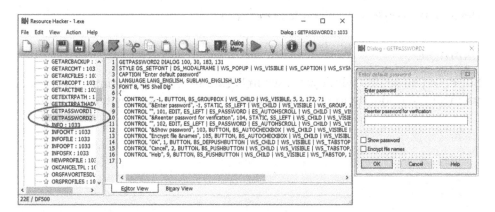

Figure 10.15: Identifying a dialog box in Resource Hacker

Mini-Lab: Windows Calculator

To try your hand at using Resource Hacker, try rebranding the Microsoft Calculator. As shown in Figure 10.16, the Calculator window is titled Calculator. Try changing this value to something else.

To start, open the `calc.exe` executable in Resource Hacker. Then, search for the word *Calculator*, as shown in Figure 10.17.

Figure 10.16: Microsoft Calculator

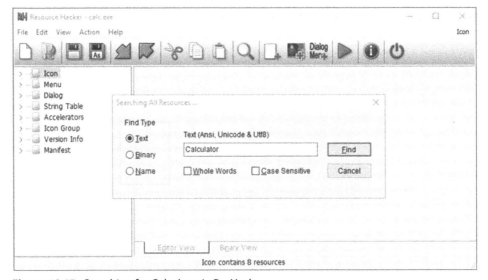

Figure 10.17: Searching for *Calculator* in ResHack

The main Calculator window may not be the first result. Keep on searching until you find the code defining the Calculator dialog box, as shown in Figure 10.18.

In Figure 10.18, the CAPTION string determines the title on the application window. Change this string to rebrand the application as your own.

After changing the CAPTION, click the green arrow button shown in Figure 10.19. This will compile the modified Calculator application.

After the application has been compiled, the updated version of the window should be shown in the window preview. This should include the modified caption, as shown in Figure 10.20.

Compiling the application doesn't automatically save the modified version. To do so, select File ➪ Save, as shown in Figure 10.21.

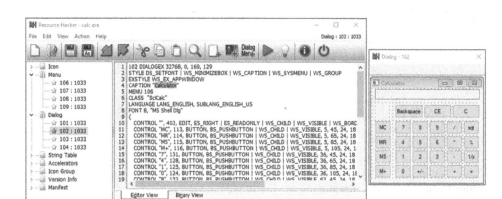

Figure 10.18: Calculator window in Resource Hacker

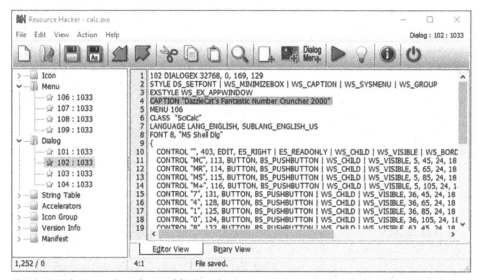

Figure 10.19: Compiling the modified application

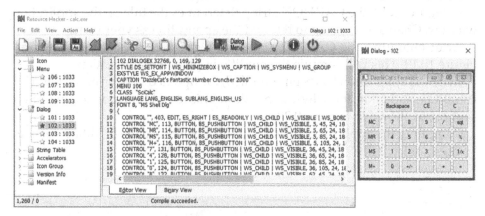

Figure 10.20: Modified window in Resource Hacker

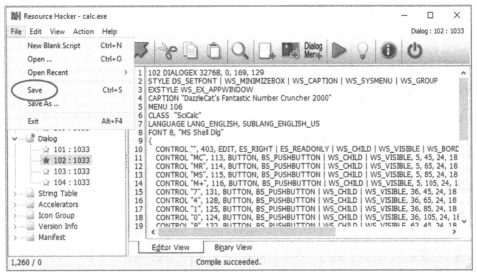

Figure 10.21: Saving the modified application in ResHack

At this point, you've successfully rebranded Windows Calculator. For more of a challenge, try the following:

- Use Resource Hacker to resize the window to accommodate your new name.
- Modify the available buttons.
- Modify the calculator background.
- Open and edit other programs in your VM.

Patching

Patching involves modifying a compiled binary to modify code affecting its execution. Depending on the situation, sometimes the easiest thing to do is patch an application to circumvent its security.

Patching vs. Key-Genning

In some cases, advanced integrity checks or obfuscation might make patching difficult. For example:

- Patching an encrypted/packed program on disk is not feasible.
- Patching around dynamic integrity checks (e.g., continuously validated checksums) may be too cumbersome.
- The logistics of distributing a patched executable may not be desirable.

In these situations, you may choose to fall back on key generators instead. Otherwise, patching a program to remove its key checks (or any other logic you want to avoid) is often the easier approach, when possible.

Where to Patch

Patching can be done in two different places: in memory or on disk.

Patching in memory modifies the machine code in memory. This is useful for reverse engineering attempts because you may need to try dozens (or hundreds. . .or more. . .gasp) of things before one works. In-memory patching affects only the current execution of the application. Each time you restart the application, any in-memory patching will be lost.

Patching on disk modifies the machine code in the compiled binary. This is useful once you know what works and affects all future executions of the application. It makes the modifications persistent and will be there every time the application is launched.

NOPs

Recall the instruction nop. It is a one-byte instruction (0x90) that does nothing.

When patching applications, it is critical to not move the code. In fact, modifying the size or simply deleting code will crash the application. To remove sections of code yet maintain the same size, fill the space with nops.

For those of you who are curious why simply deleting code doesn't work, there are many factors to this, but the most important is that some x86 code is relative and some of it is absolute references. Looking at the relative case first: this means some code translates to relative things like "jump forward 40 bytes from where I am now." In cases like this, if you remove code between the jump and its destination 40 bytes away, you've messed up the jump. It will continue to jump 40 bytes ahead, except that now it may land in the middle of an opcode or skip critical instructions, which then results in a crash. If the code you remove is outside of that 40-byte bubble and the jump forward 40 bytes still lands in the same spot, then it would have no effect.

Now, consider absolute references. These types of references would look like "use the data value at address 0x1234567." If you remove code anywhere in the binary before that address, you've caused everything to shift. So, when any absolute reference goes to grab its values or perform an absolute jump, all of the locations will be wrong, even if all you did was remove 1 byte from the binary.

This means relative references are affected only by adding/removing bytes if they occur in between where the reference is made and the destination. However, all absolute references are destroyed if you shift the application even by

1 byte. This is why it's critical in patching to maintain the size (unless of course causing everything to crash is your goal, in which case smash away!).

Circling back to `nop`, if you want to remove a piece of code, such as causing software to skip a key checker, instead of deleting the code, you simply replace it all with `nop`s. This maintains the application's byte alignment but causes nothing to happen when it reaches the undesirable code.

Other Debuggers

For reverse engineering with dynamic analysis on Windows, there are numerous popular choices. Here are a few:

- OllyDbg
- Immunity
- x64dbg
- WinDbg

Which of these to use depends on the situation and user preference. All of them have similar features, and skills in one typically translate to the others as well. You'll dip your toes into a few different pieces of software throughout the book; the goal is to give you a taste of many so you can get a feel for when each is useful.

OllyDbg

OllyDbg is an immensely popular and powerful debugger. While most debuggers focus on debugging, Olly has extended features, including the following:

- Extensibility, plugins, scripting
- Execution tracing system
- Code patching features
- Automatic parameter descriptions for most Windows functions
- Emphasis on binary code analysis (i.e., not based around source debugging)
- Small and portable

These features make OllyDbg excellent for the following:

- Writing exploits
- Analyzing malware
- Reverse engineering

However, while OllyDbg is a powerful and popular tool, it does have its limitations. One of these is that it works only for 32-bit executables, which admittedly are a dying breed but not dead yet.

The other is that the OllyDbg interface often takes some getting used to and does not feel robust or intuitive at first. However, you should definitely stick with it, as it is a powerful dynamic analysis tool.

Immunity

Immunity is a fork of OllyDby, meaning that it has many of the same capabilities. It also introduces many additional features that make it popular for exploit developers, such as support for Python scripting.

However, like OllyDbg, Immunity can be used only to debug 32-bit executables. Also, it inherits OllyDbg's unintuitive user interface.

x86dbg

x86dbg is a replacement for OllyDbg that supports both 32-bit (x86dbg) and 64-bit (x64dbg) applications. This wider support means that it is commonly the tool of choice when reversing or debugging 64-bit applications.

WinDbg

WinDbg is a debugger that is universally applicable, has strong support, and offers excellent debugging symbol support (but which is less useful with RE). However, it has a debugging focus and lacks some features of RE-focused tools.

Debugging with Immunity

Because of time and space constraints, exploring all of these debuggers is infeasible in this book. Immunity was selected because of its popularity for reverse engineering and exploit development. However, it's important to remember that all of these debuggers have similar features, and skills learned in one will often translate over to others.

Figure 10.22 shows how Immunity looks in Windows. From the top-left and moving clockwise, the four windows show the program's disassembly, registers, stack, and memory.

Immunity: Assembly

Figure 10.23 shows a program's disassembly in Immunity. Note that it shows the memory address, machine code, and x86 assembly.

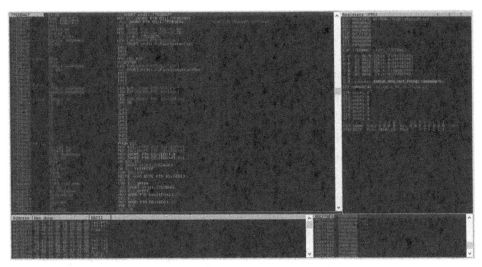

Figure 10.22: Immunity debugger window

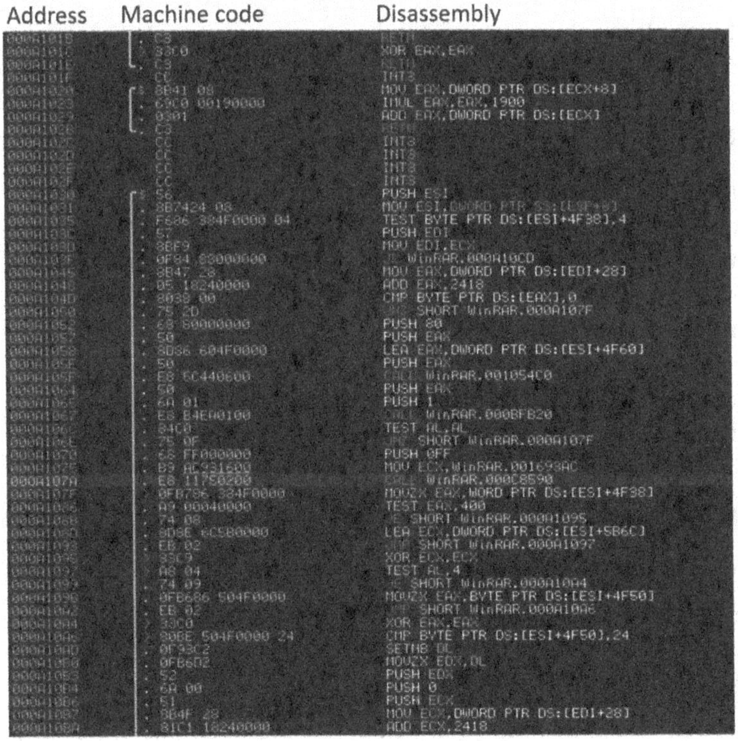

Address   Machine code   Disassembly

Figure 10.23: Assembly code in Immunity debugger

To select a line of code, click it. Once a line is selected, Immunity offers various keyboard shortcuts, including the following:

- **;:** Add a comment to the selected line. This is the most important part of reverse engineering; it helps you keep track of your work.

- **ctrl-a:** Auto-analyze the program. Immunity can do a fairly good job of adding comments and guessing function parameters.

- **<enter>:** Navigate to the selected function. For example, if you see the assembly `call 0x1234` and want to find out what the function at 0x1234 does.

- **-:** Go back to the previous location. For example, after you've analyzed function 0x1234 and want to return to where you were.

- **+:** Go to the next location (after pressing -). For example, if you returned to the calling function with -, but then want to go back to function 0x1234.

- **ctrl-r:** Find cross-references to the selected line. For example, if you have a string selected in the memory dump window and want to know who uses that string; or if you have the top of a function selected in the disassembly and want to find out who calls that function.

- **Double-click address:** Set a debugging breakpoint at this address.

Immunity: Modules

In Immunity, you can load the list of executable modules by pressing the e button. This shows all the code—including dynamically loaded libraries—that you can debug, as shown in Figure 10.24. After opening the list, you can double-click a module to go to that code.

When you start Immunity, see what module you are currently looking at by checking the `eip` register. In nearly every case, you will want to start by debugging the main executable, not a shared library like `ntdll`. You can use the modules window to switch to the main executable.

Immunity: Strings

It is often useful to find what code is using a certain string in the executable. To find all the strings that a program is using, right-click and select Search For ⇨ All Referenced Text Strings, as shown in Figure 10.25.

In the strings window, right-click and select Search For Text to find a specific string, as shown in Figure 10.26. Then, right-click again, and select Search For Next to find the next reference to that string. You can double-click a string's address to go to the location where it is used in the disassembly.

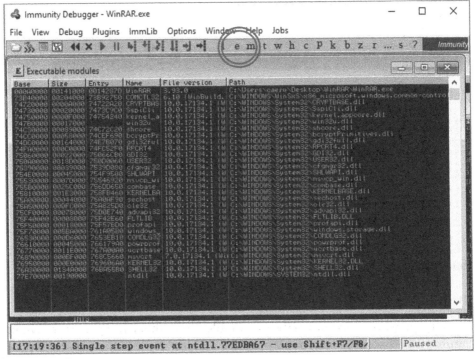

Figure 10.24: Executable modules in the Immunity debugger

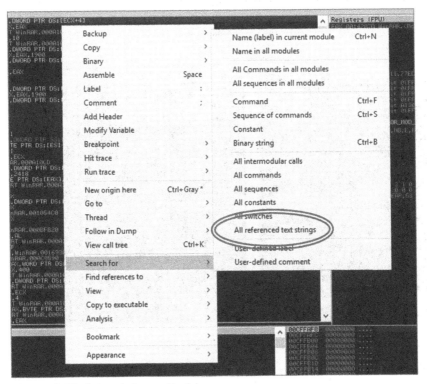

Figure 10.25: Strings in Immunity debugger

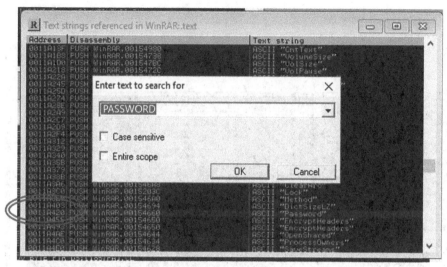

Figure 10.26: String references in Immunity debugger

Immunity: Running the Program

Click the play arrow to launch the executable under the debugger, as shown in Figure 10.27. Execution can be stopped by clicking the X to the left of the play arrow or can be paused using the pause button to its right. Execution can be restarted via the button with two left-facing arrows.

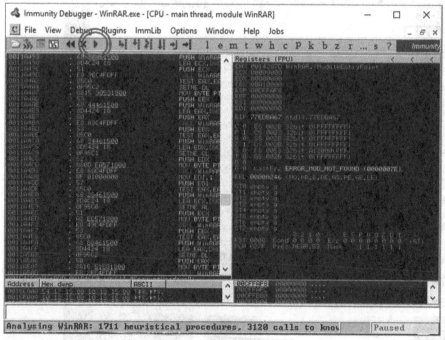

Figure 10.27: Launching an executable in Immunity debugger

After execution has been halted by a breakpoint or the pause button, you can click Step Into to progress the program one instruction, as shown in Figure 10.28. Alternatively, if you are stopped on a function call but already know or do not care about what the function does, click overstep Over, as shown in Figure 10.29, to continue debugging after the function returns.

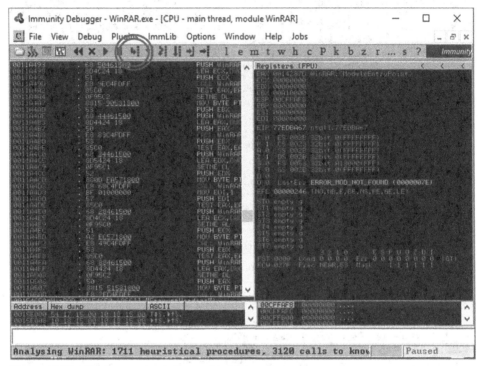

Figure 10.28: Single-stepping in Immunity debugger

Immunity: Exceptions

Many applications generate exceptions as part of normal execution. For example, a try {} except {} block will generate an exception if anything goes wrong in the try block. As a debugger, dynamic analysis tools like Immunity typically intercept the exception first to see if you want to do anything with it.

But for reverse engineering, you generally don't want to interfere with normal execution. Instead, you want to let the application handle the exception the way it normally would. This means you almost always want to pass the exception from the debugger to the application.

As shown in Figure 10.30, exceptions are reported at the bottom of the Immunity window, but each debugger is slightly different. In Immunity, press Shift+F9 to pass the exception and continue execution.

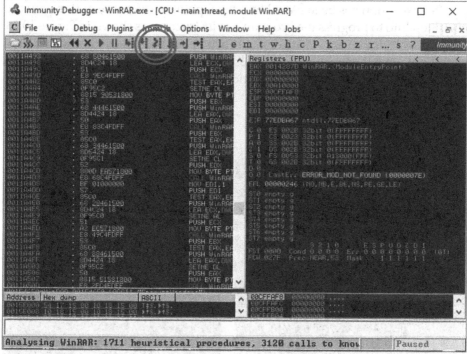

Figure 10.29: Stepping over instructions in Immunity debugger

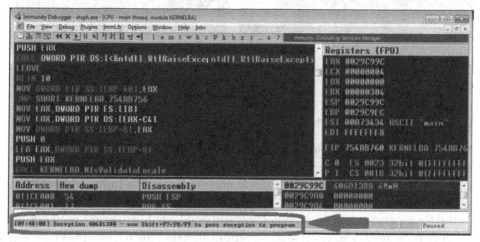

Figure 10.30: Exceptions in Immunity debugger

Immunity: REwriting the Program

Immunity has many features to aid in the development of patches to modify software behavior. For the purposes of software cracking, this includes making program edits to remove key checks, nag screens, etc.

In your first cracks, you will use the process of "noping" out code to remove it from the program. This involves replacing program instructions with nop instructions.

To do so in Immunity, first select the instruction(s) that you want to remove. Then, right-click and select Binary ➪ Fill With NOPs, as shown in Figure 10.31.

This will replace the selected instruction(s) with a series of nops, as shown in Figure 10.32.

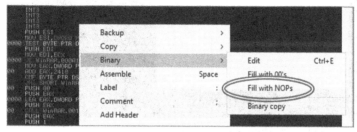

Figure 10.31: noping out code in Immunity debugger

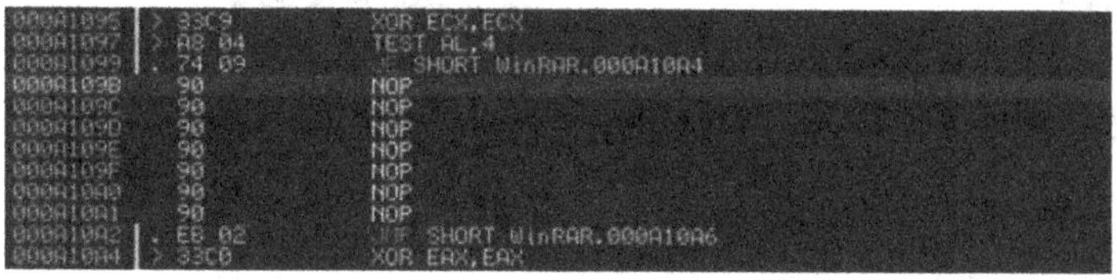

Figure 10.32: noped code in Immunity debugger

After modifying the program, test the patch by rerunning the program. If you patched the correct portion of code, you should find that the nag screen (key check, etc.) has disappeared.

However, if the patch crashes or failed to remove your target, you can easily revert your changes and try again. To do so, select the patch button to bring up the patches window. Then, right-click your patch and select Restore Original Code, as shown in Figure 10.33, to revert your patch and try again.

Once you have identified a working patch, save your changes to the executable to make it permanent. As shown in Figure 10.34, right-click and select Copy To Executable ➪ All Modifications. When a confirmation window appears, select Copy All.

A modified executable window should appear, showing your changes. Close the window, and select Yes to save your file. Give your file a new name, such as cracked.exe.

If you are confident in your modification, you can run cracked.exe directly. If you want to keep debugging with these new changes, you'll need to reload cracked.exe into Immunity.

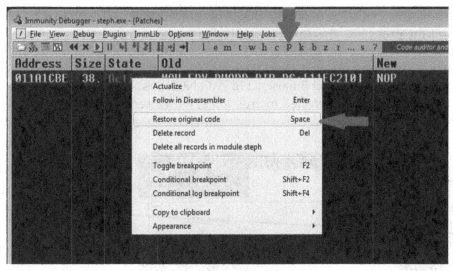

Figure 10.33: Reverting modified code in Immunity debugger

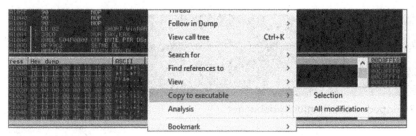

Figure 10.34: Saving a modified file in Immunity debugger

Lab: Cracking with Immunity

This lab provides hands-on experience with cracking programs using a debugger. Labs and all associated instructions can be found in their corresponding folder here:

```
https://github.com/DazzleCatDuo/
X86-SOFTWARE-REVERSE-ENGINEERING-CRACKING-AND-COUNTER-MEASURES
```

For this lab, please locate Lab Cracking with Immunity and follow the provided instructions.

Skills

This lab practices reverse engineering, patching, and circumventing software protections using Immunity and Resource Hacker. Some of the key skills tested include the following:

- Reverse engineering x86

- Patching
- Static versus dynamic analysis

Takeaways

Software can be easily modified to add, change, or remove functionality. These same techniques can be used to circumvent anything from trivial to advanced protections, as long as you understand how the software works.

Summary

Key checkers are intended to protect against the distribution and use of unlicensed and cracked copies of software, but no defense is perfect. Tools like Procmon, Resource Hacker, and debuggers can be used to understand these defenses and defeat them through the use of key generators or patching.

Patching and Advanced Tooling

The previous chapter introduced software cracking and patching. This chapter provides a more in-depth look at patching and some of the more advanced tools that can be used for reversing and cracking.

Patching in 010 Editor

It is often useful to be able to view and edit the hex of a file. If you've ever tried to open a binary in a text editor, you saw a lot of crazy symbols and blank space. This is because the text editor is trying to interpret everything in the file as ASCII, which it's not. Instead, we need an editor that will display as hex, not ASCII. There are many different *hex editors* capable of doing this. One of our favorites is 010 Editor. (Find links in the Tools section of our GitHub site at `https://github.com/DazzleCatDuo/X86-SOFTWARE-REVERSE-ENGINEERING-CRACKING-AND-COUNTER-MEASURES`).

Open any file (executable, data file, image, music, etc.) to view its hex. Figure 11.1 shows a sample executable in 010 Editor.

Figure 11.2 shows the Inspector pane. This shows the various different possible interpretations of the data at your cursor.

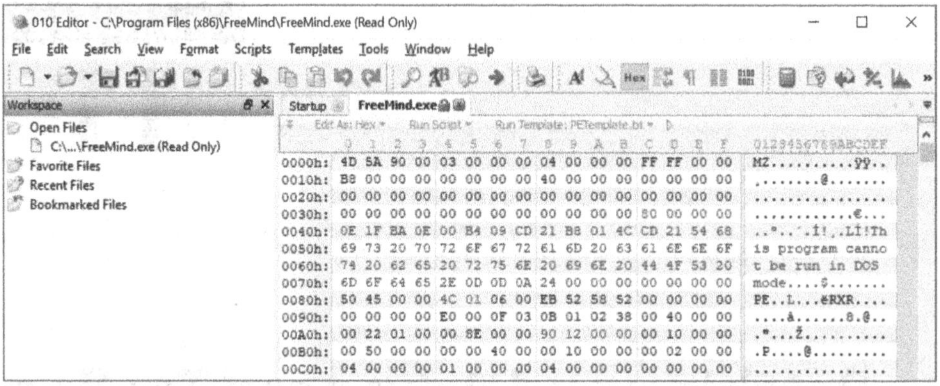

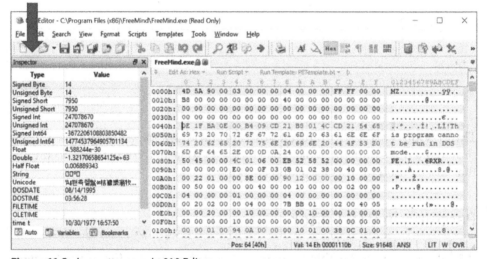

Figure 11.1: Viewing a file in 010 Editor

Figure 11.2: Inspector pane in 010 Editor

If you know what you're looking for, you can search for it, as shown in Figure 11.3. You can search for many different types of data, including the following:

- Text
- Hex bytes
- ASCII string
- Unicode string
- EBCDIC string
- Signed/unsigned byte
- Signed/unsigned short

- Signed/unsigned int
- Signed/unsigned int64
- Float
- Double
- Variable name
- Variable value

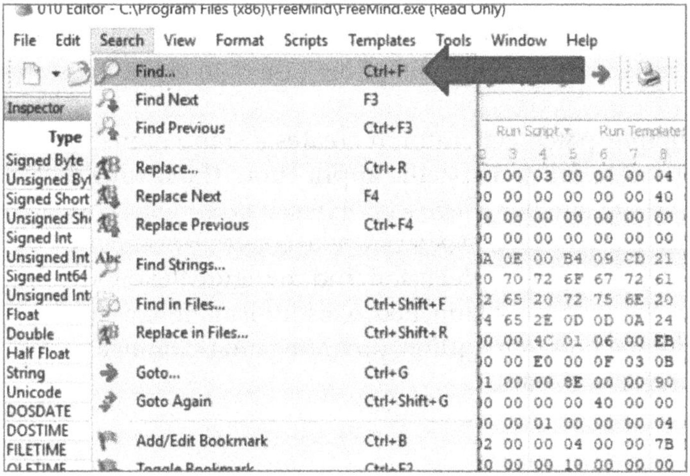

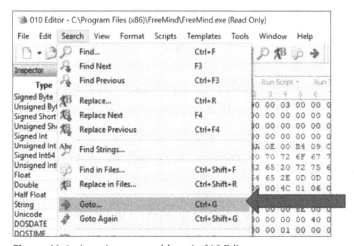

Figure 11.3: Searching in 010 Editor

You can jump to a specific address if you know where you need to go, as shown in Figure 11.4. This location of "where to go" can be specified as a byte, line number, sector, or short.

Figure 11.4: Jumping to an address in 010 Editor

In 010 Editor, you can directly modify the hex. Simply place your cursor and start typing to overwrite.

However, 010 Editor understands how important it is to maintain file size. When you type values, in 010 Editor it *overwrites* existing values at that location. It does not insert them, which would make the file larger.

CodeFusion Patching

After a researcher figures out how to crack a program, the next step is often to create a patcher/cracker utility. This will allow others to crack the same program.

CodeFusion is a popular patch generator. It creates a stand-alone executable file that can be used to crack a specific application. (Find links in the tools section of our GitHub site here: `https://github.com/DazzleCatDuo/` `X86-SOFTWARE-REVERSE-ENGINEERING-CRACKING-AND-COUNTER-MEASURES`).

To start creating a patcher, launch CodeFusion, and configure the information that will appear when the patcher is launched. This information is shown in Figure 11.5 and includes the program caption, program name, comments, icon, etc. These can be whatever you want.

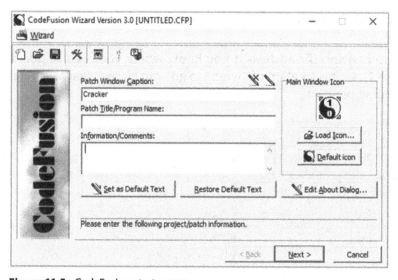

Figure 11.5: CodeFusion start screen

On the next screen, add the files to be patched, as shown in Figure 11.6. This is the executable that you want to crack.

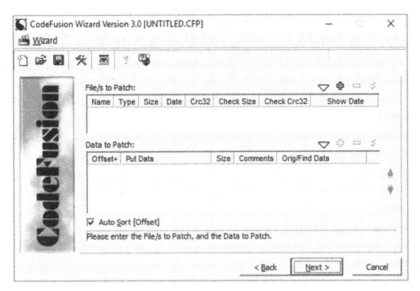

Figure 11.6: Loading a file in CodeFusion

Next, add the patch information by clicking the + icon shown in Figure 11.7. This is typically the information you learned from Immunity, Cheat Engine, IDA, etc. It usually includes an offset to patch, and the bytes to replace. Often, the bytes to patch with are 0x90 (nops). On the next page, click Make Win32 Executable to create an EXE file to patch the target application.

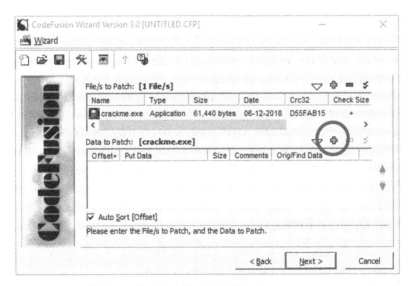

Figure 11.7: Adding patch information in CodeFusion

CodeFusion will add a new executable alongside the target application. As shown in Figure 11.8, run this executable, select the target, and click Start to apply the patch and crack the application.

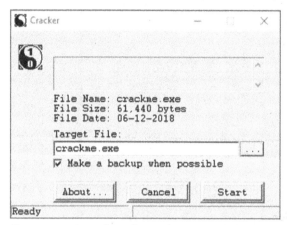

Figure 11.8: Launching the patched executable in CodeFusion

This cracking executable is what a cracking group would often redistribute. It is much smaller and more portable than the full, cracked app. Someone just needs to have the application installed, download your small patcher, and run it, and it will perform the patching to the genuine executable.

Cheat Engine

Cheat Engine is a popular and powerful open-source memory scanner, hex editor, and debugger. While the tool is primarily used for cheating in computer games, it can also often be valuable for quick dynamic analysis in software cracking. (Find links in our tools section on our GitHub here: `https://github.com/DazzleCatDuo/` `X86-SOFTWARE-REVERSE-ENGINEERING-CRACKING-AND-COUNTER-MEASURES`).

Cheat Engine enables searches for values input by the user with a wide variety of options. These allow the user to find and sort through the computer's memory.

Cheat Engine: Open a Process

Unlike other tools, reversing with Cheat Engine doesn't start with opening an executable. Instead, you select a running process to edit.

First, run the program that you want to crack. Then, start Cheat Engine and click Select A Process To Open, as shown in Figure 11.9. The Process List window appears, and you can select the process to crack and click Open.

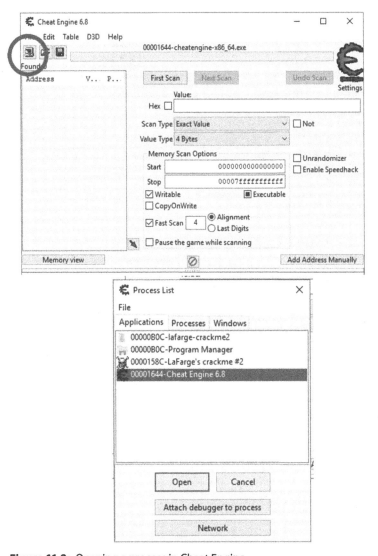

Figure 11.9: Opening a process in Cheat Engine

Cheat Engine: View Memory

Cheat Engine is based heavily around the idea of memory scans.

The main Cheat Engine window is primarily used for scanning memory. However, for now, focus on some simpler functionality: memory view. As shown in Figure 11.10, click Memory View to view the process's memory.

The memory view provides an easy and powerful way to view, scan, and modify a process's memory. As shown in Figure 11.11, memory view includes the disassembly at the top of the screen, an instruction reference in the middle, and a hex dump at the bottom.

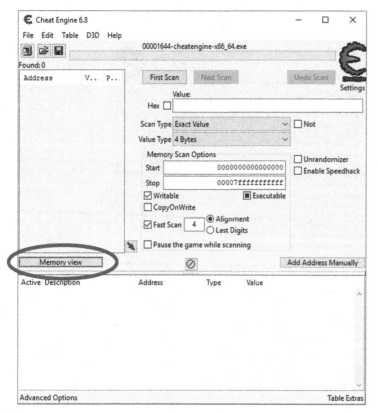

Figure 11.10: Viewing memory in Cheat Engine

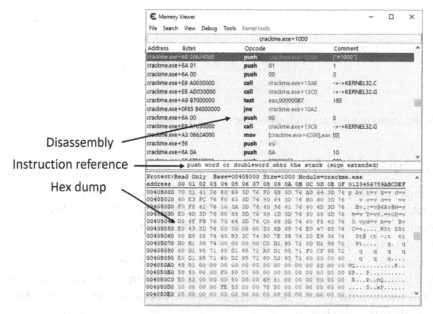

Figure 11.11: Memory Viewer pane in Cheat Engine

Cheat Engine: String References

As discussed, examining the strings in an executable can provide invaluable hints regarding its functionality. To view strings in Cheat Engine, select View ⇨ Referenced Strings to get a list of all of the strings used by the program.

Figure 11.12 shows the window that will pop up, where you can click on a string to view its cross references. Double-click on a cross-reference address to go to where the string is used in the disassembly.

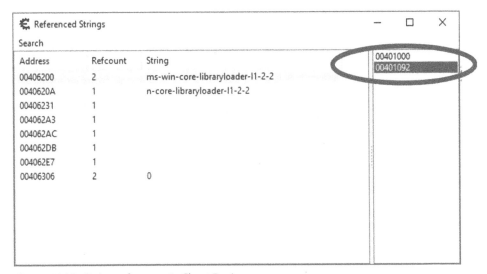

Figure 11.12: String references in Cheat Engine

Cheat Engine: REwriting Programs

Recall that noping out a chunk of code is the safest and easiest way to remove it without affecting the rest of the program. Cheat Engine makes this easy. To bypass an instruction (such as a final conditional jump in a key check), right-click the instruction and select Replace With Code That Does Nothing, as shown in Figure 11.13.

Cheat Engine is highly interactive. You can immediately try your modification in the running program! If your modification didn't work or if you want to undo it, right-click the modified code and select Restore With Original Code, as shown in Figure 11.14.

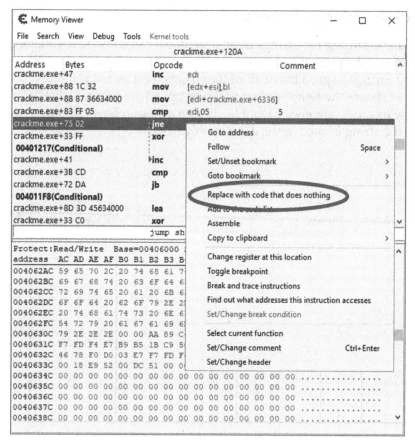

Figure 11.13: noping out instructions in Cheat Engine

Cheat Engine: Copying Bytes

Once you've found a working patch, the next step is to copy that patch over into an executable file rather than a running process. As shown in Figure 11.15, you can right-click the patch location and select Copy To Clipboard ➪ Bytes Only to copy those bytes for use by other tools.

Cheat Engine: Getting Addresses

To make a patch, you need to know where in the file the data to patch is. Cheat Engine is all about runtime analysis, so it does not know where in the file the data is.

To find an address, use 010 Editor to perform a search for the machine code you are replacing. That address is the file offset to patch for use in CodeFusion or other patchers.

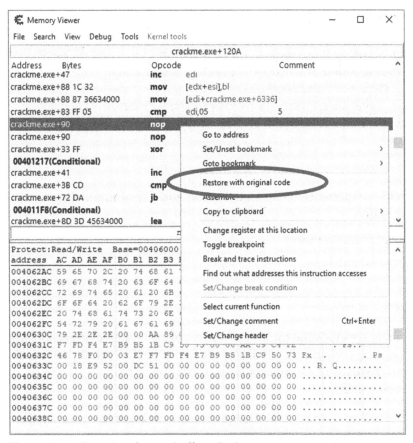

Figure 11.14: Reverting changes in Cheat Engine

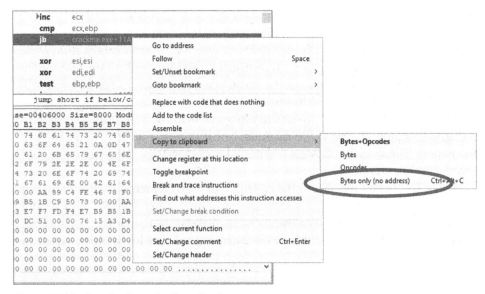

Figure 11.15: Copying bytes in Cheat Engine

Lab: Cracking LaFarge

This lab practices using these tools to patch programs. Labs and all associated instructions can be found in their corresponding folder here:

https://github.com/DazzleCatDuo/

X86-SOFTWARE-REVERSE-ENGINEERING-CRACKING-AND-COUNTER-MEASURES

For this lab, please locate Lab LaFarge and follow the provided instructions.

Skills

This lab provides experience using CodeFusion and Cheat Engine to practice the following skills:

- Reverse engineering x86
- Patching and patchers

Takeaways

A variety of tools are available for reverse engineering and cracking; choosing the "right" one depends on the challenge at hand and personal preference. Crackmes are a (usually) safe, always legal, incredibly addictive way to practice your cracking skills.

IDA Introduction

If you've ever googled reverse engineering tools, IDA is guaranteed to come up. It's the Cadillac of reverse engineering tools.

IDA, aka the Interactive Disassembler, allows for binary visualization of disassembly. It is available under a freemium model where limited features are available for free, while some of the more powerful features (or more obscure architectures) require a paid license.

Figure 11.16 shows the process of loading a new file in IDA. IDA automatically recognizes many common file formats, but if it gets it wrong, you can select the generic Binary File. IDA also offers a Processor Type drop-down menu to change architectures.

One of IDA's greatest strengths is its graph view, which shows a visual representation of an executable's x86 assembly and control flows. Figure 11.17 shows this view and some of the most useful components of it, including a memory map of the executable, a list of functions, the logic block view, and a graph window.

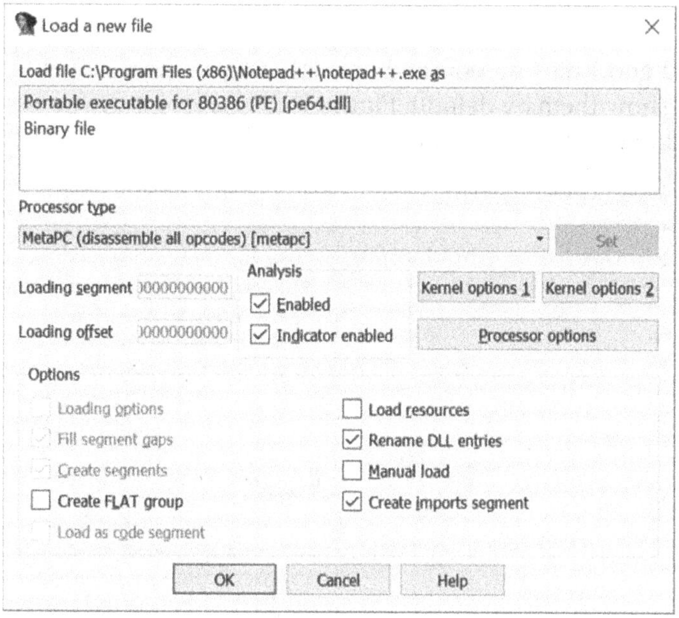

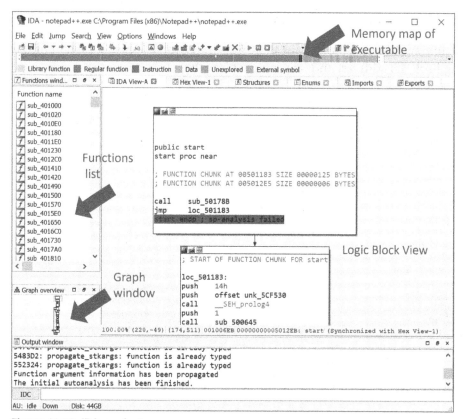

Figure 11.16: Loading a file in IDA

Figure 11.17: IDA graph view

IDA: Strings

As always, strings are a good starting point when analyzing a new executable. However, IDA doesn't show them by default. Figure 11.18 shows how to access the String view by clicking View ⇨ Open Subviews ⇨ Strings.

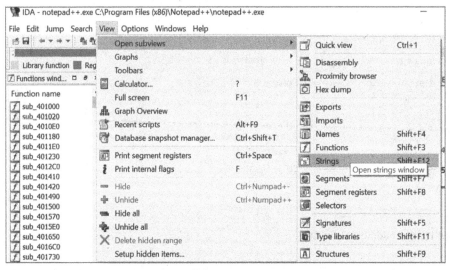

Figure 11.18: Opening strings view in IDA

Figure 11.19 shows the full list of strings in IDA. IDA shows the text of the string itself, its address, and its predicted length.

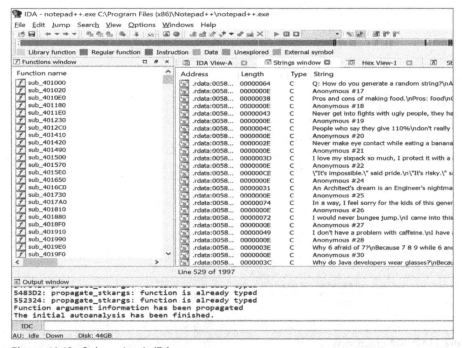

Figure 11.19: Strings view in IDA

Click a string to highlight it. Then, press X or right-click and select Jump To Xref To Operand. This will open up a window showing all of the locations where the string is used in the program, as shown in Figure 11.20.

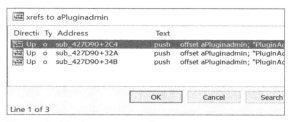

Figure 11.20: String cross-references in IDA

Following one of these cross-references will show the disassembly where the string is used. As shown in Figure 11.21, IDA understands how string references work. When it sees one, it shows the string as a comment.

```
push    offset aPlugin  ; "Plugin"
mov     [ebp+var_1C], ebx
push    offset aPluginadmin ; "PluginAdmin"
lea     ecx, [eax-14h]
mov     [ebp+var_5C], edi
mov     [ebp+nHeight], ecx
lea     ecx, ds:0FFFFFFE2h[eax*2]
lea     eax, [ebx+0Ah]
mov     [ebp+var_50], ecx
mov     [ebp+var_58], eax
lea     eax, [ebx+1Eh]
mov     ebx, dword_5ED884
add     eax, ecx
mov     [ebp+Y], eax
lea     eax, [ebp+var_D4]
mov     [ebp+var_54], esi
push    offset aPlugin_0 ; "Plugin"
mov     esi, [ebx+23564h]
mov     ecx, esi
push    eax
mov     [ebp+var_D8], ebx
call    sub_452F10
mov     [ebp+var_4], 0
lea     eax, [ebp+var_BC]
push    offset aVersion ; "Version"
```

Figure 11.21: Strings in IDA code view

IDA: Basic Blocks

IDA's graph view shows code in basic blocks. A basic block is a contiguous sequence of instructions uninterrupted by a branching instruction or branching reference.

Consider the following simple program in pseudocode. Figure 11.22 shows what this program looks like when disassembled in IDA.

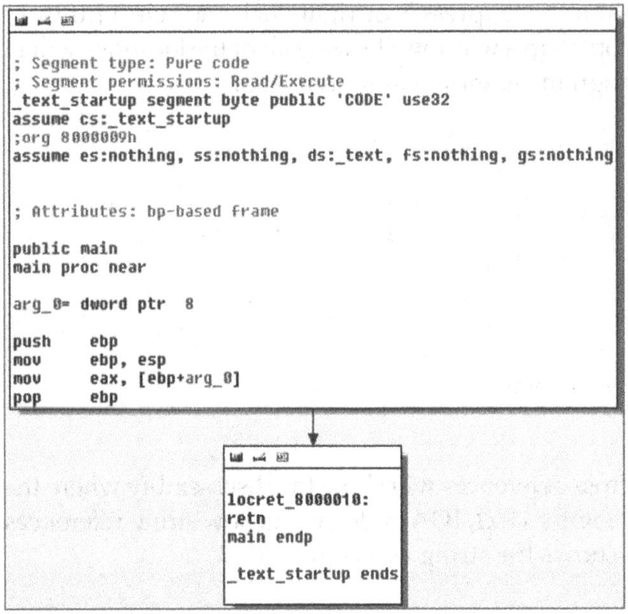

```
; Segment type: Pure code
; Segment permissions: Read/Execute
_text_startup segment byte public 'CODE' use32
assume cs:_text_startup
;org 8000009h
assume es:nothing, ss:nothing, ds:_text, fs:nothing, gs:nothing


; Attributes: bp-based frame

public main
main proc near

arg_0= dword ptr   8

push     ebp
mov      ebp, esp
mov      eax, [ebp+arg_0]
pop      ebp
```

```
locret_8000010:
retn
main endp

_text_startup ends
```

Figure 11.22: Basic blocks in IDA

```
int main(int argc, char* argv[])
{
     return argc;
}
```

IDA: Functions and Variables

IDA understands many calling conventions, including cdecl. It will recognize cdecl and knows the first argument always starts at ebp+8. IDA renames that offset to *arg_0* to make it easier to read. It will do this renaming with all of the input variables (*arg_X*), as shown in Figure 11.23.

This understanding also extends to how local variables are handled on the stack. For example, as shown in Figure 11.24, IDA will rename local variables to *var_X*.

Knowing how IDA labels arguments and variables can greatly aid in function analysis. For example, with the function shown in Figure 11.25, we can very quickly tell it has one local variable and six input variables because we recognize how IDA does its naming conventions.

Often, IDA has no information about the intent or context in which these variables are used, so it labels them sequentially. As you learn about an argument, variable, or function, you can rename it by pressing N or right-clicking the variable label and selecting Rename.

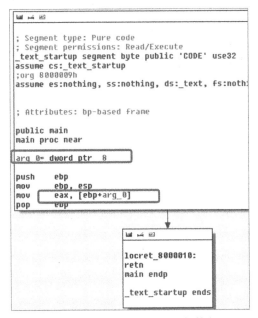

```
; Segment type: Pure code
; Segment permissions: Read/Execute
_text_startup segment byte public 'CODE' use32
assume cs:_text_startup
;org 8000009h
assume es:nothing, ss:nothing, ds:_text, fs:noth:


; Attributes: bp-based frame

public main
main proc near

arg_0= dword ptr   8

push    ebp
mov     ebp, esp
mov     eax, [ebp+arg_0]
pop     ebp
```

```
locret_8000010:
retn
main endp

_text_startup ends
```

Figure 11.23: Function arguments in IDA

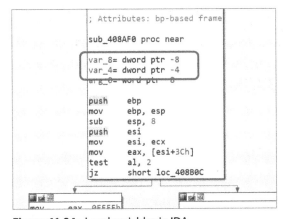

```
; Attributes: bp-based frame

sub_408AF0 proc near

var_8= dword ptr -8
var_4= dword ptr -4
arg_0= word ptr  8

push    ebp
mov     ebp, esp
sub     esp, 8
push    esi
mov     esi, ecx
mov     eax, [esi+3Ch]
test    al, 2
jz      short loc_408B0C
```
```
mov     eax, 0FFFFh
```

Figure 11.24: Local variables in IDA

```
sub_408FB0 proc near

var_4= dword ptr -4
arg_0= dword ptr   8
arg_4= dword ptr   0Ch
arg_8= dword ptr   10h
arg_C= dword ptr   14h
arg_10= dword ptr  18h
arg_1C= dword ptr  24h

push    ebp
mov     ebp, esp
```

Figure 11.25: Local variables and function arguments in IDA

IDA: Comments

When reversing an application, it's essential to be able to track what you've figured out and done so far. In IDA, pressing ; opens up a box to enter comments, as shown in Figure 11.26.

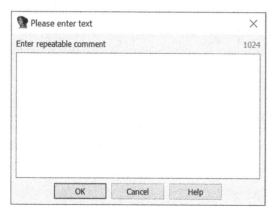

Figure 11.26: IDA comment window

One tip is to put an identifier like "_x" in all of your comments. This gives you something to search for to find all comments.

To start a search for comments, select Search ▷ Text, as shown in Figure 11.27. Then, search for "_x" while selecting Find All Occurrences to find all of the comments that you've placed in the program.

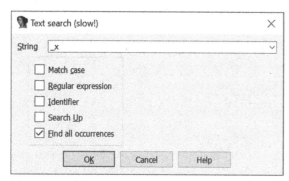

Figure 11.27: Searching for comments in IDA

By using a consistent commenting style and searching for comments, it's easy to find places in the code that you've already explored. For example, as shown in Figure 11.28, you can quickly identify locations that were marked "TODO" for later analysis.

Address	Function	Instruction
.text:00408DB9	sub_408DB0	mov edx, [ebx+20h] ; _x TODO figure out what this does
.text:00408DC2	sub_408DB0	cmp [ebx+38h], eax ; _x this looks like a count check
.text:00408DC5	sub_408DB0	jnb short loc_408DCA ; _x prompt for username

Figure 11.28: Search results in IDA

IDA: Paths

IDA shows three types of paths between basic blocks:

- **Red:** Path taken if a conditional jump is not taken
- **Green:** Path taken if a conditional jump is taken
- **Blue:** Guaranteed path (no conditionals)

For example, consider the following code sample containing a simple `if` statement:

```
int main(int argc, char* argv[])
{
        if (argc > 1)
                return 0;

        return argc;
}
```

Figure 11.29 shows how this code would look in IDA. After the conditional block, the paths diverge. The colors aren't shown in this book, but the left path, which is red in IDA, shows what happens if the jump is not taken. The right path, which is green in IDA, is followed if the conditional resolves to false.

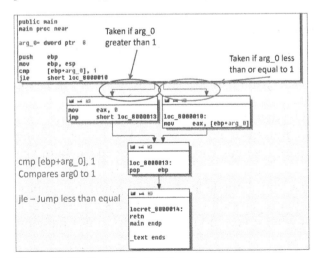

Figure 11.29: Code paths in IDA

Below this point, several more arrows indicate transitions between basic blocks. Since none of these involves conditionals, they will all be blue in IDA.

IDA Patching

IDA is another tool that can be used to patch executables. As an example, consider the following code:

```
printf("please enter the password\n");
scanf("%s", user_entered_password);
if (strcmp(user_entered_password, correct_password) == 0)
{
        printf("SUCCESS\n");
}
else
{
        printf("Failure\n");
}
```

This code implements a simple authentication system. It asks a user to enter a password and checks the answer. If the answer is correct, it prints SUCCESS; otherwise, it prints Failure. While it's a simplistic example, keep in mind this flow of checking the password and going one way if it's wrong and one way if it's right is very common. In IDA, you can patch the application to defeat this password verification.

By default, IDA does not show the machine code in graph view. Unless you're patching, it doesn't serve much purpose. But when you start to desire patching, you'll want to see it. To show machine code, select Options ⇨ General to open the window shown in Figure 11.30. Then, specify the number of opcode bytes to show in graph view (most opcodes don't exceed 8 bytes, so it's a good practice to set it to 8).

Figure 11.31 shows the application's password-checking logic in IDA. As shown, the left (red) path is taken if the passwords match, while the right (green) path is taken if they don't.

The instruction that decides which jump to take is jnz. Recall that jnz stands for "jump not zero."

This password check could be defeated in a couple of different ways. One option is to try to figure out what needs to be "not zero." This means figuring out what two values it's comparing so you can potentially make a valid key or a cracker.

An easier alternative is to use your knowledge of x86 to patch the application. As is, the application evaluates a condition and performs a jnz (0x75) if the password is incorrect. But what if you did the exact opposite? Changing this `jnz` to a `jz` (`0x74`) will reverse the logic, causing the application to accept only *incorrect* passwords. With the logic flipped, an incorrect password would result in success and a correct one would result in failure.

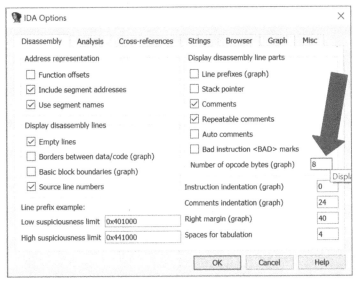

Figure 11.30: Showing opcode bytes in IDA

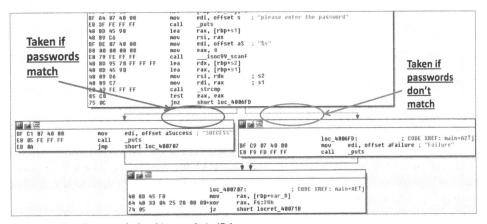

Figure 11.31: Password-checking code in IDA

To change the instruction, highlight it and click Edit ⇨ Patch Program ⇨ Change Byte. Then, in the Patch Bytes window shown in Figure 11.32, change the first value from 74 to 75.

Figure 11.33 shows how the application will look after the patch is applied. The single bit that was changed will be highlighted in IDA, and the meaning of the two paths after the jump will be reversed. Now, the application will work for anything *except* the correct password.

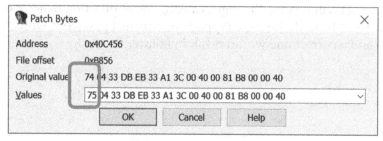

Figure 11.32: IDA Patch Bytes window

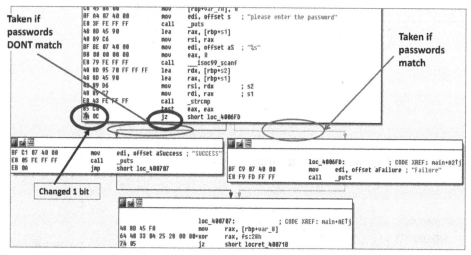

Figure 11.33: Password-checking logic in IDA after patching

Lab: IDA Logic Flows

This lab provides an introduction to using IDA for reversing. The lab files are on the Windows VM in the `ida_logic` folder on the Desktop. Inside this folder will be several binaries. Find out which of them is:

- ▪ `if`
- ▪ Multipart `if` (i.e., `if (cont1 && cond2)`)
- ▪ `while` loop
- ▪ `for` loop
- ▪ `do while` loop

Skills

This lab provides practice using IDA to reverse engineer control flow graphs. The goal is to learn to quickly identify high-level coding constructs based on their control flow patterns.

Takeaways

Analyzing a program's control flow can make it easier to quickly understand what is happening inside of code. Getting good at recognizing these flows quickly can vastly improve your reverse engineering ability.

Ghidra

Ghidra is a static analysis tool released in 2019 by the NSA. It has many similarities to IDA, but unlike IDA, it is free and open source. In many situations, Ghidra is an adequate replacement to IDA.

IDA has a much longer reputation in the space, but Ghidra is also immensely powerful and in many cases has a lot of the same features. This example demos IDA given its long history in the reverse engineering space, but everything shown can also be done in Ghidra. The tools are similar enough that skills in one will often transfer over. Try Ghidra out for some of the later, open-ended labs in this book and your own practice.

Lab: Cracking with IDA

This lab takes a look at a more complex application in IDA. Labs and all associated instructions can be found in their corresponding folder here:

```
https://github.com/DazzleCatDuo/
X86-SOFTWARE-REVERSE-ENGINEERING-CRACKING-AND-COUNTER-MEASURES
```

For this lab, please locate Lab Cracking with IDA and follow the provided instructions.

Skills

This lab practices using IDA to crack large, real-world applications. The goal is to learn to quickly identify points of interest and to prioritize multiple cracking approaches.

Takeaways

Real-world programs are too large for uniform, fine-grained analysis. Triage is critical to finding the points of interest.

Multiple opportunities are usually available to a cracker. Selecting which to pursue can save (or cost) significant time.

Summary

This chapter explored some of the most widely used tools for reversing and cracking. Take the time to become familiar with them. It'll pay off in the long run!

Defense

How do you defend against cracking? To start, it's essential to have a good key check design (don't pull a *Starcraft/Half-Life*). From there, you can implement additional defensive options.

However, it's important to remember that there is no such thing as uncrackable software. As a defender, your job is to slow attackers down in the critical parts of your software and make them frustrated enough they go to a different target.

Like many things in cybersecurity, you just don't want to be the low-hanging fruit. "When swimming in shark-infested water, you don't have to be the fastest. . .just faster than the guy next to you."

Obfuscation

Obfuscation is the practice of hiding the intended meaning of code by purposefully making logic ambiguous and unclear. It can be valuable for slowing reverse engineering to do the following:

- Slow cracking
- Slow tampering
- Protect intellectual property

Done well, obfuscation can make code essentially unreadable. For example, the following C code (available from www.ioccc.org/1988/phillipps.c), when compiled and run, prints out the lyrics to the entire 12 days of Christmas song. It was one of the IOCCC winners, which is a competition to hand-obfuscate code. Looking at it makes my brain hurt, and I can't guess at how long I'd have to reverse engineer the code before I figured out what it did.

```
#include <stdio.h>
main(t,_,a)
char
*
a;
{
        return!
 0<t?
t<3?
 main(-79,-13,a+
main(-87,1-_,
main(-86, 0, a+1 )
 +a)):
 1,
t<_?
main(t+1, _, a )
:3,
 main ( -94, -27+t, a )
&&t == 2 ?_
<13 ?
 main ( 2, _+1, "%s %d %d\n" )
 :9:16:
t<0?
t<-72?
main( _, t,
"@n'+,#'/*{}w+/w#cdnr/+,{}r/*de}+,/*{*+,/w{%+,/w#q#n+,/#{l,+,
        /n{n+,/+#n+,/#;\
#q#n+,/+k#;*+,/'r :'d*'3,}{w+K w'K:'+}e#';dq#'l q#'+d'K#!
        /+k#;\
q#'r}eKK#}w'r}eKK{nl]'/#;#q#n')}#}w')}{nl]'/+#n';d}rw'
        i;# ){nl]!/n{n#'; \
r{#w'r nc{nl]'/#{l,+'K {rw' iK{;[{nl]'/w#q#\
\
n'wk nw' iwk{KK{nl]!/w{%'l##w#' i; :{nl]'/*{q#'ld;r'}{nlwb!/*de}'c ;;\
{nl'-{}rw]'/+,}##'*}#nc,',#nw]'/+kd'+e}+;\
#'rdq#w! nr'/ ') }+}{rl#'{n' ')# }'+}##(!!/")
:
t<-50?
_==*a ?
putchar(31[a]):
 main(-65,_,a+1)
:
```

```
main((*a == '/') + t, _, a + 1 )
:
0<t?
main ( 2, 2 , "%s")
:*a=='/'||
main(0,
main(-61,*a, "!ek;dc i@bK'(q)-[w]*%n+r3#l,{}:\nuwloca-O;m .vpbks,
     fxntdCeghiry")
,a+1);}
```

The concept of obfuscation has also made its way into popular culture. The following quotes are from a scene in one of the James Bond movies, *Skyfall* when Q is attempting to get into Silva's laptop.

- ▪ "There are algorithms and encryptions and asymmetrics!"
- ▪ "Looks like obfuscated code to conceal its true purpose. Security through obscurity!"

Obfuscations can be applied by hand or automatically to a program at various stages of its life cycle, including the following:

- ▪ Source code
- ▪ Bytecode
- ▪ Object code
- ▪ Binary executable code

Evaluating Obfuscation

When evaluating options for obfuscation, there are a few different factors to consider:

- ▪ **Potency:** How much obfuscation is applied to the program
- ▪ **Resilience:** How well-obfuscated code holds up to attack from reverse engineering tools
- ▪ **Stealth:** How well-obfuscated code blends in with the rest of the program
- ▪ **Cost:** Performance penalty of an obfuscated application

In general, these factors tend to work against each other. For example, the more potent the obfuscation is, the less stealthy it typically is.

In practice, performance cost is often the limiting factor. However, almost all obfuscations allow some degree of scaling/tuning based on requirements.

Automated Obfuscation

Obfuscation can be performed manually. However, it's almost always better to use tools to obfuscate the code. Some of the common obfuscation techniques include the following:

- Name mangling
- String encryption
- Control flow obfuscation
    - Control flow flattening
    - Opaque predicates
- Instruction substitution

Name Mangling

Name mangling involves obfuscating function and variable names. This can be done a few different ways, including the following:

- Replace with gibberish (get_key -> aVJ230AM)
- Replace with misleading name (get_key -> draw_screen)
- Replace with nondescriptive name (get_key -> a)

After mangling, the purpose of functions and variables is no longer immediately apparent. For example, consider the following code sample:

```
public static void SelectionSort <T> (T[] data, int size)
        where T: IComparable
{
        for (int num1 = size - 1; num1 >= 1; num1--)
        {
                T local1 = data[0];
                int num2 = 0;
                for (int num3 = 1; num3 <= num1; num3++)
                {
                        if (data[num3].CompareTo(local1) > 0)
                        {
                                local1 = data[num3];
                                num2 = num3;
                        }
                }
                T local2 = data[num2];
                data[num2] = data[num1];
                data[num1] = local2;
        }
}
```

After mangling, this might look something like the following:

```
public static void a <a> (a[] A_0, int A_1) where a:IComparable
{
        int num1 = A_1 - 1;
Label_004D:
        if (num1 < 1)
        {
                return;
        }
        a local1 A_0[0];
        int num2 = 0;
        int num3 = 1;
        while(true)
        {
                if (num3 <= num1)
                {
                        if (A_0[num3].CompareTo(local1) > 0)
                        {
                                local1 = A_0[num3];
                                num2 = num3;
                        }
                }
                else
                {
                        a local2 = A_0[num2];
                        A_0[num2] = A_0[num1];
                        A_0[num1] = local2;
                        num1--;
                        goto Label_004D;
                }
                num3++;
        }
}
```

In the original, it is relatively easy to determine that the code is a sort algorithm even without the function name. However, doing so after mangling is much harder.

String Encryption

Another obfuscation technique is for the obfuscator to encrypt strings when the executable is built. A decrypt function in the code will then decrypt individual strings as needed at runtime. This renders tools like IDA's string view unusable.

String encryption can have a dramatic effect on code readability. Consider the following code:

```
public a() {
        this.a = "Hi, my name is Paul."
}
```

```
public static void a() {
      a a1 = new a();
      Console.WriteLine("Enter password: ");
      string text1 = Console.ReadLine();
      if (!text1.Equals(a1.a))
      {
            Console.WriteLine("Incorrect password.");
      }
      else
      {
            Console.WriteLine("Correct password.");
      }
      Console.ReadLine();
}
```

After string encryption, this code might look like this:

```
pubic a() {
      int num1 = 5;
      this.a =
a("\ue6ad\u9eb1\u94b3\uc1b7\u9ab9\ud2bb\uadbf\ua7c1\ue4c
      3\uafc5\ubbc7\ueac9\u9ccb\uafcd\ua5cf\ubed1\ufad3", num1;
}


public static void a()
{
      int num1 = 13;
      a a1 = new a();
      Console.WriteLine(a("\uf3b5\ud6b7\uceb9\uccbd\ue0bf\ub2c1\ua5c3\u
            b5c5\ubbc7\ubdc9\ua3cb\ubccd\ub4cf\ue8d1\uf4d3, num1));
      string text1 = Console.ReadLine();
      if (1text1.Equals(a1.a)) {
                  Console.WriteLine(a("\uffb5\ud8b7\ud3bb\uccbd\ub2bf\ua7c1
                        \ua7c3\ub2c5\ue8c7\ubac9\uadcb\ubdcd\ua3cf\ua5d1\ubb
                        d3\ua4d5\ubcd7\uf4d9", num1));
      }
      else
      {
                  Console.WriteLine(a("\uf5b5\ud7b7\uc8b9\ucebb\ua3bf\ub6c1
                        \ue4c3\ub6c5\ua9c7\ub9c9\ubfcb\ub9cd\ubfcf\ua0d1\ub0
                        d3\uf8d5", num1));
      }
      Console.ReadLine();
}
```

In the original, the strings make it easy to determine that this is authentication code (which is often very interesting to attackers). Without these strings,
the logic of the code is much more difficult to figure out. Keep in mind one of
the biggest struggles to cracking an application is finding the relevant code. In a

binary with hundreds of thousands of lines of code, only five might be related to the key checker, and using tools like strings is a powerful way to quickly hone in on those five lines. Taking away strings is quite painful to the reverse engineer.

Control Flow Flattening

With this obfuscation technique, the control flow of each function is "flattened." This includes the following steps:

1. The function is collapsed into a `switch` statement within an infinite loop.
2. Each basic block of the original flow is assigned a state number.
3. A `switch` statement selects between basic blocks, dispatching them in the correct order.

Figure 12.1 shows how the flattening process transforms an application in IDA. While the logic is the same, the control flow is much harder to analyze.

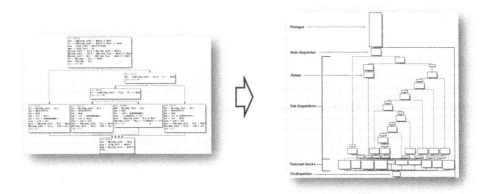

Figure 12.1: Control flow flattening in IDA

Opaque Predicates

Opaque predicates add junk code interleaved with real code. The junk code never executes, while the real code always executes. However, to a reverse engineer, this is a good way to distract them with useless code, making them spend hours reverse engineering junk code that is essentially irrelevant. Figure 12.2 shows an example of this in IDA.

The path is determined by an `if` statement that always resolves to the same value. However, it can take time to identify (an "opaque predicate"), slowing analysis.

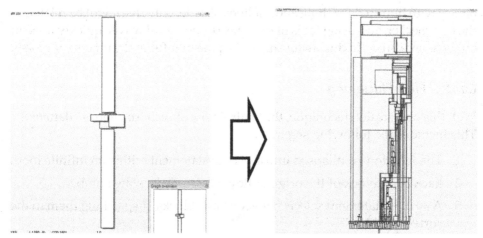

Figure 12.2: Opaque predicates in IDA

Consider the following statement:

```
if ( (a<<1)%2 ) { b = a * b + a; } else { a = a + b; }
```

Where is the junk code here?

Instruction Substitution

Instruction substitution involves replacing easily identified instructions with complex ones that perform the same action. For example, consider the following code:

```
sub edx, 0x192A6C72
neg ecx
sub edx, ecx
add edx, 0x192A6C72
```

What was the original operation?

Obfuscators

Obfuscators typically provide "knobs" that allow the developer to tweak the level of obfuscation. The reason for this is that more obfuscation is not always better. In general, increasing obfuscation decreases execution speed and increases file size. Also, drastically increasing obfuscation does not substantially increase the difficulty of reverse engineering. Balancing usability and security requires finding a middle ground.

If you manage to do that, obfuscation can be a valuable tool, especially for code that is otherwise trivial to decompile (such as the JIT languages discussed earlier, e.g., .NET, etc.). However, it's also important to ensure that the tool you are using does not also provide an easily accessible de-obfuscator.

For general-purpose obfuscation, OLLVM can be a good starting point. This tool has a few benefits, including the fact that it works with the LLVM intermediate representation (IR) and supports all LLVM front ends (gcc, clang) and many source languages (C, C++, C#, Lisp, Fortran, Haskell, Python, Ruby, etc.).

The use of OLLVM is not recommended for production code. However, it can be a good basis for custom obfuscators or simply learning/playing with obfuscation.

In addition to OLLVM, there are numerous language-specific obfuscator tools and tricks. Some examples include Dotfuscator for C# and Proguard for Java.

For JavaScript programs, tools such as YUICompressor and UglifyJS can be used for obfuscation. In general, minimizers, simply as a byproduct, introduce some reasonable level of obfuscation.

Python code can be compiled to bytecode to remove some variable names and comments. Then, the bytecode can be obfuscated and released with a custom interpreter. Some Python obfuscators include Tigress, BitBoost, and Opy, but these are less popular than the ones mentioned earlier.

Defeating Obfuscators

Obfuscators are designed to protect against reverse engineering by making it more difficult and time-consuming to perform. However, obfuscation isn't perfect, and as stated many times previously, motivated crackers can eventually defeat it.

Some of the ways that a reverse engineer can speed up the process of analyzing an obfuscated binary include the following:

- Run traces to identify real versus fake code
- Use symbolic analysis to simplify complexity
- Write custom scripts to remove obfuscations

Lab: Obfuscation

This lab explores obfuscation techniques. T Labs and all associated instructions can be found in their corresponding folder here:

```
https://github.com/DazzleCatDuo/
X86-SOFTWARE-REVERSE-ENGINEERING-CRACKING-AND-COUNTER-MEASURES
```

For this lab, please locate Lab Obfuscation and follow the provided instructions.

Skills

This lab provides experience in circumventing obfuscation techniques using objdump. The goal is to understand the impact of common code defense techniques.

Takeaways

Obfuscation techniques will slow down—but not defeat—cracking. However, remember that sometimes slowing down is enough. Advanced reverse engineers often have tools to automatically circumvent common obfuscations.

Anti-Debugging

Debugging is often the fastest way to reverse engineer an executable. Anti-debugging is a series of techniques to try to stop someone from having the ability to dynamically analyze your application with a debugger. There are many techniques in this space, but most of them are geared at trying to check for the presence of a debugger. A few common anti-debugging checks include the following:

- Memory checks
- CPU checks
- Timing checks
- Exception checks
- Environment checks

As with most security controls, there are usability trade-offs to anti-debugging, code size and performance being the two most painful side effects. Because of this, anti-debugging functionality is often added only selectively, reserving its use for the code most likely to be attacked (key checkers, sensitive IP addresses, etc.). But as with all security there are pros and cons; if you build a bunch of anti-debugging checks around your sensitive code, you're also painting a bull's-eye telling an attacker exactly where the interesting stuff is. So, while they might not be able to debug it, they now know exactly where to focus with static analysis techniques. But that doesn't mean it's not worth doing; static analysis might take 100x longer than dynamic, so even if you paint arrows to your sensitive code, forcing them to do it statically can still be a powerful tool.

The main goal with anti-debugging is to identify when a debugger is attached and take an action. The most commonly used actions include the following:

- Forcibly disconnecting the debugger
- Exiting the program
- Executing red herring code to waste an attacker's time

IsDebuggerPresent()

`IsDebuggerPresent` is a memory check for a debugger. The function `IsDebuggerPresent`, which is located in `Windows.h`, returns `true` if a program is being run under a debugger. The following code shows an example of how it is used to exit an application if a debugger is attached:

```
if (IsDebuggerPresent())
    exit(1);
```

A check using IsDebuggerPresent can be defeated by placing a breakpoint at the instruction right after the function returns. When the breakpoint triggers, set the value of *eax* to 0, which tells the program that no debugger is attached. Remember that *eax* holds the return value. Returning a 1 is undesirable, because that means it detected the debugger, so instead make it return a 0. While that seems trivial, keep in mind the game is to just make it harder. If your code has 100 of these checks, attackers wanting to debug have to track each of these down and either manually breakpoint and change the return value every time or start to get custom scripts going to do this change for them. Is that annoying as an attacker? Yup.

Debug Registers

An application can also make use of the CPU's debug registers to perform a check for a debugger. Recall that the debugging section discussed software and hardware breakpoints. A hardware breakpoint uses CPU hardware registers to set itself.

These hardware breakpoints use debug registers (in x86: DR0, 1, 2, 3, 6, 7) instead of memory modifications. It's possible to detect debugging by examining these registers.

For example, consider the following code sample. It checks to see if any of the debug registers are set, indicating a hardware breakpoint.

```
if (GetThreadContext(hThread, &ctx))
    if ((ctx.Dr0 != 0x00) || ... || (ctx.Dr7 != 0x00))
        exit(1);
```

The call to GetThreadContext() is crucial to this anti-debugging technique. For those looking to bypass this technique, place a breakpoint after this call and modify the context structure, setting the observed values of all of the debug registers to 0x0. Again, is it doable to bypass? Yes. Is it annoying to an attacker to have to keep doing these modifications? Yup. An annoyed attacker equals success to a defender! Also recall we discussed that IDA 6.3 and above support hardware breakpoints. These breakpoints don't use the debug registers and instead use page permissions. In other words, this type of anti-debugging check won't catch a hardware breakpoint.

RDTSC

RDTSC stands for the x86 instruction Read Timestamp Counter. This counter can be used to read a timestamp from the CPU. This has lots of interesting uses, but one of them is to perform a timing check for a debugger.

When running an application (with no debugger), the CPU is very fast, but when a debugger is attached, it isn't. Even if you're not stepping and you're just letting the code run, it's orders of magnitude slower than just letting the CPU go. And it's even slower if you're doing something like single-stepping through the code. With RDTSC, an application can take timestamps before and after a block of code and measure how long the code took to execute. If the delta is large, it's likely that the code hit a breakpoint or was being manually stepped through with a debugger.

The following pseudocode shows how RDTSC could be used to detect a debugger:

```
a = __rdtsc();
keycheck();
b = __rdtsc();
if (b - a > 0x10000)
    exit(1);
```

To defeat this type of anti-debugging check, you could break on the second call to RDTSC. You could then modify the value of either a to be closer to b or b to be closer to a. Essentially, make the difference between the two very small so it assumes execution went as planned. Bypassable? Yes. Annoying to have to patch every time you debug? Yes!

Invalid CloseHandle()

The use of an invalid call to CloseHandle is an example of an exception check for a debugger. The Windows CloseHandle function throws an exception if called with an invalid handle while running under a debugger (and not otherwise). An application can use this knowledge to call CloseHandle on an invalid handle to detect the presence of a debugger.

The following code demonstrates how CloseHandle can be used to detect a debugger:

```
HANDLE hInvalid = (HANDLE)0xDEADBEEF;
__try { CloseHandle(hInvalid); }
__except (EXCEPTION_EXECUTE_HANDLER) { exit(1); }
```

To defeat this check, set a breakpoint on CloseHandle. When the breakpoint is triggered, modify the argument to INVALID_HANDLE_VALUE.

Directory Scanning

Directory scanning is an environment check for a debugger. It involves scanning the file system for installations of common debuggers and cracking tools. If these tools are found, then the application can choose to exit.

However, this is an indiscriminate search, and these tools may not be actively debugging the application. As a result, it hurts legitimate users of these tools.

To defeat this check, set a breakpoint on the directory traversal. Then, mask out the tool directories so that the application doesn't see or search them.

Offensive Anti-Debugging

Anti-debugging techniques need not be passive detection of debuggers. Many "active defense" approaches exist, including the following:

- `NtUserBlockInput`: Block keyboard input to the attached debugger.
- `NtUserFindWindowEx`: Get a handle to the debugger window.
- Debugger-specific attacks: For example, IDA versions older than 7.0 crash at about 10,000 instructions without a branch.

Many more options exist. For offensive anti-debugging, first you need to recognize the debugger is there, and then you take some type of offensive action. Open-source plugins are available to help, including some used in the following lab.

For defensive anti-debugging, it's important to remember that you don't need to reinvent the wheel. Ready-made solutions are available, including free, open-source Windows anti-debugger checks.

Defeating Anti-Debugging

Like other software defenses, anti-debugging code can be defeated (though if done right, it's painful). The first step is to find and reverse engineer the anti-debug check. Often, this is accomplished by working backward from where you got caught using the debugger.

Once you've identified the anti-debug code, you have a few different options for defeating it, including the following:

- Removing the check via `nops`
- Placing a breakpoint on the check and modifying memory/registers to mask the debugger
- Using built-in debugger plugins or scripts

In general, it's stealthier to mask the debugger immediately at the anti-debug check. For example, if an application is using `IsDebuggerPresent`, modify the return value of `IsDebuggerPresent` rather than messing with the `if` statement or exit code designed to use that value.

Lab: Anti-Debugging

This lab provides practice in defeating anti-debugging techniques. Labs and all associated instructions can be found in their corresponding folder here:

```
https://github.com/DazzleCatDuo/
X86-SOFTWARE-REVERSE-ENGINEERING-CRACKING-AND-COUNTER-MEASURES
```

For this lab, please locate Lab Anti-Debugging and follow the provided instructions.

Skills

This lab uses x64dbg to circumvent anti-debugging techniques. The goal is to understand the impact of common defensive coding techniques.

Takeaways

Again, slowing down a reverse engineer is often enough; defenses don't need to be perfect. However, skilled reversers will have tools to overcome common defensive techniques.

Summary

Developers want to defend themselves and their code against reversers and crackers. This chapter explored some of the common methods for accomplishing this, including obfuscation and anti-debugging protections.

CHAPTER 13

Advanced Defensive Techniques

The previous chapter presented some basic techniques for protecting an application against reverse engineering and cracking. This chapter demonstrates some more advanced techniques that are more difficult to defeat, including tamper-proofing, packing, virtualization, and the use of cryptors.

Tamper-Proofing

One of the powerful cracking techniques we've covered is patching, both for long-term cracking but also in the aid of reverse engineering. Tamper-proofing is a series of techniques geared toward making software more difficult for an attacker to modify. Some common approaches include the following:

- Hashing
- Signature
- Watermark
- Software guards

All of the following techniques have ways of being defeated, but (and I can't stress this enough) just because they have ways of being defeated doesn't mean they are not worth doing. Each of them provides a layer of defense in depth, and even if the method for defeating them fits into a few sentences, this doesn't mean it's easy in practice.

Hashing

An application can use hash functions to implement tamper-proofing via the following steps:

1. Compute a hash of the software.
2. Embed the hash in the software.
3. Have the software check its own hash before executing.
4. Any modifications to the software modify the hash.

The defense relies on the fact that changes to the application will cause the hash check to fail. To defeat this, an attacker will need to make their changes and then recompute the hash after modifications and changing the checked value or removing the hash check entirely.

Signatures

Digital signatures can provide strong data integrity and authenticity protections. They use public key cryptography where a public and private key pair is generated. To use them for tamper-proofing, follow these steps:

1. Sign the software with a private key, creating a signature.
2. Embed the signature in the software.
3. Have the software check its signature with your public key before executing.
4. Any modifications to the software make the signature invalid.

One of the key benefits of digital signatures is that it is effectively impossible to generate a valid signature without knowledge of the private key. To defeat this type of protection, an attacker would have to remove the signature check entirely or get ahold of the private key so they can regenerate a valid signature.

Watermark

To implement watermarking, each purchaser of your software receives a unique version of the executable, where modifications are made to the following:

- Instruction order
- Function names
- Parameter order
- Instruction substitution
- Etc.

The specific changes "watermark" that instance, allowing you to trace it back to its owner, as well as detect modifications. Also, any modifications to the software taint the watermark, making them obvious.

For an attacker to defeat this protection, they will need to identify watermarked sections. Then, replace them with an alternate mark to hide the source of the modified software.

Guards

With guards, code inside the program checks sensitive areas for modification. For example, the code may specifically look at a critical jump to make sure it still jumps to the intended location. Common areas to monitor with guards include key checks, jump instructions, other guards, etc.

Any modifications to these sections are caught by the guards. The guards will then change the software's behavior (exit, change paths, undo modifications, etc.).

This defense relies on the fact that the guard is present and able to modify the software as needed. If an attacker wants to defeat this technique, they will need to remove the software guard code.

Packing

Packing is a broad term referring to techniques commonly used on executables to compress and obfuscate their contents. Some common packing techniques include the following:

- Compression/encryption of data sections
- Scrambling code sections
- Compression/encryption of code sections
- Anti-reverse engineering

One of the main advantages of packing is that it makes reverse engineering harder. For example, a packer may include features that address many of the common reverse engineering threats, including the following:

- **Anti-debugging:** Packers can conceal the use of `IsDebuggerPresent`, making it more difficult to detect.
- **Anti-virtualization:** Packers can detect when an application is being virtualized in a platform such as VMware and conceal detection code.
- **Anti-dumping:** Packers can erase headers in memory, making it difficult to dump memory.

▪ **Anti-tampering:** Anti-tampering can be implemented via checksums. This includes both common ones (rolling checksum, CRC32, MD5, and SHA-1) and others (Tiger, Whirlpool, MD4, Adler).

Packers can use encryption to conceal their code. Often, this involves simple algorithms, such as bitwise operators (XOR/ROL/...), LCG, RC4, and Tea. However, more advanced encryption algorithms (DES, AES, Blowfish, Trivium, IDEA, ElGamal, etc.) can also be used. If an application has been packed in such a way that its code and data sections are encrypted, if you were to drop it into one of the disassemblers or hex editors, you'd see only a small section of code and a lot of nonsensical junk. The tiny section of code that is available is the unpacker. For the code to run, it will need to unpack itself in memory at runtime, but this means static analysis can't see the rest of the code.

Packers can also use mutators (obfuscation), which alter code while keeping the same instruction set and architecture. Some mutations that might be used include reflowing and oligomorphism, or other obfuscation techniques discussed in Chapter 12, "Defense."

How Packers Work

The packer (a stand-alone tool) packs an executable (compresses, obfuscates, etc.). Then, the packer adds an unpacker to the beginning of executable. When the executable is run, the unpacker will be the first code that is run, and it will unpack the original code and data into memory (and only memory).

Figure 13.1 shows what a packed executable will look like in IDA. IDA sees the initial jump to the unpacker; however, the rest of the code looks like data.

```
.text:0805C050
.text:0805C050                    public start
.text:0805C050 start              proc near
.text:0805C050                    jmp     start_0
.text:0805C050 start              endp
.text:0805C050
.text:0805C050 ; ------------------------------------------------------------
.text:0805C055                    db 0B3h, 58h, 12h
.text:0805C058                    dd 7A2EF958h, 73DE6856h, 297708BCh, 41272C37h, 492E3AE1h
.text:0805C058                    dd 0BB91C39Fh, 17072049h, 0B6572788h, 26CD82A6h, 0B6B2FBB8h
.text:0805C058                    dd 0D7D87B3h, 0EEA8772Ch, 0A5E71B1Bh, 0E5E1B170h, 1AA084B1h
.text:0805C058                    dd 0F67F9497h, 27E22E54h, 0D2EF54E5h, 5FC8B0FCh, 107274EDh
.text:0805C058                    dd 33DF407Ch, 3321B16Eh, 9054A231h, 25097B7Ah, 0C959BE98h
.text:0805C058                    dd 0FA156FA4h, 3A6C5D35h, 482937C8h, 4BD4AEBh, 51CE4A8h
.text:0805C058                    dd 0AFC3DC5h, 28340E28h, 0F8732F8h, 0F67A534h, 8C997059h
.text:0805C058                    dd 7C092F51h, 0F9C12512h, 41D3B406h, 413DA6AEh, 48A47C67h
.text:0805C058                    dd 9DCCFC00h, 472B12C6h, 4C19D2A2h, 472E7E3Eh, 509B602h
```

Figure 13.1: Packed code in IDA

Is This a Strong Protection?

In the following sections, we will talk about some protection techniques and ask the question of if they are a strong protection. The assessments are meant to, at a very high level, bucket which areas each protection has the strongest impact. The focus of our book is predominately offensive, but we felt it important to take a quick look at some of the defenses. In each section, to evaluate the effectiveness of an anti-cracking defense, we will use something called the CIA triad (CIA stands for confidentiality, integrity, and availability). For those not familiar with this, it's a common way to think about security controls, as not all security controls cover all three parts of the triad, so it's important to know which is useful in each pillar. *Integrity* is the authenticity of something. Is it as it was originally intended, or has it been modified? *Confidentiality* is the ability of something to be accessible to only authorized parties. *Availability* is the level to which something is available to perform its intended function. These three together are commonly known as the CIA triad. Evaluating packers against the CIA triad:

- **Confidentiality:** Yes, aside from the unpacking portion of the code, the rest of it is in nonreadable format.

- **Integrity:** Yes, modifications to the binary would cause corruption of the packed sections, causing likely application failure.

- **Availability:** Packers can have a negative effect on performance, which can affect availability. However, if configured carefully, this effect can be minimized.

Defeating Packing

So, how can packers be defeated? Debug the program and watch for the program to decrypt in memory. Once it is unpacked in memory, you can analyze it, but any patching done will be viable only on the unpacked binary. Patching can't be saved back to the packed binary.

One natural thought that occurs to people is once it's unpacked in memory, can't I just memory dump that out to a new unpacked binary? This is technically possible but difficult to do. Applications include a lot of startup code, and getting it loading in the right spot in memory, setting up the stack, etc., doesn't naturally come from dumping memory and just calling it an EXE.

Another option is to see if you can unpack the program. Some of the common packers out there have unpacking tools that can be used to reverse the protections put in place; some examples include UPX, MEW, and ASPack.

However, there may be no stand-alone unpacker, and the unpacking code exists only in the packed executable. However, that doesn't mean we're stuck! There are a number of great plugins and tools built specifically for this purpose, such as OllyDumpEx and ImpRec, which aim to reconstruct the import table. This is a complex but doable process, but not the focus of our book. However, if this is of interest, there are some great blogs to be found online on import reconstruction.

PEiD

Often when approaching a file, it can be difficult to figure out what types of manipulations were done to it. If you somehow know out of the gate it was packed with a certain tool, then it's easy to start down that path. But cracking doesn't typically come with a handy playbook telling you what defenses are in place. PEiD is a tool to detect most common packers, cryptors, and compilers for portable execution files (e.g., applications). It can detect the signatures of more than 470 different obfuscation tools. Another more recent tool in this space is Detect it Easy.

As we've mentioned, many defensive tools such as packers and cryptors have unpackers and decryptors as well. Identifying the one used can reduce analysis time by an order of magnitude by allowing you to strip away many of an application's protections.

Figure 13.2 shows an example of using PEiD. To start, select the file to check. PEiD will then show the details of its packing, crypting, and compiling.

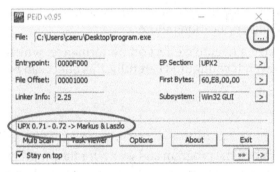

Figure 13.2: Identifying packers with PEiD

Lab: Detecting and Unpacking

This lab explores how to detect and defeat the use of a common packer. Labs and all associated instructions can be found in their corresponding folder here:

```
https://github.com/DazzleCatDuo/
X86-SOFTWARE-REVERSE-ENGINEERING-CRACKING-AND-COUNTER-MEASURES
```

For this lab, please locate Lab Detecting and Unpacking and follow the provided instructions.

Skills

Packers are a common protection against reversing. This lab explores the use of IDA, Cheat Engine, and PEiD to test the following skills:

- Detecting the presence of packers
- Unpacking programs with existing tools
- Unpacking programs with advanced debugging

Takeaways

Off-the-shelf unpackers are available for many packers (don't reinvent the wheel). When unpackers are not available, the unpacked, original program can still be manually recovered from memory.

Virtualization

Virtualization provides a form of obfuscation and packing. It translates a program into a custom machine language and generates a virtual environment/machine (VM) to interpret it. The VM is embedded into the application and runs when the application is executed. Note that in this case we're not talking about typical large virtual machines such as Windows or Linux running in a hypervisor. Virtualization in this case can quite simply mean a layer of abstraction/interpretation being added between the host (x86) and the code.

For example, consider the following simple "hello world" program:

```
#include <stdio.h>
int main(void)
{
        printf("hello, world!\n");
        return 0;
}
```

This program could then be compiled to an arbitrary machine language. For example, this is what it looks like in Brain$#@!:

```
++++++++[>++++[>++>+++>+++>+<<<<-]>+>+>->>+[<]<-]>>.>---
.+++++++..+++.>>.<-.<.+++.------.--------.>>+.>++.#
```

The application is then packaged with an interpreter written in the target architecture (i.e., x86).

```
#include <stdio.h>

char data[30000];
char program[30000];
int ip=0; /* instruction pointer */
int dp=0; /* data pointer */

char read_byte(void) { return getchar(); }
void write_byte(char b) { putchar(b); }

int main(void) {
```

```
int i=0; char b;

do {
  b=read_byte();
  program[i]=b;
  i++;
} while (b!='#');
while (1) {
  b=program[ip];
  if (b==0) {
    break;
  } else if (b=='>') {
    dp++;
  } else if (b=='<') {
    dp--;
  } else if (b=='+') {
    data[dp]++;
  } else if (b=='-') {
    data[dp]--;
  } else if (b=='.') {
    write_byte(data[dp]);
  } else if (b==',') {
    data[dp]=read_byte();
  } else if (b=='[') {
    if (!data[dp]) {
      int c=1;
      do {
        ip++;
        if (program[ip]=='[') { c++; }
        else if (program[ip]==']') { c--; }
      } while (c);
    }
  } else if (b==']') {
    if (data[dp]) {
      int c=1;
      do {
        ip--;
        if (program[ip]=='[') { c--; }
        else if (program[ip]==']') { c++; }
      } while (c);
    }
  } else {
    /* do nothing */
  }
  ip++;
}
return 0;
}
```

This adds a layer of abstraction that a cracker or reverse engineer must get through. First, reverse engineer the intermediate VM language. For those familiar with the programming language Java, Java runs inside of a VM, called the Java virtual machine (JVM). While that was done for portability, not security, it does add a layer of complexity. There are other languages that run inside of a VM, but you can also create your own (as with the example).

How Code Virtualization Works

Unlike in the simplistic example, a good virtualizer will create a unique, arbitrary machine language on the fly, as opposed to using a static or known language. This makes it more difficult to develop devirtualization tools.

In this case, the program logic is translated to a custom instruction set. As a result, reversing tools are not immediately applicable because they are unable to recover/analyze program logic. Then, the VM is compiled to the native architecture (i.e., x86).

Reversing the application requires both of these:

- Reversing the VM to decipher the custom instruction set
- Reversing the application logic in the new instruction set

This process is complicated and tedious because your access to debugging is limited. You cannot debug the target program logic directly, only the VM. Some tools that aid in accomplishing this include Themida and VMProtect.

Layered Virtualization

Virtualization protections can be layered as in the following process:

- Virtual machine VM0 implements the custom instruction set IS0.
- IS0 runs the virtual machine VM1, which implements custom instruction set IS1.
- IS1 runs the original application.

An example of layered virtualization may include the following:

1. Compile the C source code to a custom language, such as DazzleZ.
2. Write the DazzleZ interpreter in a custom language such as CatCat.
3. Write the CatCat interpreter in x86.
4. Run the program on the regular x86 platform.
5. Reversing requires backing out all layers of virtualization.

Issues with Virtualization

Virtualization can be an effective tool to slow reversing and cracking. However, it does have its downsides, including the following:

- **AV detection:** Often, malware will use virtualization to conceal itself, so many antivirus programs will automatically flag applications using it.

- **File bloat:** An application using virtualization needs to have the VM built in, which increases file sizes.

- **Slowed execution:** Virtualized applications need to run both the VM and the virtualized code, slowing the application's execution.

Layering multiple VMs compounds these size and speed issues exponentially.

Is This a Strong Protection?

Evaluating virtualization against the CIA triad has the following results:

- **Confidentiality:** Yes, the original code is abstracted through layers of virtualization.

- **Integrity:** Yes, modifications to any of the layers will likely cause a ripple effect of failures, making it difficult to patch.

- **Availability:** Each layer added into this setup has an effect on performance. Too many layers can dramatically affect speed and availability of code, data fetches, etc.

Defeating Virtualization

Virtualization can be an effective defense because defeating it is time-consuming and difficult. In general, the following process can be used to defeat virtualization:

- **Reverse the code-dispatch scheme:** VMs typically follow the familiar fetch-decode-execute cycle of a CPU, which makes it possible to understand how code is dispatched.

- **Reduce complexity:** Use pattern matching, symbolic analysis, and similar techniques to remove unnecessary complexity.

- **"Devirtualize" the program:** Attempt to recover a representation of the original code. However, this is not always a simple "inverse" for complex VMs and may not be possible to recover original code, forcing you to reverse engineer the virtualized code.

- **Reverse the recovered code:** Use traditional tools to reverse the recovered code. You may need to rely on static analysis if a functioning program cannot be recovered.

Virtualization can be defeated by reverse engineering the virtual machine and then transforming the application back into x86 machine code for analysis. Some tools that aid in accomplishing this include Themida, VMProtect, and Tigress.

Cryptors/Decryptors

Cryptors encrypt the application code sections (a subset of the techniques discussed in earlier section on packers), often to avoid malware detection. Many anti-malware tools will analyze a piece of software prior to running and block software based on API calls to suspicious operating system functions. By encrypting the code section, the malware makes it impossible for anti-malware programs to inspect the content of the application before execution.

In general, encrypted software must decrypt itself prior to execution. Typically, this means the decryption key is somewhere within the software. Therefore, reverse engineering should be able to find the key and decrypt the software.

However, there are some exceptions to this. For example, node-locked software may derive a key from the specific system on which it resides. Alternatively, malware may beacon to a server to retrieve a decryption key on the fly.

Is This a Useful Protection?

The benefits that cryptors provide include the following:

- **Confidentiality:** Yes, encryption always adds a layer of confidentiality. Only under the right circumstances will it decrypt.
- **Integrity:** Some, most encryption algorithms add a layer of integrity protection here because modifying the encrypted data yields corruption versus translating to modification of the end code.
- **Availability:** None; this has no effect.

Defeating Cryptors

Most encryptors have supporting decryptors, which are tools that can automatically restore the original software. Often these decryptors are just the encryptor itself with a different input flag

If you are reversing a crypted application, decrypting will get you back to the original binary. Since this will be much easier to analyze, see if there is an available decryptor before you begin your Reverse Engineering. Some common cryptors to check include Yoda's Cryptor, Morphine, and PGMP.

Summary

In looking at defense options, there is no silver bullet. Most anti-reversing techniques also have downsides.

Obfuscation incurs performance impact and complicates legitimate debugging. However, at reasonable levels, it can be a good option for slowing down RE, especially of decompilable languages.

Anti-debugging has relatively low impact on RE time (many debuggers have plugins to circumvent all common anti-debugging tricks) and complicates legitimate debugging. However, it may be sufficient to thwart novice crackers. Packers again raise the bar in level of difficulty to reverse engineering and pack, but, that said, beware of commercial off-the-shelf (COTS) packers, which typically have corresponding, publicly available unpackers.

Cryptors and decryptors significantly complicate RE. This makes them useful for protection of software. However, if not used carefully, they can flag common AV as when used maliciously it can also help protect malware.

When considering if/when to use anti-reversing tools, you should weigh the trade-offs of potency, resilience, stealth, and cost. Consider your adversary and their goals:

- Competing company (IP theft)
- Casual cracker (low-hanging fruit)
- Professional cracker (big/high-value targets)

Also, consider what needs to be defended:

- Key check? Entire program? Most defenses can be applied to specific functions.
- Consider that adding defenses can call attention to a target.

A common falsehood is that "everything is hackable and can be reverse engineered if someone tries hard enough, so we shouldn't bother [protecting/obfuscating/encrypting/etc.] it." This is a gross misunderstanding of what defense is supposed to achieve. Often a cracker may give up hacking, reversing, cracking, or breaking a product just because it stopped being fun.

If you can slow down reverse engineers enough, you've done your job. Often, a solid design with moderate settings of a commercial-off-the-shelf (COTS) obfuscator is the best available option. You will need to weigh each approach based on project needs.

There is no silver bullet. Don't let perfect be the enemy of good. Once a reasonable approach is settled on, obfuscators, anti-debugging, packers, etc., can be built into your DevOps.

Detection and Prevention

Application developers use various mechanisms to detect and protect against reversing and cracking. However, some of these methods are more effective than others. This chapter explores some of the most common techniques, their relative strengths and weaknesses, and how they can be defeated.

CRC

A cyclic redundancy check (CRC) is a mathematical calculation performed on the bytes of the data to be protected. The result is stored as the CRC, which is often appended to the data (i.e., `data data data data data data CRC`). To verify the data, recalculate and compare.

CRC algorithms have their advantages, including the following:

- Fast and compact
- Easy to accelerate with hardware
- Quick to calculate and compare
- Numerous options available (IEEE802.3, CRC-32, etc.)

In general, CRCs are great for detecting accidental errors or modification, such as transmission errors.

However, they are a poor defense against intentional errors or modifications. CRCs can be easily recalculated and updated by an adversary. For example, a simplistic CRC might add all of the bytes together and save the result. If a corruption were to occur in the file somewhere in the data, then the new sum would not match, and action could be taken. If the corruption occurred in the CRC portion of the file, then the sum would not match the corrupted CRC, and action could be taken. This is great for detecting if a bit got accidentally flipped while being downloaded, for example.

But because the CRC is so trivial to recalculate, it's simple for an attacker to make their modifications and simply update the CRC to include their new values.

Is This a Strong Protection?

Comparing CRCs to the CIA triad yields disappointing results:

- **Confidentiality:** None
- **Integrity:** Very little (it's too easy for an attacker to recalculate and put the new CRC into the file)
- **Availability:** None

This defense can easily be defeated by generating a new, valid CRC. Alternatively, you can simply patch out the CRC check. CRCs are powerful for detecting accidental corruption but are not useful for intentional corruption.

Code Signing

Many organizations digitally sign their code before releasing it. This is because code signing provides two main benefits:

- **Authenticity:** A digital signature can be generated only with the correct private key. This proves that software came from its alleged creator.
- **Integrity:** Changing digitally signed data invalidates its signature. Code signing proves that software hasn't been modified after release.

Code signing protects against a wide range of potential attacks. However, from a cracker's perspective, the most significant impact is that it can prevent patching if a program checks its signature before executing.

How to Code Sign

Code signing works using public key or asymmetric cryptography. These cryptographic algorithms use a pair of public and private keys. To code sign, you first need to generate a public/private keypair.

Digital signatures are validated using your public key; however, you need a way to prove that a particular public key belongs to you. This is where public key infrastructure (PKI) comes into the picture. Using the generated public key, you apply for a certificate from a code signing certificate authority (CA). The CA will verify your identity and issue a digital certificate, which contains your public key and validates your ownership of this.

With this certificate, you can now generate digital signatures. To do so, you would generate a hash of the executable and encrypt that hash with the private key. Then, when you distribute the executable, you would bundle the resulting signature and your digital certificate with the executable.

While you can go through this process manually, many build tools will do this for you. You still would need to buy a certificate and load it into your build tool, but then you can ask the build tool to sign the application. If this is your first exposure to PKI, know that this is intentionally just scratching the surface of it; there are many books dedicated to just this concept.

How to Verify a Signed Application

A code signature is essentially an encrypted hash of the executable. After verifying that the public key is valid using the associated certificate, you can decrypt the executable's hash. Then, you independently calculate the hash of the application using the same hash function as the application developer. If you compare the two hashes and they match, the application is authentic and unmodified. If they differ, the application is fake or has been tampered with.

Most operating systems will verify code signatures for you. The OS will also generate a warning if the public key used to generate the code signature is unverified, as shown in Figure 14.1. However, most people will click Run anyway.

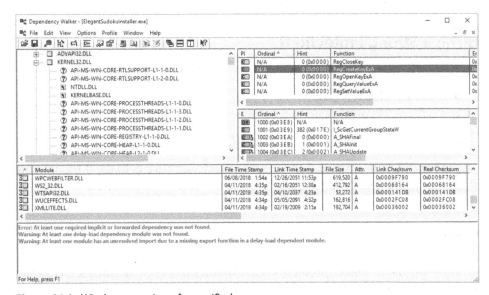

Figure 14.1: Windows warning of unverified program

Is Code Signing Effective?

Does code signing stop all patching attacks? No.

The reason for this is that there must be a piece of unsigned code that does the sign checking. This includes performing a few actions:

1. Calculate the hash of the code.
2. Check if this is what it should be.

   2a. If the answer is correct, run code.

   2b. If the answer is incorrect, don't run code.

This signature verification code can't be included in a code signature because it needs to contain (or access) the hash value to compare against. It's impossible to predict what this value would be without hashing the application. If you hashed the application (which includes this value) and included the hash in the application, then the modified application would have a new hash.

Since the signature verification code can't be signed, there is a different location that could be patched to bypass code signing. However, code signing is hands down one of the best techniques for securing software integrity against both accidental and intentional modifications.

Code Signing vs. CRC

CRCs are commonly used to detect bit errors in data sent over a network. However, they provide protection only against accidental changes, not intentional ones. CRCs are easily recalculated by an adversary.

Code signing is as strong as your protection of the private key. Without the private key, an attacker cannot regenerate a valid signed hash.

Is This a Strong Protection?

Code signing does a lot better than CRCs when compared to the CIA triad.

- **Confidentiality:** None
- **Integrity:** Yes! Fantastic
- **Availability:** None

A more difficult approach to defeating code signing is to steal the private signing keys and use them to digitally sign a modified version of the application.

RASP

Runtime application self-protection (RASP) embeds security into the running application. It does so by intercepting system calls and verifying that they are from an expected source. It also intercepts data manipulations and verifies that they are coming from authorized sources.

RASP is a reactionary defense. It can be configured to "stop" attacks live. For example, RASP can do the following:

- Drop/delete a call it deems malicious, such as a suspicious SQL call into an application.

- End a user session.

- Halt execution.

Function Hooking

One technique that RASP uses is function hooking. This involves overwriting the first few bytes of a function's code with a jump to the RASP code.

The RASP code will include checks to verify that the call is legitimate. This can include the following:

- Checking the parameters and context of the call

- Checking the code has not been modified (might compare a hash of the function with a known good hash)

At the end of the RASP code, it will then execute the overwritten code before jumping back to the original function.

Risks of RASP

If RASP detects an attack, it can stop execution. However, this may not be acceptable depending on the use case of your software. For example, in hospitals, manufacturing, critical infrastructure, automobiles, and similar environments, an application suddenly halting can pose a significant risk to health and safety.

RASP can also have its downsides even in the absence of an attack. Some effects include the following:

- **Speed:** Because of the function hooking, RASP has a nontrivial effect on speed.

- **Size:** Function hooking and lookup tables help to assure security; however, they also bloat binaries.

Is This a Strong Protection?

RASP provides mixed results when compared against the CIA benchmark:

- **Confidentiality:** No

- **Integrity:** Yes (for the sections that RASP is protecting, the context checking at runtime is a very powerful check)

- **Availability:** No (in fact can be negative)

If RASP is correctly configured, it can be difficult to defeat. You can't easily patch the application if code signing is enabled, and you can't easily reverse the application if anti-debugging is enabled.

However, RASP does open a potential avenue for an attack against availability. If you can identify an input that it perceives as an "attack," you can potentially make it shut itself down.

Allowlisting

Allowlisting, sometimes called whitelisting, is providing the execution environment with a list of "good" things. For example, a computer may allow only allowlisted applications to run.

There are numerous commercial products that provide allowlists. For example, the Windows operating system has built-in *software restriction policies*.

From a cracking perspective, allowlisting can prevent the use of cracking and reverse engineering tools. For example, tools such as Procmon, debuggers, Cheat Engine, ResourceHacker, Dependency Walker, and other reversing and cracking applications are unlikely to be included in the allowlist.

Allowlisting is difficult to get right. It can be difficult to know all of the various libraries that your application needs. When generating a whitelist, a great deal of testing must be performed to ensure that all required applications and libraries are included on the allowlist.

How Allowlisting Works

There are two main approaches to allowlisting. A list can be based on a process's name or on its hash. These lists are applied only when an application is first launched.

Breaking Name-Based Allowlists

Allowlists keep track of the names of processes or applications allowed to execute. To bypass this type of list, name your malicious application a whitelist-approved name. For example, you determine that `solitare.exe` is allowlisted, so you name your malicious app `solitare.exe`.

Breaking Name and Hash-Based Allowlists

If an allowlist uses both application names and hashes, it can't be bypassed by renaming an application. The hash of the malicious app wouldn't match that of the legitimate one.

However, these allowlists can be defeated through process injection. Once an allowlisted application is running, if you can get code execution, you can inject malicious libraries. And while that's easily said, getting code execution is not often trivial. So, this is one of those cases where it sounds easy because it can be said in a sentence, but in reality having a prerequisite of code execution in a whitelisted process may be a full roadblock for a cracker.

If you have gotten the elusive code execution in an allowlisted application, there are numerous techniques for loading into the process. In Windows, you can use `LoadLibrary()` or `SetWindowsHookEx()`. In Linux, you can use `ptrace()`/`PTRACE_POKEDATA`/opcodes for `uselib()` syscall.

An application's hash is checked prior to application launch. Modifications to the application after it is launched won't be detected by the allowlist.

Example: Metasploit

Metasploit is a popular hacking tool. Its main goal is to exploit an application and inject a meterpreter, which provides the attacker with remote access to the infected computer. (See the "Tools" section of our repository for links.)

With Metasploit, no new applications are started; a meterpreter injects into the hacked process. From there it can "pivot" into any other running application.

Is This a Strong Protection?

Allowlisting provides limited protection:

- **Confidentiality:** No
- **Integrity:** Yes (if paired with the name and hash; however, the integrity checking is generally done only at application start time)
- **Availability:** No

Allowlisting can be defeated in a couple of ways. A malicious program can impersonate a legitimate application to defeat a name-based whitelist or use code injection to defeat an allowlist that uses both names and hashes.

Blocklisting

Blocklisting, sometimes referred to as blacklisting, is the exact opposite of allowlisting. Instead of specifying everything that is permitted, it is a list of all the things that are not allowed. The blocklist can be based on names, keys, or hashes.

Blocklists are easy to make but difficult to maintain. For example, consider a blocklist including the malicious executable `virus1.exe`. What happens next week when `virus2.exe` comes out?

From a more cracking perspective, you might blocklist keys that you know to be bad (i.e., cracked). Depending how your key generation works, it may be possible to blocklist whole subsets of keys.

Alternatively, a program can also refuse to run if certain other applications are seen. For example, the application may not run if a debugger is installed.

Many antiviruses use this approach to identify and block known malware. They include a list of "signatures" of known bad applications. If something matches the signature, it's flagged as bad.

Is This a Strong Protection?

A blocklist provides less protection than a whitelist:

- **Confidentiality:** None
- **Integrity:** Some (if paired with hashes or keys)
- **Availability:** None

The means of defeating a blocklist depend on the information that it uses to identify malicious applications. If it is name-based, change the name. If it stores the hashes of known-bad programs, mutate it by making a small change to the application's code or data to change its hash.

Remote Authentication

For most anti-reversing and anti-cracking strategies, the attacker has all of the pieces that they need to overcome the defense. With enough time, they can reverse engineer and/or patch the application.

Remote authentication requires the application to retrieve something remotely in order to work. For example, it might get a key from a remote server that it uses to decrypt some crucial code.

Most attackers will reverse engineer a system "offline." They don't want it reaching out to your servers because they don't want you to have their IP address or to know that they are running your software. Keep in mind when attempting to crack a piece of software, you're likely launching and running the startup and checking code frequently. Whereas a legitimate user would likely launch the application at max a few times a day. That type of behavior is really easy to spot on a remote authentication server. A user who is authenticating 100 times a day is likely doing something nefarious.

Architecting the application in such a way that it can't run without information from a server helps prevent reverse engineering. The attacker will either need to reverse it "online" or give up.

Remote Authentication Example

One possible approach to implement remote authentication is to encrypt every part of the application except for the loaders. The loader sends system information, a hash of the software, and the activation key to the server.

The server will verify the expected hash and the activation key. If they validate, it uses an algorithm to produce a decryption key, which it will send back to the application. The loader can then decrypt the application, enabling it to run.

An attacker will not be able to "mimic" your remote server and algorithm without access to the server-side code. The only way to research the software will be to activate it online. The application can have decryption code be resident in memory only. This way, each startup requires server interaction.

The main challenge of this approach is that implementing cryptography and enterprise key management solutions is not trivial. A mistake may allow a cracker to bypass the validation code and generate their own decryption keys. As discussed with packed applications, once it's unpacked in memory, you could take a memory dump of it for future static analysis. However, that memory dump can't easily (or sometimes not at all) be turned into a decrypted application capable of running. The memory dump won't be useful for patching or testing modifications but never discount the value of static analysis.

Is This a Strong Protection?

Remote authentication provides mixed reviews when compared against the CIA triad:

- **Confidentiality:** Some (the application will eventually be decrypted in memory, but the binary at rest is restricted)
- **Integrity:** Yes (the server should be doing some type of integrity checking prior to releasing the response)
- **Availability:** Possibly negative

One possible attack against a remote server is to set up a fake server. To start, activate the application online and capture all communication between the application and server.

Then, stand up a fake server with appropriate responses. The application's code will be decrypted and can be saved to disk.

This approach does require a single online application to get the decrypted code. However, this allows a full, decrypted binary to be created, making further online authentication unnecessary. But note that this approach can't always work if the application does good due diligence in requiring certain certificates from the server or if the challenge/response from the server is not always the same (i.e., changes with time or date).

Lab: ProcMon

This lab shows that there is more than one possible way to crack a program. Head back to the book's GitHub page (https://github.com/DazzleCatDuo/X86-SOFTWARE-REVERSE-ENGINEERING-CRACKING-AND-COUNTER-MEASURES) and locate the ProcMon lab.Skills.

This lab uses ProcMon and IDA to understand opportunities for alternative cracking solutions. Some key skills being tested include the following:

- Analyzing program behavior dynamically
- Identifying indirect approaches to circumventing software defenses

Takeaways

Watching what a process does from the outside can be quicker/easier than watching it from the inside (that is, debugging is not always the best approach).

There are usually many ways to crack a program; finding the best takes practice.

Summary

This chapter presented various methods of protecting against software cracking and reversing. Some techniques are generally ineffective, while others can work but also have some downsides.

It's important to remember that almost any defense can be defeated given enough time and effort. The goal is to slow an attacker down and, ideally, make them frustrated enough to give up.

In an "Introducton" the legal implications and considerations of reverse engineering and cracking were explored at a high level. This section provides a more in-depth discussion of relevant U.S. laws and their impacts and interpretations.

> **WARNING** As a disclaimer, we are not lawyers, and this is not legal advice. If you need legal advice, please contact any reputable lawyer or the Electronic Frontier Foundation at www.eff.org, which has deep specialization in the security space.

U.S. Laws Affecting Reverse Engineering

Laws regarding copyrights, hacking, etc., vary based on jurisdiction. This section covers some applicable laws in the United States. If you are located elsewhere, check your local laws and restrictions.

The Digital Millennium Copyright Act

Digital rights management (DRM) is a solution designed to protect intellectual property. DRM solutions can track and control protected content after it reaches the marketplace.

The Digital Millennium Copyright Act (DMCA) was passed by Congress in 1998. It brought the United States into compliance with international copyright agreements.

Computer Fraud and Abuse Act

The Computer Fraud and Abuse Act (CFAA) was enacted in 1984. It is a federal anti-hacking statute that prohibits unauthorized access to computers and networks.

Lawmakers wrote the law so poorly that creative prosecutors have been abusing it ever since. However, in recent years, efforts have been made to protect security researchers from being prosecuted under it. Wired.com said this about the CFAA in a 2014 article:

> *A high profile case involving misuse of the statute occurred in 2008 when three MIT students were barred from giving a presentation at the Def Con hacker conference. The students had found flaws in the electronic ticketing system used by the Massachusetts Bay Transportation Authority that would have allowed anyone to obtain free rides. The MBTA sought and obtained a temporary restraining order to bar the students from speaking about the flaws. In granting the temporary gag order, the judge invoked the CFAA, saying that information the students planned to present would provide others with the means to hack the system. The judge's words implied that simply talking about hacking was the same as actual hacking. The ruling was publicly criticized, however, as an unconstitutional prior restraint of speech, and when the MBTA subsequently sought a court order to make the restraining order permanent, another judge rejected the request, ruling in part that the CFAA does not apply to speech and therefore had no relevance to the case.*

> www.wired.com/2014/11/
> hacker-lexicon-computer-fraud-abuse-act

A second high-profile, and very sad, abuse of the CFAA resulted in a high-profile suicide. This came after a U.S. attorney used CFAA to launch a heavy-handed prosecution against Internet activist Aaron Swartz for what many considered a minor infraction. Swartz, who helped develop the RSS standard and was a cofounder of the advocacy group Demand Progress, was indicted after he gained entry to a closet at MIT and allegedly connected a laptop to the university's network to download millions of academic papers that were distributed by the JSTOR subscription service. Swartz was accused of repeatedly spoofing the MAC address of his computer to bypass a block MIT had placed on the address he used.

Although JSTOR did not pursue a complaint, the Justice Department pushed forward with prosecuting Swartz. U.S. Attorney Carmen Ortiz insisted that "stealing is stealing" and that authorities were just upholding the law. Swartz, in despair over his pending trial and the prospect of a felony conviction, committed suicide in 2013. In response to the tragedy, two lawmakers proposed a long-overdue amendment to the law that would help prevent prosecutors from overreaching in their use of it. The amendment, referred to as Aaron's law, was introduced months after Swartz's death by Rep. Zoe Lofgren (D-Calif.) and Sen. Ron Wyden (D-Oregon). The amendment would exclude breaches of terms of service and user agreements from the law and also narrow the definition of unauthorized access to make a clear distinction between criminal hacking activity and simple acts that exceed authorized access on a minor level. Instead, the amendment proposes to define unauthorized access as "circumventing one or more technological measures that exclude or prevent unauthorized individuals from obtaining or altering" information on a protected computer. The amendment also would make it clear that the act of circumvention would not include a user simply changing his MAC or IP address to gain access to a system.

Copyright Act

Under the Copyright Act of 1976, a copyright for a computer program comes into being as the source code for the computer program is being written by the programmer. The program does not need to be complete or even functional for copyright protection to come into being. Copyright case law treats the copyright of the source code and object code as equivalent.

If you are not the copyright owner, it is typically not legal to perform any of the following actions without permission:

- Copying a program, or parts of programs, to give or sell to someone else
- Preloading a program onto the hard disk of a computer being sold
- Distributing a program over the Internet
- Circumventing controls that prevent access to copyrighted material

However, there are many exceptions and nuances to this. The first copyright for software was in 1964. The justification for why to begin granting protection of software was they now viewed a computer program like a "how-to book." The Copyright Act of 1976 officially calls out software as copyrightable.

So, when a piece of software gets copyright protection, what exactly is copyrighted? The copyright protects the expression of an idea, not the idea itself. For example, if you develop the concept of a lemonade stand game, you can copyright your implementation of it but not the idea of a lemonade stand game. Second, the protection protects the object (executable) program, not the source code. Lastly, it protects the screen displays produced by the program while it executes.

The source code of software is generally kept as a trade secret and not released under a copyright to the public.

Important Court Cases

In addition to laws, court precedent is important to determining what is and isn't legal in the United States. A couple of important court cases include the following:

- **Apple Computer v. Franklin Computer:** Established that object programs are copyrightable.

    - In the early 1980s Franklin Computer corporation started to produce the Franklin Ace computer to compete with the Apple II. The Franklin ACE was compatible with Apple 2 programs. To do that, the Franklin Ace had copied some of the operating system functions directly from the ROM on an Apple II. Apple sued Franklin Computers for copyright infringement because they copied their object code. Apple won.

- **Sega v. Accolate:** Established that disassembling object code to determine technical specifications is fair use.

    - A video game maker, Accolate, wanted to make some of its games for the Sega Genesis. However, Sega didn't share the technical specs for the system, so Accolade disassembled the object code of a Sega game to determine how it worked. Sega sued Accolade for infringing on their copyright. However, this time the court ruled in favor of Accolade, because Accolade's actions constituted fair use of the software.

What was gained from these two court cases was that reverse engineering was OK as long as you didn't infringe on the copyright. Recall Franklin Computer infringed on the copyright by copying some of Apple's code. Where Accolate did not infringe the copyright, they didn't copy any copywritten material; they just learned from it.

One way to make sure you fall in the OK use like Accolate and not in the copying situation like Franklin Computers is to use something known as a *clean room software strategy*. This consists of having two teams that are separated; each do different parts of the work. The first would research the competitor system or program and write technical specifications of how it performs. The second team would use that specification to develop the new system.

If Franklin Computer had taken this approach, it would have had some team members figure out how the Apple system worked and describe the functionality. Then, if a second team implemented it themselves, never having seen the Apple implementation, it potentially could have changed the outcome of the event. If they had approached the situation this way they likely would have been fine from lawsuits because they would not have used any of Apple's code.

The key is to avoid the unconscious copying of code. If the team that researched the Apple II had also been the team to implement the specification, they would likely have suffered from a predisposition to use code like that in Apple's system because that's what they had seen already.

Fair Use

Sometimes it is legal to reproduce a copyrighted work without permission. In general, courts consider four factors when evaluating whether something falls under the fair use exceptions:

- **Purpose and how it's used:** If the purpose is criticism, commentary, news reporting, teaching, or research, then it is likely permissible. However, commercial use likely isn't.

  How about for character of use? The most important consideration is how much the work has been transformed from the original. If the new author has added new expressions or meaning, then it's potentially a candidate for fair use.

- **Nature of work:** Fair use is granted more favorably to works of nonfiction than of works of fiction.

- **Amount of work being copied:** A brief excerpt is more likely to be OK than copying an entire book or an entire chapter.

- **Effect on market for copyrighted work:** For example, copying out-of-print material doesn't have the same material effect as copying a newly written and printed work.

According to the Copyright Act, 17 U.S.C. § 107, reverse engineering falls under "fair use" when done for ". . .purposes such as criticism, comment, news reporting, teaching (including multiple copies for classroom use), scholarship, or research. . . ." However, this is weighed against "the effect of the use upon the potential market for or value of the copyrighted work."

DMCA Research Exception

In October 2016, DMCA added a good-faith security research exception to the law. It states that "accessing a computer program solely for purposes of good-faith testing, . . .where such activity is carried out in a controlled environment designed to avoid any harm to individuals or the public, . . .and is not used or maintained in a manner that facilitates copyright infringement."

This also can apply to reverse engineering and cracking. It states ". . .researchers can circumvent digital access controls, reverse engineer, access, copy, and manipulate digital content which is protected by copyright without fear of prosecution—within reason."

This is not a get-out-of-jail-free card or a blank permission to go hack and crack everything. This represents an evolution in the industry to recognize that security research done for the right reasons is a good thing and that the law will now protect those who are doing good faith research.

Legality

Copyright law in relation to reverse engineering and code modification heavily emphasizes intent and effects. When proceeding on your own, consult with a lawyer. . .or keep it to yourself. This isn't meant in a sneaky way, but recall that a part of fair use is the effect your work has on the market. If you're tinkering and cracking for education or for research and your outcomes stay with you, they don't really affect the potential market for the work. That's a key factor in fair use. The second you use your knowledge to make a keygen that you put online that causes a vendor to lose money, then it's no longer considered fair use. But if you're keeping it all to yourself in a way that doesn't affect the market or others, then you've gone a long way to fall under fair use.

> **WARNING** To repeat, we are not lawyers, this is not legal advice, and this is our interpretation and understanding of the regulatory landscape in the United States that affects reverse engineering.

Summary

This chapter covered some of the legal considerations of reverse engineering and cracking, but we are not lawyers. For legal advice, we recommend contacting the EFF.

Advanced Techniques

Up to this point, this book has covered the core tools and skills used for reverse engineering and cracking. However, this is an evolving field, and new methods are being developed to make it faster and easier. This section describes at a high level some advanced techniques and tools on the cutting edge of reverse engineering. Our goal with this chapter is that if at this point you're still loving software cracking and looking to take it even further to the next level, we want to present you with a plethora of rabbit holes to go down. Depending on what interests you, we hope the following will point you in the right directions to go deeper.

Timeless Debugging

Timeless debugging is also known as reverse debugging. The core idea is: "what if we could go backwards when debugging?"

Consider the case where something went wrong while debugging. Maybe a patch failed, you missed an anti-debug check, you don't know how you got here, etc.

There are a few different tools designed for timeless debugging, including the following:

- Visual Studio Ultimate (.NET)

- rr

- gdb

To get started, check out George Hotz @ Enigma in his 2016 USENIX Enigma talk at www.youtube.com/watch?v=eGl6kpSajag.

Binary Instrumentation

Binary instrumentation is when you inject code to watch or modify a process as it executes. This can be useful for finding memory leaks, tracing key checks, performing anti-anti-debugging, etc.

Some tools for binary instrumentation include the following:

- PIN
- DynamoRIO
- Frida
- Valgrind
- QBDI

For an introduction to binary instrumentation, check out the 2015 Blackhat USA talk "Augmenting Static Analysis Using Pintool: Ablation" at www.youtube .com/watch?v=wHI1NRK_HiQ.

Intermediate Representations

Normally, for reversing and cracking, it's necessary to learn and write tools for each new architecture. The idea of intermediate representations is to translate all assembly code for all architectures to the same language. That way, you can learn and write tools for just that language.

There are a few different tools that can be used to work with intermediate representations, including the following:

- Binary Ninja
- REIL
- VEX
- BNIL
- Ghidra PCode
- IDA microcode
- LLVM IR

To get started with intermediate representations, check out "Finding Bugs with Binary Ninja" by Jordan Wiens from LevelUp 0x03 at www.youtube.com/ watch?v=55gClG-sjWc.

Decompiling

The idea of decompiling is to recover original source code from advanced automated analysis of assembly code. Some tools that offer decompilation include the following:

- IDA's Hex-Rays
- Ghidra
- Binary Ninja
- Snowman Decompiler

To learn more about decompiling, check out "Decompiling a Virus using IDA Pro" at www.youtube.com/watch?v=gYkDcUO9otQ.

Automatic Structure Recovery

Automatic structure recovery involves automatically finding patterns and links in memory to make inferences about the data types used. Some tools for this include the following:

- dynStruct
- Cheat Engine

To learn more about automatic structure recovery, check out the dynStruct idea and paper at https://github.com/ampotos/dynStruct.

Visualization

Code listings and text can be difficult to think and reason about. Visualization can be used to deepen your understanding of file structure and execution.

Some reversing tools that offer useful visualizations include the following:

- BinWalk
- Hopper
- IDA plugins
- Veles
- ..cantor.dust..
- Cheat Engine

A good starting point for understanding how visualization can be used for reversing includes the Derbycon talk "Dynamic Binary Visualization" from Christopher Domas at www.youtube.com/watch?v=4bM3Gut1hIk.

Deobfuscation

Obfuscation is designed to slow down reversing in an attempt to get a cracker to give up. The idea is to use tools to automatically remove obfuscations from programs using tools like Tigress Protection.

Check out "Lets break modern binary code obfuscation" at `www.youtube` `.com/watch?v=TDnAkm6ZTYw`.

Theorem Provers

Theorem provers use mathematics to analyze code, including reduction, deobfuscation, boundaries, inputs, etc. Some theorem proving tools for reversing include the following:

- Z3
- STP
- Boolector
- Yices

To see how theorem provers can be used, watch "Using z3 to find a password and reverse obfuscated JavaScript" at `www.youtube.com/watch?v=TpdDq56KH1I`.

Also check out the yearly SMT-COMP!, which has some really interesting benchmarks on many unique solvers at `https://smt-comp.github.io/2023`.

Symbolic Analysis

The idea behind symbolic analysis is trying to find inputs that cause interesting results. For example, what inputs could cause a crash, pass a key check, unlock a secret, etc.

Symbolic analysis tools will trace user input through a program. At each branch, they ask a theorem prover which user input would go down the taken path. What user input would go down the not-taken path?

For example, consider the following code:

```
if (strlen(username) > 10)
        if (key_1^sum(username)==key_2)
                printf("key passed");
```

A symbolic analysis tool will automatically identify the combination of *username*, *key_1*, and *key_2* that will pass the checks and reach the "key passed" print statement.

Some symbolic analysis tools include the following:

- Angr
- Mayhem
- KLEE
- Triton
- S2E

To see an example of symbolic analysis with Angr, check out the DEF CON 23 talk by Shoshitaishvili and Wang, "Angry Hacking: The next gen of binary analysis," at `www.youtube.com/watch?v=oznsT-ptAbk`.

Summary

At this point, the best way to improve your reversing and cracking skills is via more hands-on practice. On the Windows VM, the `allthethings` folder on the Desktop contains a variety of different crackmes to practice with sorted by difficulty level.

Bonus Topics

This last chapter of this book introduces software reversing and cracking. It is primarily focused on understanding how a program works and bypassing or modifying undesirable functionality (like key checkers).

This chapter takes this knowledge and applies it to real-world hacking. Stack smashing and shellcoding both use an understanding of how a program and the stack works to run malicious code within a program.

Stack Smashing

Stack smashing, also known as *stack-based buffer overflows*, is one of the most classic attacks against software. It takes advantage of the fact that non-memory-safe languages such as C/C++ have no built-in protection that prevents an application from accessing or overwriting data in other parts of memory. For example, C/C++ doesn't automatically check that the data written to an array fits within the bounds of that array. If you don't know C, don't worry. As long as you know any programming language, you should be able to follow along.

Because stack smashing has been around for such a long time, there are numerous compilers that have built-in automatic guards that are put into compiled code to prevent this. While it's not as easy of an attack as it used to be, everyone should fully understand how the attack works, because:

- Some facets of it still work.
- It's the foundation of other types of attacks.
- Not every application has stack protections.

For any of the following C code examples, if you build them with `gcc`, you must use the flag `-fno-stack-protector` to turn off these protections. Making the full command line for using `gcc` to build in Linux: `gcc myfile .c-fno-stack-protector`.

For example, consider the following simple C program:

```
void function(int a, int b, int c) {
    char buffer1[5];
    char buffer2[10];
}

void main() {
    function(1,2,3);
}
```

After this application has been compiled and the object has been dumped from memory, it results in the following assembly code:

```
function:
        push ebp
        mov esp, ebp
        sub ebp, 20   (*stack shown here)
        leave
        ret
main:
        push ebp
        mov ebp, esp
        push 3
        push 2
        push 1
        call function
        add esp 0xc
        leave
        ret
```

After executing the first three instructions under `function`, including `sub ebp, 20`, the stack will look like the following table with addresses increasing from the top of the table going down:

NAME	SIZE
buffer2	10
buffer1	5
ebp	4

NAME	SIZE
ret	4
a	4
b	4
c	4
ebp	4

Now, consider the following example code:

```
void function(char *str) {
   char buffer[16];

   strcpy(buffer,str); //Copies incoming str to buffer
}

void main() {
  char large_string[256];
  int i;

  for( i = 0; i < 255; i++)
    large_string[i] = 'A';  //creates a string of 255 'A's

  function(large_string);
}
```

In this code, the main function builds a string that consists of 255 As. It then passes a pointer to that buffer to function, and function allocates 16 bytes for a local buffer but then copies (using strcpy) the input buffer blindly with no length checks. This means the input buffer that was 255 As will overflow the local buffer that was allocated only 16 bytes.

If you run the code, the result will be Segmentation fault (core dumped). A segmentation fault occurs when an application attempts to read, write, or execute an invalid memory address. Let's dig deeper to figure out what happened.

After assembly, the code is transformed into the following assembly code:

```
0804840c <function>:
 804840c:    55                      push    ebp
 804840d:    89 e5                   mov     ebp,esp
 804840f:    83 ec 28                sub     esp,0x28
 8048412:    8b 45 08                mov     eax,DWORD PTR [ebp+0x8]
 8048415:    89 44 24 04             mov     DWORD PTR [esp+0x4],eax
 8048419:    8d 45 e8                lea     eax,[ebp-0x18]   ;[1]
 804841c:    89 04 24                mov     DWORD PTR [esp],eax
 804841f:    e8 cc fe ff ff          call    80482f0 <strcpy@plt>
 8048424:    c9                      leave
 8048425:    c3                      ret
```

Looking at this, you can see that ebp-0x18 is the address at the start of the buffer (marked as [1] in the previous code). Looking at the function preamble, with the stack setup, you can see that 0x28 bytes were allocated for the stack. Recall that ebp points to the bottom of the stack and esp the top. Therefore, ebp = esp+0x28.

So, at the time of function setup, the start of the array, in terms relative to esp, starts at esp+0x10. While this seems complicated, all it means is that the buffer is 0x10 bytes away from the end of the function's allocated stack, which makes sense. Recall that 0x10 is 16 in base 10, and the function is allocated 16 bytes.

To see the effects of the stack smashing in action, run the application in gdb and set a breakpoint right before the strcpy operation. At the breakpoint, printing memory at the stack pointer should show something similar to Figure 17.1.

```
(gdb) x/16x $esp
0xffffd120:    0x00000000    0xf7fdab18    0x00000000    0x00000000
0xffffd130:    0x00000000    0x00000003    0xf63d4e2e    0x000003f3
0xffffd140:    0x00000000    0xf7e25938    0xffffd278    0x08048470
0xffffd150:    0xffffd16c    0x00000000    0x00000026    0xf7e4a95d
```

Figure 17.1: Function stack frame before strcpy

In this image, the allocated buffer takes up the row indicated by address 0xffffd130, and 0x10 bytes after that is the end of the function's stack frame. That is then followed by the saved value of the previous stacks ebp, and lastly the return address. The value of the saved *ebp* (previous functions stack frame) register is 0xffffd278, and the return address is 0x08048470.

After stepping over the strcpy operation, the same region of memory will look like Figure 17.2. The strcpy operation overwrites the buffer, the saved *ebp* register, and the return address with 0x41 (A).

```
(gdb) s
6        }
(gdb) x/16x $esp
0xffffd120:    0xffffd130    0xffffd16c    0x00000000    0x00000000
0xffffd130:    0x41414141    0x41414141    0x41414141    0x41414141
0xffffd140:    0x41414141    0x41414141    0x41414141    0x41414141
0xffffd150:    0x41414141    0x41414141    0x41414141    0x41414141
```

Figure 17.2: Function stack after strcpy

When the application reaches the ret operation, it will pop the return address off of the stack and attempt to continue execution at that location. However, since 0x41414141 is an invalid address, the CPU segfaults.

This example causes the application to crash, but this is not the only possible effect. At a high level, what you have the ability to do is control the return address and the stack frame of the previous function. While stack frame manipulation has its uses, it's a lot more common to go after the return address manipulation, so we'll focus on that. In the first case, the return address was overwritten with junk, but what if we were more tactical about what we overwrite with the return address? The following code sample is designed to alter the return address to control code execution. The goal is to skip over the x=1 instruction in the following code:

```c
#include <stdio.h>
void function(int a, int b, int c) {
//do something so we skip x=1 after a return
}
void main() {
    int x;
    x = 0;
    function(1,2,3);
    x = 1;
    printf("%d\n",x);
}
```

In this code, the main function sets up a local variable x and gives it an initial value of 0. It then calls function with some fixed values. Inside of function, there is no code yet. The next step is to figure out what code is needed there to achieve the goal of rewriting the return address.

After returning from function, the main function updates the value of x to be 1 and then proceeds to print the value of x. Can we use our knowledge of cdecl and the stack setup to make it so the code never runs x=1 and instead prints x=0? Yes! The challenge is to write the contents of function in such a way that the x=1 instruction inside of the main function is skipped.

For this code, the stack inside of Function would look like the following:

NAME	ADDR
ebp	ebp
return address	ebp+4
a	ebp+8
b	ebp+12
c	ebp+16

This is your run-of-the-mill standard cdecl stack setup. You know you're going to want a buffer since this chapter is all about buffer overflows, so add a buffer to function. You're also going to want a way to manipulate certain values in the buffer, so add a pointer. You could also use syntax like buffer[z], but the pointer helps to more explicitly state memory offsets, which is helpful for learning.

```c
#include <stdio.h>
void function(int a, int b, int c) {
char buffer[16];
```

```
int *r;
r = 0x99;  //this is here so r is not optimized out
buffer[0] = 0x88; //this is here so buffer is not optimized out
}
void main() {
    int x;
    x = 0;
    function(1,2,3);
    x = 1;
    printf("%d\n",x);
}
```

When assembled, this translates to the following assembly code:

```
0804840c <function>:
 804840c:    55                        push    ebp
 804840d:    89 e5                     mov     ebp,esp
 804840f:    83 ec 20                  sub     esp,0x20
 8048412:    c7 45 fc 99 00 00 00      mov     DWORD PTR [ebp-0x4],0x99
 8048419:    c6 45 ec 88               mov     BYTE PTR [ebp-0x14],0x88
 804841d:    c9                        leave
 804841e:    c3                        ret
```

Now there are new things on the stack, the pointer and the buffer.

NAME	ADDR
buffer	ebp-0x14
r	ebp-4
ebp	ebp
return address	ebp+4
a	ebp+8
b	ebp+12
c	ebp+16

In this stack frame, the return address is at buffer+0x18. The next step is to update function's code to have the pointer point to this address in memory.

For those not familiar with C, & is "address of," so the following code sets ret to point to the address in memory where buffer+0x18 is. By drawing out the stack, you can see that this is the saved return address. At this point, the return address hasn't been changed, but we have a pointer to it. The next step is to figure out what to change it to, to skip x=1.

```
#include <stdio.h>
void function(int a, int b, int c) {
```

```
        char buffer[16];
        int *ret;

        //now we have the return value, what do we do with it?
        ret = (unsigned int)&buffer+0x18;
        buffer[0] = 0x88; //this is here so buffer is not optimized out
    }
void main() {
        int x;
        x = 0;
        function(1,2,3);
        x = 1;
        printf("%d\n",x);
    }
```

To figure out how to manipulate the return address, take a look at the assembled code for `main`:

```
0804841f <main>:
 804841f:    55                          push   ebp
 8048420:    89 e5                       mov    ebp,esp
 8048422:    83 e4 f0                    and    esp,0xfffffff0
 8048425:    83 ec 20                    sub    esp,0x20
 8048428:    c7 44 24 1c 00 00 00        mov    DWORD PTR [esp+0x1c],0x0
 8048430:    c7 44 24 08 03 00 00        mov    DWORD PTR [esp+0x8],0x3
 8048438:    c7 44 24 04 02 00 00        mov    DWORD PTR [esp+0x4],0x2
 8048440:    c7 04 24 01 00 00 00        mov    DWORD PTR [esp],0x1
 8048447:    e8 c0 ff ff ff              call   804840c <function>
 804844c:    c7 44 24 1c 01 00 00        mov    DWORD PTR [esp+0x1c],0x1;x=1
 8048454:    8b 44 24 1c                 mov    eax,DWORD PTR [esp+0x1c]
 8048458:    89 44 24 04                 mov    DWORD PTR [esp+0x4],eax
 804845c:    c7 04 24 08 85 04 08        mov    DWORD PTR [esp],0x8048508
 8048463:    e8 88 fe ff ff              call   80482f0 <printf@plt>
 8048468:    c9                          leave
 8048469:    c3                          ret
```

Normally, the return address of the function would be 0x804844C, and, looking at that instruction, that is the x=1 that we want to avoid! After this line, the next instruction starts at 0x8048454.

Now, there are two options for changing the return address. One is to use the pointer to the return address to change it to be the hard-coded 0x8048454. The problem with this approach is that the address is a virtual address chosen at build time by the compiler, and every time you launch it, it will be the same, until you recompile. When you recompile, there is a chance you will get new virtual addresses. You'd need to recompile to test this theory, so this approach is a bit rigid.

Instead, the better approach is to note that the x=1 instruction is 8 bytes long. That will always be consistent, so the stronger approach is to add 8 bytes to the current return address.

> **NOTE** When printing out assembly, gdb will often cut off the hex display, so if you're looking at the printout, you'll count only 7 bytes on the x=1 line. That is simply because it was cut off. Always do the math with the addresses to make sure you have the right byte count.

To skip the x=1 instruction, the return address should be updated by adding 8 bytes. Adding that into the code produces the following:

```
#include <stdio.h>
void function(int a, int b, int c) {
char buffer[16];
int *ret;

ret = (unsigned int)buffer+0x18; //get the return value
*ret +=0x8; //increment the return value by 8
buffer[0] = 0x88; //this is here so buffer is not optimized out
}
void main() {
    int x;
    x = 0;
    function(1,2,3);
    x = 1;
    printf("%d\n",x);
}
```

Running this code (with the compile flag -fno-stack-protector) should result in the program printing out a value of 0. This indicates that the return address was successfully modified and the program skips over the x=1 instruction. Victory!

Shellcode

The ability to modify return addresses provides control over code execution, which is powerful. One common application of this is to "pop a shell," providing the ability to run more powerful commands.

To pop a shell, you need to be able to run your own, arbitrary code within the application. To do so, you need to place *shellcode* within the buffer that is being overflowed and modify the return address to point to the beginning of this code. Shellcode quite literally means code that will launch a command prompt (shell). The shellcode can come before or after the return address depending on the amount of buffer space you have available. The goal is to get your shellcode into a buffer somewhere and then modify the return address to point to it.

The following code shows a very simple shellcode. It uses the `execve` Linux syscall to execute `/bin/sh`, which is a common shell application. `execve` is asking the Linux kernel to do something. In this case, passing in the shell application asks Linux to launch the shell.

```
#include <stdio.h>

void main() {
    char *name[2];

    name[0] = "/bin/sh";
    name[1] = NULL;
    execve(name[0], name, NULL);
        exit(0);
}
```

This simple shellcode assembles to the following assembly code:

```
0804843c <main>:
 804843c:    55                        push   ebp
 804843d:    89 e5                     mov    ebp,esp
 804843f:    83 e4 f0                  and    esp,0xfffffff0
 8048442:    83 ec 20                  sub    esp,0x20
 8048445:    c7 44 24 18 18 85 04      mov    DWORD PTR [esp+0x18],
 0x8048518
 804844c:    08
 804844d:    c7 44 24 1c 00 00 00      mov    DWORD PTR [esp+0x1c],0x0
 8048454:    00
 8048455:    8b 44 24 18               mov    eax,DWORD PTR [esp+0x18]
 8048459:    c7 44 24 08 00 00 00      mov    DWORD PTR [esp+0x8],0x0
 8048460:    00
 8048461:    8d 54 24 18               lea    edx,[esp+0x18]
 8048465:    89 54 24 04               mov    DWORD PTR [esp+0x4],edx
 8048469:    89 04 24                  mov    DWORD PTR [esp],eax
 804846c:    e8 cf fe ff ff            call   8048340 <execve@plt>
 8048471:    c7 04 24 00 00 00 00      mov    DWORD PTR [esp],0x0
 8048478:    e8 a3 fe ff ff            call   8048320 <exit@plt>
```

This code relies on standard C methods for `execve` and `exit`, which will move around in memory, making it difficult to predict their addresses and embed them in the code. Meaning that if you took this assembly code as is, dropped the opcodes into a buffer, and updated the return address to point to it, when the code reaches the `call execve` instruction, it would likely segfault. This is because the address compiled into the shellcode is where `execve` was loaded for that application (`0x8048340`), but that is not a universal address. You would need to know where `execve` is loaded for the target application (if it even has `execve` at all). This makes it necessary to find an alternative way of popping a shell that doesn't involve C libraries.

If you disassemble the `execve` and `exit` methods, you can see the underlying implementation, as shown in the following code sample:

```
mov     eax, 0xb
mov     ebx, string_addr
lea     ecx, string_addr
lea     edx, null_string
int     0x80    ;sys call for exec
mov     eax, 0x1
mov     ebx, 0x0
int     0x80    ;sys call for exit
":/bin/sh"\0
```

So that solves some of the struggle, and the C library calls distill down into the `int 0x80` syscalls covered earlier in the book. But now there is another challenge: the values of *string_addr* and *null_string* are unknown since you can't predict where they will be loaded in memory. Again, the assembled shellcode placed them in that local memory space (in this example `0x8048518` is the compiled address for `/bin/sh`), but when the shellcode is dropped into the target buffer, those addresses will be wrong.

Making the shellcode work requires figuring out another way to find the address that is relative and not hard-coded. One way to learn this value is to take advantage of return addresses in function calls; again, apply your immense knowledge of calling conventions and the stack! If a function call is placed right before the string, then the address of the string will be at the top of the stack within that function (because the string is sitting at the function's return address).

To start, add in a few place holders to the existing shellcode.

```
jmp     ??
pop     esi
mov     [esi+0x8],esi
mov     [esi+0x7],0x0
mov     [esi+0xc],0x0
mov     eax, 0xb
mov     ebx, esi
lea     ecx, [esi+0x8]
lea     edx, [0xc+esi]
int     0x80
mov     eax, 0x1
mov     ebx, 0
int     0x80
call    ??
.string \"/bin/sh\"
```

This code sample takes the initial shellcode and adds two instructions to the front and two to the end. The next step is to determine the address of the string, which is located at the end of the assembly block. Ideally, the initial `jmp` instruction should jump down to the new `call` at the bottom.

Then, this `call` should call the new `pop esi line`. Why? When using a call (instead of a jump) to get back up to the top of the code, the return address (the next address after the call) will be placed on the stack. We have no intention of doing a normal `cdecl` stack setup; this is abusing x86 knowledge to do naughty things.

After the call back up to `pop esi`, the top of the stack will have the return address, which in this case is the shell string. This address can be popped off the stack into `esi` and used in the previous shellcode.

Now, that sounds awesome, but there are currently placeholders for the jump and call. To figure out where those are going to jump to, we have to count our bytes. Here we count the compiled bytes to determine the correct offsets for `jmp` and `call`:

```
jmp     0x26                    # 2 bytes
pop     esi                     # 1 byte
mov     [esi+0x8],esi           # 3 bytes
mov     [esi+0x7],0x0           # 4 bytes
mov     [esi+0xc],0x0           # 7 bytes
mov     eax, 0xb                # 5 bytes
mov     ebx, esi                # 2 bytes
lea     ecx, [esi+0x8]          # 3 bytes
lea     edx, [0xc+esi]          # 3 bytes
int     0x80                    # 2 bytes
mov     eax, 0x1                # 5 bytes
mov     ebx, 0                  # 5 bytes
int     0x80                    # 2 bytes
call    -0x2b                   # 5 bytes
.string \"/bin/sh\"
```

This modified code solves the problem of finding the string in memory by making it all relative (no hard-coded addresses) and uses the fundamental workings of x86 to help. The final challenge is getting the code to run, which requires placing a binary representation of the code on the stack via a buffer overflow.

Stack Smashing and Stack Protection

As mentioned, by default many compilers now build in stack protections to prevent rudimentary stack attacks. As an example, gcc and g++ after gcc 4.1 have some built-in stack protection. To practice stack smashing, it's necessary to build executables using the `-fno-stack-protector` flag. So, what does stack protection look like? Let's build an example and see what it adds.

The following code sample shows a program built with stack protection enabled:

```
0804845c <function>:
  804845c:    55               push   ebp
  804845d:    89 e5            mov    ebp,esp
```

```
 804845f:     83 ec 48              sub     esp,0x48
 8048462:     8b 45 08              mov     eax,DWORD PTR [ebp+0x8]
 8048465:     89 45 d4              mov     DWORD PTR [ebp-0x2c],eax
 8048468:     65 a1 14 00 00 00     mov     eax,gs:0x14
 804846e:     89 45 f4              mov     DWORD PTR [ebp-0xc],eax
 8048471:     31 c0                 xor     eax,eax
 8048473:     8b 45 d4              mov     eax,DWORD PTR [ebp-0x2c]
 8048476:     89 44 24 04           mov     DWORD PTR [esp+0x4],eax
 804847a:     8d 45 e4              lea     eax,[ebp-0x1c]
 804847d:     89 04 24              mov     DWORD PTR [esp],eax
 8048480:     e8 bb fe ff ff        call    8048340 <strcpy@plt>
 8048485:     8b 45 f4              mov     eax,DWORD PTR [ebp-0xc]
 8048488:     65 33 05 14 00 00 00  xor     eax,DWORD PTR gs:0x14
 804848f:     74 05                 je      8048496 <function+0x3a>
 8048491:     e8 9a fe ff ff        call    8048330 <__stack_chk
_fail@plt>
 8048496:     c9                    leave
 8048497:     c3                    ret
```

The bolded lines illustrate the things added by the compiler for stack protection. The compiler added code that will save the return address on function entry and will verify that it is unchanged after a strcpy operation. The compiler knows calls like strcpy can be dangerous; this prevents the strcpy from overwriting the return address.

There are a few options for protecting against stack smashing, including gcc's built-in stack protections, the use of memory-safe languages with bounds checking, and Data Execution Prevention (DEP). However, buffer overflows are still a threat in some cases because not all compilers will support stack protection or DEP, and as you can see, there is nuance to how it protects, not adding stack guards around every single call. Yet protections are focused against specific things like strcpy. And many compilers are pretty smart about which are most dangerous and need protection.

Connecting C and x86

Any program that can be written in C (or any other language) can also be written in assembly. In fact, higher-level languages are compiled into assembly before they are run by the CPU. However, in some cases, it can be helpful to mix C and assembly code. If you're writing your own exploits/cracks, this is a powerful combination. Some things are nuanced enough that you need assembly-level control, and some things are just code that needs to happen, and it's faster to write it in C, so feel free to mix the two!

To call a function written in another language, it's necessary to know where that function is located in memory. The linker can provide this information automatically.

It's also necessary to know how to pass information to that function, i.e., its calling convention. For this case we will assume our C functions are using cdecl. Recall the following, with cdecl:

- Arguments are passed on the stack pushed from right to left.

- The caller is responsible for cleaning up the stack after the call returns.

- The function's return value is stored in *eax*.

- The *eax*, *ecx*, and *edx* registers are available to the callee. The caller should save these registers' values if needed, and the callee should save and restore the values of any other registers that they need.

If you follow the correct calling convention, you can call C functions from your assembly code.

Using C Functions in x86 Code

For x86 code to use C functions, the assembly code needs to know that the C function is defined elsewhere. This is done using the extern directive in the assembly code. For example, to call the C function, x(), in x86, use the following instructions:

```
extern x
call x
```

The first step to using C functions in assembly is to include the extern *function_name* directive at the top of the assembly file. This tells the assembler that you intend to use this function, but you don't know its location (address) yet. When you write call *function_name* in the assembly code, it will initially be assembled as call 0x????????. However, the program won't be able to run until you put it through a linker, which will fill in the appropriate address.

The next step is to call the desired function using the cdecl calling convention. For example, when calling the C function int add(int x, int y), you'd use the following assembly code. Remember, arguments are pushed from right to left, and you need to clean up the stack after the call and place the return value in eax.

```
push [y]
push [x]
call add
add esp, 8
mov [sum], eax
```

After writing the assembly code, the next step is to assemble it using nasm. Here's an example: nasm example.asm -o example.o.

At this point, everything will be in assembly except those placeholders. If you had no external functions, your code would be ready to run, but since it does, you need a linker's help. The final step is to link your assembly code to the C function. If you're using gcc and calling functions from the C library, gcc can handle this automatically. For example, gcc example.o -o example will use the linker to fill out any addresses that it knows, transforming call 0x???????? to call 0x08048320.

For example, consider the following example, which runs printf hello world 42:

```
extern printf
global main

section .text
main:

push 42
push world
push hello
call printf
add esp, 12

mov eax, 1
mov ebx, 0
int 0x80

section .data
hello: db "hello %s %d", 0xa, 0
world: db "world"
```

This assembly code can be assembled using nasm -f elf example.asm and linked with gcc -m32 example.o -o example.

It can be very helpful and powerful to be able to call simple things like printf from your assembly code while you're testing your crack/patch ideas.

Using x86 Functions in C Code

It's also possible to call assembly functions from C code. The C program must have a prototype for the x86 functions that it wants to use. For example, in C, to use the assembly function f, you need the prototype int f(void);. A prototype is a fancy way of saying that you need to declare how that function definition would look if it was in a higher-level language (what's its name, what arguments does it take, and what does it return).

To use x86 functions in your C code, they need to be *exported* from your assembly code so that the linker can find them. To export an x86 function in your assembly file, label it with the global directive, as shown in the following example:

```
global f
f:
```

```
mov eax, 0xdabbad00
ret
```

Then, assemble your assembly code with `nasm` and compile and link the complete program with `gcc`.

For example, consider the following C program:

```c
// x.c

#include <stdio.h>

int add(int,int);

int main(void)
{
    int x=add(1,2);
    printf("%d\n",x);
    return 0;
}
```

This program uses the add function, which is defined in the following assembly code:

```
; y.asm

add:
  push ebp
  mov ebp, esp

  mov eax, [ebp+8]
  add eax, [ebp+12]

  leave
  ret
```

To link and assemble this program, run the following commands:

```
nasm -f elf y.asm # produces y.o object
gcc -m32 -c x.c # produces x.o object
gcc x.o y.o -o adder # produces executable adder
# run with ./adder
```

_start vs. main()

x86 assembly programs commonly begin with a label named _start. C programs, on the other hand, start with a main() function. What's the difference?

Execution of a program (whether written in C, assembly, or any other language) doesn't really start at main. For example, consider the simplest possible C function, as shown here:

```
int main()
{
return 0;
}
```

Compiling this with gcc simple.c -o simple translates your program to assembly. As part of this process, the compiler adds a function called _start, and _start calls main.

The resulting compiled main function has the following assembly:

```
80483b4:    55              push    ebp
80483b5:    89 e5           mov     ebp,esp
80483b7:    5d              pop     ebp
80483b8:    c3              ret
```

The start function looks like this:

```
8048300:    31 ed           xor     ebp,ebp
8048302:    5e              pop     esi
8048303:    89 e1           mov     ecx,esp
8048305:    83 e4 f0        and     esp,0xfffffff0
8048308:    50              push    eax
8048309:    54              push    esp
804830a:    52              push    edx
804830b:    68 30 84 04 08  push    0x8048430
8048310:    68 c0 83 04 08  push    0x80483c0
8048315:    51              push    ecx
8048316:    56              push    esi
8048317:    68 b4 83 04 08  push    0x80483b4
804831c:    e8 cf ff ff ff  call    80482f0 <__libc_start_main@plt>
8048321:    f4              hlt
```

The start function is responsible for a few different tasks, including the following:

- Initializing the frame pointer
- Configuring the stack
- Setting up the standard arguments (parameters to main())
- Calling libc_start_main, which performs security checks, threading subsystem, init, calls your main function, and finally calls exit()

When writing pure assembly code, you write everything yourself. You don't need all of the setup C does and can write your own _start function.

When combining assembly and C, you need gcc to step in. Often, gcc wants to provide its own _start function and expects you to provide a main() function.

When writing an assembly program that will be linked against the standard C library, do the following:

1. Use main instead of _start (libc_start_main will call main() for you).

2. Set up a stack frame only, not the entire stack (_start has already configured your stack).

3. Finish with ret, not int 0x80 (ret will return to libc_start_main, which will call the C exit function, which will call int 0x80 for you).

4. Set the return value in eax before ret'ing (usually 0).

For example, consider the following stand-alone assembly program, which defines its own _start:

```
global _start

section .text
_start:
    mov   esp, stack
    mov   ebp, esp


    . . .


    mov   esp, ebp

    mov   eax, 1
    mov   ebx, 0
    int   0x80

section .data
times 128 db 0
stack equ $-4
```

When linking to libc, the program should use main instead.

```
global main

section .text
main:
    push ebp
    mov  ebp, esp


    . . .


    mov  eax, 0
    leave
    ret
```

Standard Arguments

In C, arguments can be read from the command link with `stdargs`. For example, `main()` is commonly defined as `int main(int argc, char **argv)`, which provides access to these command-line arguments. Recall that `argc` is the number of arguments passed in, and `argv` is an array that holds those arguments.

It's also possible to access command-line arguments when writing a `main` function in assembly. Your assembly version of `main` will be automatically called with `cdecl`. Recall that the following:

- Arguments are passed on the stack, pushed on from right to left.

- Arguments are at `[ebp+8]`, `[ebp+12]`, etc.

- `argc` will be the last argument and is at the top of the list of arguments on the stack, at `[ebp+8]`.

- `argv` is the first argument pushed to the stack and will be at `[ebp+12]`.

For example, the following assembly program will print the first command-line argument:

```
extern printf
global main

main:
    push   ebp
    mov    ebp, esp

    mov    eax, [ebp+12]    ; load argv into eax
    push   dword [eax+4]    ; push argv[1]
    call   printf           ; print argv[1]
    add    esp, 4           ; clean up stack
    mov    eax, 0
    leave
    ret
```

Mixing C and Assembly

In C, it's possible to switch seamlessly between C and assembly code. This is called *inline assembly*, named for the fact that the assembly is *inlined* with your source code.

Inline assembly is not part of the C specification, but most compilers will support it via an extension. However, the syntax is unique for each compiler. In `gcc`, this is the AT&T x86 syntax.

The basic form of this is `__asm__ ("assembly code here");`. When compiling, `gcc` compiles the C code to assembly and pastes in the assembly code from the `__asm__` directive.

For example, consider the following C program:

```
int main(void)
{
    // set keyboard control register

    __asm__ ("mov  $0x10010001, %eax");
    __asm__ ("out  %eax, $0x64");

    return 0;
}
```

The extended form of inline assembly lets you set advanced "constraints." These constraints can include the following:

- **Input variables:** C variables that you want to manipulate using assembly.

- **Output variables:** Values produced in the inline assembly code that you want to use in the C code.

- **Clobbered registers:** gcc translates the C to assembly and figures out which registers to use. This list ensures that the registers used by the C and assembly code won't conflict.

Extended assembly can be specified as follows:

```
__asm__ (

            "assembly"
            : input constraints
            : output constraints
            : clobber list
            );
```

The following code sample shows an example of using extended assembly in C:

```
#include <stdio.h>

int main(void)
{
    // getting the return address for the current function

    int x;

    __asm__ ("\
            movl 0x4(%%ebp), %%eax  \n\
            movl %%eax, %0          \n\
            "
            : "=r" (x)
            :
            : "%eax"
```

```
            );

    printf("%08x\n", x);

    return 0;
}
```

Inline assembly is used extensively in C for the following:

- An operating system kernel (check out the Linux kernel source).
- Embedded systems.
- Any code that needs to work with hardware.
- Any code that needs to be very fast.
- You'll see it from time to time if you ever work with C, and you may need to use it yourself.

Remember that when using inline assembly, you'll need to add a new flag to gcc. For example, the command gcc -masm=intel myFile.c tells gcc that you've written some intel assembly into your C file.

Summary

This chapter demonstrated how to use an understanding of x86 and the stack for hacking. By smashing the stack and inserting shellcode, a reverser can trick a program into running the attacker's code.

Conclusion

Wow, this has been quite a journey! We've covered offense to defense; high-level languages down to assembly; registers, control flow, reverse engineering; patching, tools, techniques, and mindset. If you've made it this far, you have an amazing baseline of knowledge to build from as you continue to move forward.

And as you do move forward, you will always encounter something new. At first, it will be assembly instructions you don't know, then defenses you've never seen, then architectures you've never heard of, and of course the latest, greatest tool-of-the-day or defense-of-the-year. But now that you have the basics, you'll find that new things become easier and easier to pick up quickly.

Now that you know `mov`, you can easily understand the string version `movs`. You've worked with bit manipulations like `not`, so negation with `neg` makes sense pretty quickly. You've mastered comparisons like `cmp`, so `cmps` isn't much of a stretch, and from there how about `cmpxchg` or `cmpxchg16b` or `lock cmpxchg8b`? The gist is: now that you have the basics, it becomes increasingly easy to understand new instructions; whether it's `ud` (undefined instruction) or `gf2p8affineinvqb` (Galois field affine transformation inverse), the fundamentals tend to be mostly the same for everything.

But of course, learning more doesn't end there. New instructions are great, but if you keep on this path, you'll soon encounter entirely new architectures. The good news is, they also tend to follow the same basic patterns, and now that you've mastered one, you'll be able to understand new ones in no time. x64 (64-bit x86) is easy now that you've done x86—just extend the registers to 64 bits (`rax` instead of `eax`, `rsp` instead of `esp`) and follow some different calling conventions (AMD64 ABI in addition to cdecl), and you'll be able to apply all the same tools and techniques to 64-bit code. From there, Arm comes pretty easily—again, it's just new registers (`r0` instead of `rax`), instructions (`b` instead of jmp), and calling conventions (Arm instead of cdecl). The underlying patterns tend to be mostly the same, so whatever your target—PowerPC, MIPS, RISC-V, MIL-STD-1750A, etc.—you can usually learn the basics in a few hours. Expanding to new architectures will also let you apply your skills to new devices. Whether it's phones, routers, cars, or satellites, the fundamentals are fairly uniform.

Naturally, as you keep advancing, you won't just encounter new architectures; you'll encounter new tools as well. The good news here, too, is that they tend to build off of the same base set of concepts. We've worked through a bevy of disassemblers, hex editors, debuggers, and decompilers. Now it's time to start exploring new options to see what clicks with you. Ghidra, Binary Ninja, and Cutter/radare2 are popular next steps that will build off of your experience with IDA and offer even more ways to dissect and understand a program. As you grow your arsenal of tools, you'll gradually build up your own scripts, workflows, and strategies to become increasingly proficient with more and more difficult targets.

And, of course, if you keep at it, you'll begin to encounter new defenses. Whether it's the latest anti-cheat in online gaming, a new opaque predicate obfuscation from academia, or creative new hashing in an esoteric keychecker, keeping up-to-date with the latest trends will help you stay sharp, whether your passion is offense or defense. Both academic journals and cracking forums can be fantastic resources here.

But whatever your end goals with this skill set, the singular key to moving forward is practice. Try writing your own keychecker, and then see if you can crack it—playing both sides at once can offer interesting insights into the challenges and limitations of an adversary. Crackmes offer a fantastic, fun, and (mostly) safe way to get experience in reverse engineering and software modification on a wide variety of languages and architectures. Whenever you have a few minutes, grab a crackme that seems in line with your experience and skill level and see if you can defeat it; if you have a few hours, find one that uses a language you don't know or defenses you've never seen. Beyond cracking, modifying simple programs can quickly offer new insights and expand your skill set. Drop your favorite 90s video game into IDA and see if you can add infinite lives; try out Ghidra on your favorite text editor and see if you can add a secret menu. Alternatively, capture-the-flag competitions can be an exciting way to push your reverse engineering skills to their limit, while simultaneously branching into new areas like binary exploitation and computer forensics.

However you proceed, stay persistent, keep practicing, and continue to push your limits into new domains. As you do, we hope that this book has helped you establish a broad baseline of skills and that you'll use them to dive ever deeper into this awesome facet of security.

Index